Britische und Irische Studien
zur deutschen Sprache und Literatur

British and Irish Studies
in German Language and Literature

Etudes britanniques et irlandaises
sur la langue et la littérature allemandes

Edited by H.S. Reiss and W.E. Yates

Band 45

PETER LANG
Oxford · Bern · Berlin · Bruxelles · Frankfurt/M. · New York · Wien

Landmarks in the German Novel (1)

Peter Hutchinson (ed.)

PETER LANG

Oxford · Bern · Berlin · Bruxelles · Frankfurt/M. · New York · Wien

Bibliographic information published by Die Deutsche Bibliothek
Die Deutsche Bibliothek lists this publication in the Deutsche
Nationalbibliografie; detailed bibliographic data is available on the
Internet at ‹http://dnb.ddb.de›.

British Library and Library of Congress Cataloguing-in-Publication Data:
A catalogue record for this book is available from *The British Library*,
Great Britain, and from *The Library of Congress*, USA

ISSN 0171-6662
ISBN 978-3-03910-927-2

© Peter Lang AG, International Academic Publishers, Bern 2007
Hochfeldstrasse 32, Postfach 746, CH-3000 Bern 9, Switzerland
info@peterlang.com, www.peterlang.com, www.peterlang.net

Printed in Germany

Contents

PETER HUTCHINSON

Introduction

Earlier volumes devoted to major novels in the German language have naturally identified rather different texts as milestones in the development of the genre. The first important post-1945 survey, for example, Benno von Wiese's two-volume *Der deutsche Roman* (1965), viewed the canon in what the twenty-first century would consider a very strange way, featuring novels which today command little attention – such as Hoffmann's *Kater Murr*, Immermann's *Münchhausen*, and Gotthelf's *Geld und Geist*. Only six of von Wiese's nineteen novels are featured in the present volume, and most of these are from the twentieth century. More surprisingly, Jost Schillemeit's popular paperback, *Interpretationen: Deutsche Romane von Grimmelshausen bis Musil* (1966) selected only three of those included here. There are actually only two novels to be included in both these older collections and the present one: Goethe's *Wilhelm Meisters Lehrjahre* and Mann's *Buddenbrooks*. What is most striking here, perhaps, is that although one might expect disagreement on more recent, twentieth-century, writing, there is in fact minimal agreement on what constitutes the most important work in earlier centuries. Such divergence is in part attributable to different editorial priorities and changing readers' expectations; but it is also in part a reflection of the large pool of important works on which editors can draw. In this respect German fiction is clearly rich, and its canon is thus bound to be dynamic, comfortably able to reflect all shifts in taste. The sketch of its history given below mentions a number of novels which, in a larger volume, would undoubtedly have commanded a place.

Until the appearance of Goethe's *Die Leiden des jungen Werthers* (1774), the novel in Germany was a relatively poor relation to other genres. Serious critical attention to poetry is evident as early as 1624 with Opitz's *Buch von der deutschen Poeterei*, but the first study of the novel did not come until 150 years later, Blankenburg's *Versuch über den Roman*, which was actually published in the same year as *Werther*. The novel's humble status was partly attributable to its subject-matter and partly to its propensity to draw inspiration – and unashamedly copy – from abroad. Early, seventeenth-century, novels tended to string together sensational and sometimes bawdy episodes, or delighted in romances of the most preposterous kind, never reaching the level of their models in France, England or Spain, and completely lacking the subtlety and sensitivity of German poetry of their age. Only Grimmelshausen's *Simplicissimus* (1669), with its broad treatment of the Thirty Years' War and a well-handled perspective of the 'innocent eye', has any claim to stand out against this background. Grimmelshausen managed to combine a fresh world view with an unusual use of language, and his novel represents the first example of something which could be seen as distinctively German. It is also the best early example of the picaresque in the German tradition, and it spawned a number of imitations. Its influence has extended as far as the final novel featured in the present volume, but it has had little appeal beyond Germany. It is clearly a partial landmark, but it cannot rank with that featured in the first essay in this volume.

Without Goethe, the history of German literature – and especially that of the novel – would have been totally different, but with his unprecedented approach and amazing capacity for empathy, Goethe gave the novel credibility as a genre. *Die Leiden des jungen Werthers* showed how a partial perspective and motivational ambiguity could provide far more satisfying reading that simple story-telling, traditional epistolary forms, or 'trustworthy' omniscient narrators. It also proved Germany could produce fiction of international significance.

The experimental drive of *Werther* is not continued in Goethe's next published novel, *Wilhelm Meisters Lehrjahre* (1795–96), but this totally different, and conceptually less exciting, work was actually to prove more significant for traditions in Germany. It established the benchmark for the *Bildungsroman*, a concept not actually popularised until Wilhelm Dilthey, who talked of 'die Schule des Wilhelm Meister' in *Das Leben Schleiermachers* (1870). The first German example is usually taken as Wieland's *Geschichte des Agathon* (1766–67), but it was Goethe's work which inspired a succession of portrayals of young (male) heroes, likeable partial failures, who almost stumble into some form of social maturity after a succession of adventures which seemingly shape their minds and character. *Wilhelm Meister* also inspired – or propelled into a contrary position – the German Romantics. It is surprising such a powerful movement, much concerned with formal experiment, did not produce a novel which one would nowadays consider a land-mark, but it is significant that the two major contenders, Novalis' *Heinrich von Ofterdingen* (1802), and Jean Paul's *Flegeljahre* (1804–05), were both unfinished. The strength of such figures as Tieck, Brentano and Eichendorff – indeed of all the Romantics – lay in shorter forms.

It may seem excessive to claim that Goethe was also to produce the third great landmark in the history of the novel in German, but *Die Wahlverwandtschaften* (1808–09) has not ceased to intrigue generations of readers: in his handling of the mysterious forces underlying Nature and human nature, Goethe is writing almost as a Romantic, but in showing the moral law in operation he is working very much in the classical spirit. The combination of these two forces creates a work of contradictions and ambiguities which resist adequate explanation, although the biographical and historical exploration undertaken in the essay by Nicholas Boyle certainly helps elucidate many of these.

The nineteenth century witnessed that growth in the novel which had come to England in the preceding century, with figures from Austria (such as Adalbert Stifter, whose *Der Nachsommer* (1857) arguably qualifies for landmark status) and Switzerland (such as Gottfried Keller, whose *Der grüne Heinrich* (first version 1854–55) clearly does). Political novels, and works engaged with the social situation of their age, became common, and historical novels, notably those by Wilhelm Hauff, Willibald Alexis, and Theodor Fontane found an eager readership. Some novelists of the period are prolific and explore the historical currents, problems and failings of their age and of the individual with frankness and skill. But between 1828, the second version of Goethe's final novel, *Wilhelm Meisters Wanderjahre* (itself virtually a landmark in its exploitation of techniques which were not again to be properly exploited in German until the twentieth century), and 1895, Fontane's subtle analysis of the need for female fulfilment against a background of Wilhelminian morals (*Effi Briest*), it is easier to speak of successful and prolific writers rather than truly distinguished ones.

The twentieth century begins with a complex work that combines the historical, economic, and social concerns of nineteenth-century writing with an element that will acquire increasing importance: Mann's *Buddenbrooks* (1901) draws on philosophers (Schopenhauer, Nietzsche) to complete its diagnosis of Wilhelminian society as the epigonic conclusion to a simpler, nobler, apparently more honest world. It is also the greatest example of realism in the German language. About the same time Arthur Schnitzler is providing a comparable analysis of Austrian (or rather Viennese) society and its rising anti-Semitism, but with the insights of psychoanalysis rather than philosophy (notably *Der Weg ins Freie*, 1908). Schnitzler's understanding of the mind was supplemented rather than formed by Sigmund Freud, but later writers rarely fail to be influenced by the latter's heavy shadow. Freud sought to explain patterns of human behaviour as the result of various sexual drives and complexes, and although most of his theories aroused controversy, their scandalising elements (particularly the Oedipus complex) led to increasing attention to mind processes and motivation in a more sophisticated way than had previously been considered necessary. Focus on the psyche thus acquires major status in the novels of Modernism, and not just on the minds of the characters: from this generation onwards there is greater concern with the reaction of the reader, and the desire to play with that reader's expectations. 'Mind games' might sum up one aspect of Franz Kafka particularly well, but it is a concept which can be applied to the increasing number of writers who turn to unreliable and self-conscious narrators, to complex strategies to encourage prognostication with regard to character interaction and plot, and to intertextuality.

The period between 1924, Mann's parody of the *Bildungsroman*, *Der Zauberberg*, and 1933, Hitler's seizure of power, is probably the richest in the history of novels written in the German language – but only one of those covered in this volume was written in Germany. Kafka's *Der Proceß* (published posthumously in 1925) was composed in Czechoslovakia, Hesse's *Der Steppenwolf* (1927) in Switzerland, Musil's *Der Mann ohne Eigenschaften* (1930) mainly in Austria, and Broch's *Die Schlafwandler* (1930–32) also in that country. Only Döblin's *Berlin Alexanderplatz* (1929) is a product of Germany itself. Although written in different parts of the German-speaking world, these novels do share certain concerns, such as the breakdown of values, problems of the psyche, and issues of free will in a world in which the individual is threatened by the forces of modernity. And they are all 'self-conscious' novels, their authors eager to ensure their readers recognise the presence of an author and his methods. With the exception of *Der Proceß*, they are all remarkably long, like most novels featured in this volume. Their authors have much to say on their subject, which they explore from various angles, and they have a tradition of length behind them. This was to be maintained by numerous writers for the rest of the century, and translations for the English-speaking market were occasionally abridged.

Many other writers were active and were highly popular during this period, and although their contribution to the development of the genre may have been slight, they consolidated various techniques and explored aspects of their changing society in a way which revealed the tensions and contradictions of the short-lived Weimar Republic – Heinrich Mann, Lion Feuchtwanger, Jakob Wassermann and, in Austria, Joseph Roth. In total contrast there was, of course, the great novel of the trenches, Erich Maria Remarque's *Im Westen nichts Neues* (1929), which compelled through its realistic presentation of what no one had dared reveal: the horrors and above all the apparent pointlessness of a war that had devastated Germany, its economic base and its social stability.

1933, and the National Socialist grip on culture, proved to be the end of major literary experiment. Exile followed for numerous progressive and Jewish writers. Liberation may have arrived in 1945, but we do not know how much literary talent had been suppressed under National Socialism and then destroyed by warfare. This is the simple explanation for the meagre output of the period up to 1959 and a 'missing generation' of young novelists. And some exiles never returned to Germany – most notably Thomas Mann, whose *Doktor Faustus* (1947) was, of course, written in the USA. Survivors like Heinrich Böll (born 1917) wrote for a different society, some of whom were only now coming to grips with works which had been suppressed under National Socialism, and many of whom were content with credible characters and well-constructed narratives which dealt with the recent past and the present. In a less devastated period it seems unlikely that Böll would have found as much acclaim. Likewise, those who had survived war partly because of their age (e.g. Nossack, Koeppen) wrote for a society that was in search of stability and secure forms: experiment was modest. Unlike the aftermath of the First World War, however, serious presentations of the deprivations and depravities of conflict emerged fairly quickly, one of the most successful actually being written in English (and first published in the USA) by one who had fled Hitler in 1933: Stefan Heym's *The Crusaders* (1948). Yet alongside Heym's anti-fascist (and pro-socialist) work, one of the most popular novels of the immediate post-war period was the restorative Ernst von Salomon's *Der Fragebogen*, which showed the foolishness of the British gestures at 'de-Nazification', the attempt to remove Nazi elements from post-war society, or at least limit their influence. In Switzerland Max Frisch, untouched by war, could devote himself to problems raised by the question of identity in the modern world. His *Stiller* (1954) may have been superseded in its technique and exploration of the problem, but for many years it remained a central document of post-war striving for construction of the self.

A totally different approach to fiction was evident in the GDR, with its distinctly Marxist-Leninist cultural politics. Ruthless elimination of any remaining vestiges of National Socialism, wholehearted acceptance of Soviet views on literature, and total control of publishing and marketing led to a uniformity and predictability in state-endorsing fiction which was produced in large print-runs. Many returning exiles found the new conditions in the East uncomfortable. Brecht, for example, was to settle in East Berlin in 1949, but he wrote little of importance in his final years. Stefan Heym returned at the turn of 1951–52, but his major novel about the GDR of the 'fifties, *Der Tag X*, was refused publication. Anna Seghers had returned as early as 1947, but her major work of this period, *Die Entscheidung* (1959), completely lacked the vitality of her earlier writing and presented a highly schematic view of East and West. GDR writing only became interesting through its exceptions, such as Bruno Apitz's semi-autobiographical *Nackt unter Wölfen* (1958), perhaps the best depiction in either East or West of the concentration camp. It was not until the early seventies that GDR literature began to flourish, with the dissident and experimental movement actually being given partial respectability by an unexpected (and later regretted) speech given by Erich Honecker, the new General Secretary of the Socialist Unity Party.

If one passes over the brilliant, Joyce-inspired, creations of Arno Schmidt, which appealed principally to intellectuals, it is ironic that the first great experiment of post-war fiction was written by an East German – who could find a publisher only in the West. Uwe Johnson's *Mutmaßungen über Jakob* (1959) treated division, problems of identity, and inter-German understanding in a complex structural and narrative mode. Johnson's difficult work will be featured in the second volume of this series. The two other major novels of 1959 were Böll's *Billard um halb zehn*, an engagement with vestiges of National Socialism in the Federal

Republic, and Grass's *Die Blechtrommel*, which dealt with some of its more repulsive aspects during the Third Reich. The latter has proved to be the most important novel written in German since Mann's *Doktor Faustus*, and it may well prove to be the most lasting of the second half of the twentieth century.

The final forty years of that century witnessed the continued dominance of the novel over other genres and a steady flow of experimental, satirical, philosophically questioning, self-conscious and often highly entertaining works. The more important of these will be featured in *Landmarks in the German Novel* Volume II.

As with the preceding volumes in this series, the essays produced here were initially delivered as lectures in the University of Cambridge. I am again grateful to my colleagues and our visiting lecturers for their enthusiasm and co-operation, and I am equally grateful to Gar Yates, Co-General Editor of the Series, for his unfailing encouragement, his immediate response, advice and comments.

ROGER PAULIN

Goethe, *Die Leiden des jungen Werthers*

The case for *Werther* as a landmark in German fiction does not need to be made. This is the one German novel of all time that was a European-wide sensation, one that has moved, seized and convulsed readers over the generations since then and which still packs a mighty punch for readers even now. Today's reader may need some induction into this 230-year-old text, but if he or she is willing to enter into its spirit, it will do the rest.

But I must issue a couple of caveats. First: this is a novel to be taken seriously and read carefully or not at all. I say this in the light of a recently published history of German literature which reduces it to a sub-Freudian case-study.[1] There, what is wrong with Werther is his mammary fixation (that bow that Lotte wears at her bosom and that he wants to be buried with). Now, Werther doesn't need a course of therapy because he wants a mother. He is a man intent on destroying himself to gain in heaven the object of the love denied him on earth. No session on the therapist's couch can cure this sickness unto death that he calls it, and we should not trivialise something that takes us into such wild regions of the mind. Perhaps the extravagant language of Werther's second-to-last letter to Lotte causes today's readers to overlook the overt sexual connotations of what Werther calls 'ewige Umarmungen',[2] but Goethe's first readers certainly didn't. Psychoanalytic readings are fine, but the example I have cited is a trivialisation of such analysis. What Werther is lacking is not so much a mother as his reason. 'ich wähne nicht!' ('I'm not mad!') that same terrible letter says. Plainly he is.

---

1   David Wellbery, 'Pathologies of Literature', *A New History of German Literature*, ed. by David Wellbery and Judith Ryan (Cambridge, Mass., London, 2004), pp. 386–393, esp. pp. 389f.

2   All quotations from the first edition of *Werther* (1774) are identified by date or by context.

Second: when later in my remarks I draw attention to a theme hitherto rather neglected in studies of *Werther*, friendship, I am applying it as a means of interpretation, to test how far it helps us with reading the novel. I am not saying that the presence of a friend might have saved him from his fate. The physical absence of a friend may well be yet another factor that contributes to the underlying theme of death. But nothing can hold back or save a man who says 'ich soll, ich soll nicht zu mir selbst kommen' (30. November) and 'Es ist beschlossen [...] ich will sterben'.

But I run ahead of my subject. We are at the outset of a series on the German novel. In the two centuries since *Werther* was written, notions of what a novel is perceived to be have undergone many changes. I want to begin with a quotation from 1799. I do this because the author of the work I am citing, Johann Adam Bergk, *Die Kunst, Bücher zu lesen*, quotes long passages from *Werther* to illustrate various points and shows himself to be sympathetic to the general sentiments expressed in Goethe's novel.[3] Bergk defines what he believes to be the right state of mind to approach the reading of a novel in these terms:

> Wie müssen wir nun Romane lesen, um unsern Geschmack zu bilden und unsre Kenntniß der Welt und der Menschen zu vermehren? Ein empfängliches und reizbares Gemüth, Lust, Kraft und Muth zum Selbstdenken und ununterbrochene Aufmerksamkeit sind die Erfodernisse, welche wir von unserer Seite mit zur Lektüre eines Romanes mitbringen müssen:[4]

In its turn:

> der Roman muß reich an Gedanken, Empfindungen und Gefühlen, Bildern und Schilderungen, Charakterzeichnungen und Handlungen seyn, um uns Interesse einzuflößen und unsere aufgewandte Mühe nicht unbelohnt zu lassen.[5]

There is nothing remarkable in these passages, especially their contention that the main purpose of a novel is to increase and deepen our

---

3   *Die Kunst, Bücher zu lesen. Nebst Bemerkungen über Schriften und Schriftsteller* [Jena, 1799] (Leipzig, 1966). My attention was drawn to this text by Robert Darnton, 'Readers Respond to Rousseau: The Fabrication of Romantic Sensibility', in *The Great Cat Massacre and Other Episodes in French Cultural History* [1984] (Harmondsworth, 2001), pp. 115–156, 179–282.

4   Bergk, op. cit., pp. 212f.

5   Ibid., p. 213.

knowledge of humankind and the world, and to cultivate our taste. But it is nevertheless a statement of what today we call 'Wirkungsästhetik', setting out not only what is the avowed aim of the work of art but its projected reception, postulating indeed requiring of us a particular readiness to receive and be moved and a strenuousness of mind and reflection upon what we have read. It comes therefore not exactly as a surprise that Bergk has accounts of two eighteenth-century novels, one very brief and succinct, the other much longer and backed up with extensive quotations. Both require that special state of sympathetic readiness to enter into the spirit of the text: Rousseau's *La Nouvelle Héloïse* of 1760 and Goethe's *Die Leiden des jungen Werthers* of 1774. Rousseau, he says, 'dringt' 'in das Innerste unsers Herzens'.[6] But of *Werther* we read:

> Welches Gefühl wollte nun der Dichter vorzüglich durch sein Werk erregen? Obgleich die Gefühle des Schönen und Furchtbaren, Feierlichen u.s.w. oft in uns während der Lektüre erregt werden, so tragen doch die meisten Schilderungen und Handlungen den Charakter des Erhabenen: ein Mensch, der das Leben nicht achtet, der sich über die tausend elenden Kleinigkeiten des menschlichen Lebens hinwegsezt [...] regt das Gefühl des Erhabenen in uns auf, welches in Werthers Leiden das Hervorstechendste ist.[7]

In support of this Bergk quotes, roughly in this order, the passages whose first lines read 'Das volle warme Gefühl meines Herzens an der lebendigen Natur' (18 August),'ich bin in einem Zustande, in dem jene Unglüklichen müssen gewesen seyn, von denen man glaubte, sie würden von einem bösen Geiste umher getrieben' (Part II, 8 December), 'Daß das Leben des Menschen nur ein Traum sey' (22 May), 'Ohngefähr eine Stunde von der Stadt liegt ein Ort, den sie Wahlheim nennen' (26 May), 'Unglüklicher! Bist du nicht ein Thor?' (30 August), 'Eine wunderbare Heiterkeit hat meine ganze Seele eingenommen' (10 May) and 'Ossian hat in meinem Herzen den Homer verdrängt' (12 October). Bergk, who has no time for so-called 'empfindelnde Romane',[8] subsumes all of these passages under one mode: the sublime. Expressing various sentiments, ranging from joy to exultation, to doubt and despair, in Berg's account they relate the range of Werther's experience of humanity and nature to

6   Ibid., p. 302.
7   Ibid., p. 217.
8   Ibid., pp. 262–66.

one over-arching way of seeing. There is of course no doubt that there is much in *Werther* that can be related to the various theories of the sublime current in the eighteenth century – and this is not the time or place to enter into a detailed discussion of them – but they are seen by our author as leading to a heroic view of Werther's character, as one who puts the tribulations of life behind him and makes the decision to end it all. What I find interesting about this passage is the way that Goethe's novel, which caused so much éclat and scandal when it first came out in 1774, is here being integrated into aesthetic and moral discussions that seem closer to the debate on Hamlet in Goethe's next novel, *Wilhelm Meisters Lehrjahre*, of 1795–6. It reminds us that successive generations read their own emphases into a text that appeals beyond the time and circumstances of its first appearance.

I do not, I said, wish to read this novel through the notions of the sublime set out by Burke or Kant or Schiller, rewarding as that exercise might be. One does, however, note that Bergk, in using selected passages from *Werther* to illustrate manifestations of it or states of mind conducive to it, is breaking up the sequent account of the decline of a young man's state of mind. The great rhetorical – sublime – set pieces, which are one of the novel's most extraordinary features, cannot satisfactorily be read out of sequence. We need to know exactly where they are in the novel. We note that the 10 May passage is the second letter in the novel, already proclaiming in absolute terms that 'Eine wunderbare Heiterkeit hat meine ganze Seele eingenommen' (utter plenitude right at the beginning, and a kind of pantheism). But it is part of a trajectory from spring to late summer that, twenty-five letters later, announces that "Das volle warme Gefühl meines Herzens' (18 August) has given way to a view of nature as a self-consuming and destructive organism. This process has only taken a few weeks of 'real' time, from May to August. These passages stand out in an inexorable process, almost imperceptible at first, but which gains momentum, swells like a stream (one of the images in the novel) until we reach the last few pages of the text with things so terrible that the narrator cannot release them except in extract and with commentary.

We are dealing therefore with a novel structured very largely around letters, a so-called epistolary novel, and the reader of 1799 (Bergk's notional reader) or 2006 misses its point if it is merely reduced to a series of selected passages, however extraordinary and compelling they may be. I want therefore to say something more about letters, a subject that interested and fascinated Goethe, not only around the time of *Werther*'s composition but also later. When Goethe in 1804 announced his forthcoming edition of Johann Joachim Winckelmann's correspondence, he referred to the letters left by representative men as individual pieces of evidence of the great 'sum of life', 'die große Lebensrechnung'[9] that also includes deeds and writings. This quotation, referring to a real person, Winckelmann, can by extension also be applied to Werther, an imaginary person, because his letters as we have them in the novel of 1774 are 'die große Lebensrechnung'; they constitute almost everything, but not quite all, of what we know about him. Thus if we are to understand the essential structures of this novel, we need to examine the way Goethe uses letters, real or fictitious, and the way letters and fiction at the time are seen to relate.

Why did Goethe want to edit Winckelmann's letters and not his works, which today we would regard as the 'essential' part of a great writer's achievement? The eighteenth century saw this issue rather differently. It has been described as the 'century of letters'.[10] Letters have a special status.[11] They are the subject of theoretical discussion. They are seen as the genuine representation and expression of the inner self, speaking from the heart to the heart, breaking down barriers of time and distance and physical or even social distinctions, going 'directly' to their recipient and into his or her inner being. Thus the letters of a poet are a sine qua non of his image and of his self-presentation. Klopstock, the only living poet among Werther's trinity of Homer and Ossian and Klopstock, is of course read for his poetry but also for his letters that are collected and copied by others and circulated. A whole circle of readers

---

9   *Werke*. Weimar Edition, Section 1, Vol. 46, p. 391.
10   Cf. Reinhard Wittmann, 'Das Jahrhundert des Briefs', *Einladung ins 18. Jahrhundert. Ein Almanach aus dem Verlag C. H. Beck im 225. Jahr seines Bestehens*, ed. by Ernst-Peter Wieckenberg (Munich, 1988), p. 151.
11   On eighteenth-century letter culture see especially *Vom Verkehr mit Dichtern und Gespenstern. Figuren der Autorschaft in der Briefkultur*, ed. by Jochen Strobel (Heidelberg 2006); of particular interest is the opening essay by Jochen Strobel (pp. 7–32) and that by Robert Vellusig, 'Gellert, der Husar, ein Brief und seine Geschichte. Briefkultur und Autorschaft im 18. Jahrhundert' (pp. 33–59); see also Nikolaus Wegmann, *Diskurse der Empfindsamkeit. Zur Geschichte eines Gefühls in der Literatur des 18. Jahrhunderts* (Stuttgart, 1988).

knows about the circumstances of his wife's death and their hope for a reunion after death. Letters, expressing 'nature', 'the writings of the heart', are cultivated as a means of self-improvement: the need to communicate one's inward self or a state of mind receptive to feeling, to sympathy, to friendship, to pity, to confession, to the subjective way of seeing. These are all notions central to the eighteenth-century culture of feeling known as 'Empfindsamkeit', and they are virtues, we should not forget, that are enshrined in Werther's letters. In a letter, one may drop one's guard, have a greater freedom of expression, speaking (that is, writing) directly, but as if the interlocutor were there present and were able to communicate in the rhythms of normal speech.

That is one side. The other is the formal institutionalising of the letter as a form of social and literary discourse where accepted norms of taste and private forms of expression coincide. The century is not lacking in practical instruction in this so-called 'authentic' and 'direct' way of writing. Christian Fürchtegott Gellert's *Practische Abhandlung von dem guten Geschmacke in Briefen* (1751) is but the best-known. (An inattentive young Goethe sat at his feet as a student in Leipzig.) He stresses the 'natural' way of writing that enables the gap in time or space to be bridged, that brings the presence of the other across to the other correspondent.[12] Others, closer in time to *Werther*, stress above all the expression of feeling, 'die Sprache der Freundschaft, der Wahrheit und der Natur', as one voice of 1768 puts it.[13]

There are here several implications for our consideration of *Werther* and its reception. The public dissemination of letters – in various forms, one yet to be discussed – is seen by proponents of the idea of a 'Leser-evolution' around 1750 as an important component, as part of the opening up of the private sphere to a wide circle of recipients.[14] For Habermas or Koselleck, the advocates of the notion of 'bürgerliche Öffentlichkeit', the emergence of a self-aware reading public, letters, in whatever form and in whatever mode of distribution, contribute to this process of mature discourse and debate. Letters, although not specifically

12   See Vellusig, loc. cit., pp. 43–47.
13   [Friedrich Justus Riedel], *Brieftheorie des 18. Jahrhunderts. Texte, Kommentare, Essays*, ed. by Angelika Ebrecht and others (Stuttgart, 1990), p. 122.
14   On this, see Darnton, 'Readers respond to Rousseau', pp. 249–51. I share the doubts he expresses there.

mentioned, form part of Niklas Luhmann's theory of love and passion, whereby religious experience in the eighteenth century is disassociated from its anchorage in ecclesiastical institutions and becomes a matter of individual experience and feeling[15] (there is of course nothing new here that Ian Watt's theory of the rise of the English novel in Puritanism didn't already say). However we stand to these ideas, we see that letters are not a marginal concern of the eighteenth century. Thus one of the century's favoured forms for the reading and reception of letters is the epistolary novel, the novel in letters.[16] What is valid for real letters, private or public, also applies to imagined and invented correspondence. For novels in letters also make the claim to be expressing – in direct form – the individuality of the correspondents and the natural language of the heart. We the readers are seen as party to an exchange of letters that drop the conventional barriers from person to person and set out their inward thoughts and motives and give vent to their emotions – and tears. The 'confessional' quality of letters so conceived means that the distinction between reading and living may become blurred, a willing suspension of belief that enables the reader to share in the dialogue of two (or more) other persons, the epistolary world and real experienced life merging. Such a novel is *Julie, ou La Nouvelle Héloïse. Lettres de deux amans, habitans d'une petite ville au pied des Alpes, recueillies et publiées par J.J. Rousseau* (1760), that novel that our informant Johann Adam Bergk says 'dringt' 'in das Innere unsers Herzens'. In this extended title, the author is telling us that this is not really a novel but merely a collection of letters under his editorship, 'true', not 'fictitious'. The preface, with its appeal to the like-minded to flee the 'monde',[17] polite taste and society, and find refuge in solitude – in effect choosing its readership – and its avowal that these letters are expressing directly the feelings they invoke, thus homes in on the essentials that author and

---

15   *Liebe als Passion. Zur Codierung von Intimität* [1982], suhrkamp taschenbuch wissenschaft 1124 (Frankfurt a. M., 1995), especially p. 130.

16   See especially Wilhelm Vosskamp, 'Dialogische Vergegenwärtigung beim Schreiben und Lesen. Zur Poetik des Briefromans im 18. Jahrhundert', *Deutsche Vierteljahrsschrift*, 45 (1971), 80–116; and Darnton, 'Readers respond to Rousseau' pp. 227–34 (on *La Nouvelle Héloïse*).

17   *Oeuvres Complètes*, ed. by Bernard Gagnebin and Marcel Raymond, 5 vols. (Paris, 1959–1995), Vol. 2, p. 21.

readers may share. And so readers of *La Nouvelle Héloïse* actually believed that the characters really existed, and corresponded directly with Rousseau, creating a dialogue between writer and recipient analogous to that between Julie and her lover Saint-Preux.[18] *La Nouvelle Héloïse* remains an extreme case. But a novel written much closer in time and space to *Werther,* Sophie von La Roche's *Geschichte des Fräuleins von Sternheim* (1771–72) (subtitle 'von einer Freundin derselben aus den Originalpapieren') indulges the fiction that the editor, instead of communicating letters in longhand, is now distributing them in print, to make more widely available the 'Nutzen' proper to 'Schriften von derjenigen Gattung, worunter Ihre Sternheim gehört'. Phrases from the preface like 'mein Herz erwärmte sich', 'Adel der Seele', 'dieses zärtliche, mitleidsvolle, wohltätige Herz', 'Stärke der Lebhaftigkeit',[19] demonstrate the claim to authenticity that Rousseau makes much more extravagantly. But the editor in this case is not the author: it is Christoph Martin Wieland, standing in as an intermediary instead of the unnamed Sophie von La Roche.

An irony of life enmeshed Goethe briefly in a relationship with Sophie's daughter Maximiliane, in 1772, just after the even more unfortunate episode in Wetzlar. She went on to become the mother of Clemens and Bettine Brentano, and he to become the author *of Die Leiden des jungen Werthers*. On the surface, the opening of Goethe's novel seems to conform to the same conventions as Maxe's mother's, with her *Fräulein von Sternheim*, or even of Rousseau's:

> Was ich von der Geschichte des armen Werthers nur habe auffinden können, habe ich mit Fleiß gesammlet, und leg es euch hier vor, und weis, daß ihr mir's danken werdet. Ihr könnt seinem Geist und seinem Charakter eure Bewunderung und Liebe, und seinem Schicksaale eure Thränen nicht versagen.
>
> Und du gute Seele, die du eben den Drang fühlst wie er, schöpfe Trost aus seinem Leiden, und laß das Büchlein deinen Freund seyn, wenn du aus Geschick oder eigner Schuld keinen nähern finden kannst.

---

18   Darnton, 'Readers respond to Rousseau', pp. 233, 244–49.
19   *Geschichte des Fräuleins von Sternheim*, ed. by Fritz Brüggemann, *Deutsche Literatur in Entwicklungsreihen, Reihe Aufklärung*, Vol. 14 (Leipzig, 1938), pp. 20f., 24.

We have here two things: the claim to authenticity by an unnamed and unidentified editor (unnamed, because the title page of 1774 has no author) collecting 'all he can' about the unhappy hero (most of which will be in the form of letters, but not all); and the appeal across the intervening divide directly to the reader: not any kind of reader, but he or she who can evince 'Bewunderung und Liebe' for what he was (his 'Geist' and 'Charakter') and who also can indulge the free expression of the emotions — in tears. Were it not for that word 'arm', one might think that this was taken from some exemplary 'Life' with religious connotations, some martyrology even; as it stands, it prepares us for extraordinary associations with religion later in the account. The letters thus refer to the past (what has happened) and to the present (the reaction of the reader). But the preface also narrows its readership down specifically to 'du gute Seele', the reader perhaps tempted to 'go and do likewise', who is not just sympathetic like 'ihr' but psychologically implicated. Let this book be your friend. I wish to return in a moment to this extraordinary formulation: 'laß das Büchlein deinen Freund seyn'.

Seen thus, Goethe's novel may be perceived as conforming to patterns of the epistolary novel as the eighteenth century conceived them: letters that are the nearest thing to conversation with an absent friend; the bridging of the gap in space and time (and circumstances); the claim of authenticity, the preface and (later on) the editorial intervention glossing the last letters that cannot stand without comment; the foreshortenings in time through selection, so that the period May 1771–December 1772 appears as a sequence different from 'real time'; the intertextuality between real letters and invented correspondence. I think that we can take most of these overlaps as read, but it is questionable whether the novel would have had the impact it did if it had merely conformed to readers' expectations.

Let me examine two of those assumptions. Take, for instance, the question of time. It has been claimed (rightly) that the novel extends from the lead-up to the longest night (16 June 1771) to the shortest day (24 December 1772), that the whole text is embedded in a system of time whereby tone and content of each episode correspond more or less exactly to the time of year.[20] Certainly, the second version of the novel,

---

20   See Wegmann, *Diskurse der Empfindsamkeit*, pp. 92–96.

of 1787, underlines this with the interpolated section 'Wie die Natur sich zum Herbste neigt, wird es Herbst in mir und um mich her' (4 September). From the perspective of 1774, however, these events seem recent, up-to-date, 'hot off the press'. But I would maintain that the rhythm of the novel is in fact different. Part One has, as I already mentioned, that extraordinary trajectory from May 1771 (with its climactic passage of nature and love) to August 1771 (that talks of 'das All der Natur' , but not, as on May 10, of its cycle) to the night of 10 September, that should be the approach of autumn but instead is the great sentimental passage inspired by Klopstock's poem *Die Sommernacht* and is the climax of the first part – and, in Werther's decision to leave, its moral triumph. With that, in Part Two and the descent into despair and mental aberration, the winter is almost forgotten as the account of Werther's unsuccessful re-integration into society takes over. May 1772, by contrast, is the scene of forlorn hopes, while 3 November still mentions 'diese herrliche Natur' of which he no longer feels a part. November and December do bring us the mad clerk and the flood in Wahlheim, but the latter is also a preparation for the Ossian passage, as are Werther's nocturnal wanderings. 'So traure denn, Natur', written on 24 December, 'dein Sohn, dein Freund, dein Geliebter naht sich seinem Ende', recalling as it does a union with nature, contrasts precisely with the horrors of the November and December days when nature shows its unfriendliest aspect. The great set pieces framed in nature are in fact against all nature or they manipulate nature, in that they superimpose poetic surrogates (Klopstock twice, for instance) or states of mind ('pantheism', 'All der Natur' and its obverse side). In other words, Goethe is subverting any claim to chronological authenticity by allowing Werther to interpret the course of time as he ordains it — even out of time and (so he believes) into eternity. The novel thus essentially takes place in private time that is dated 1771–72.

The question of the alleged intertextuality between real letters and fiction, or, we might say, the congruity between the personality of the writer and the letter of feeling, the sentimental letter and its formal articulation, is in Goethe's case much more difficult to address and is perhaps ultimately insoluble. Klopstock's letters, collected and published during his lifetime, would demonstrate the link between sentiments expressed in notes to friends and their later formulation in poetry. For contemporary readers, this would augment the 'authenticity' of the poetry. In 1774, Goethe's letters were not yet being collected in that way, but they soon would be. Any attempt to establish intertextuality must therefore be post factum, posthumous even. Forty years ago, Albrecht Schöne established such a parallel, between Goethe's letters to his friend Behrisch in 1767, and certain formulations in *Werther*.[21] He proves conclusively that the 'confessional' style of letter simulating a correspondence with the absent friend and 'communicating' straight on to the page, can also be found in the novel. It is a useful corrective for modern readers who might claim that the often disjointed and over-wrought letters of this novel, with their unfinished periods, exclamations and dashes, their lack of reflective distance, are 'artificial' constructs, Goethe's manipulation for artistic purposes of the sentimental culture, 'Empfindsamkeit', that for a brief period was his second nature. But Schöne has not, in my view, been able to show any link between Goethe's real letters and the great 'set pieces' that are enshrined in Johann Adam Bergk's book as models of the sublime. Nor indeed are there any to be found, except perhaps this:

> Der unglückliche Jerusalem. Die Nachricht war mir schröcklich und unerwartet, es war grässlich zum angenehmsten Geschenck der Liebe diese Nachricht zur Bey-lage. Der unglückliche. Aber die Teufel, welches sind die schändlichen Menschen die nichts geniessen denn Spreu der Eitelkeit, und Götzen Lust in ihrem Herzen haben, und Götzendie[n]st predigen, und hemmen gute Natur, und übertreiben und verderben die Kräffte sind schuld an diesem Unglück an unserm Unglück hohle sie der Teufel ihr Bruder. Wenn der verfluchte Pfaff sein Vater nicht schuld ist so ver-zeih mirs Gott dass ich ihm Wünsche er möge den Hals brechen wie Eli. Der arme iunge! wenn ich zurückkam vom Spaziergang und er mir begegnete hinaus im Mondschein, sagt ich er ist verliebt. Lotte muss sich noch erinnern dass ich drüber lächelte. Gott weis die Einsamkeit hat sein Herz untergraben, und – seit sieben Jahren kenn ich die Gestalt, ich habe wenig mit ihm geredt, bey meiner Abreise nahm ich ihm ein Buch mit das will ich behalten und sein Gedencken so lang ich lebe.[22]

It is, of course, Goethe's letter of early November 1772 to Johann Christian Kestner in Wetzlar. Kestner had reported in extensive and

21 'Über Goethes Brief an Behrisch vom 10. November 1767', *Festschrift für Richard Alewyn*, ed. by Herbert Singer and Benno von Wiese (Cologne, Graz, 1967), pp. 192–229.

22 *Der junge Goethe*. New edition in 5 vols, ed. by Hanna Fischer-Lamberg (Berlin, 1963–74), Vol. 3, p. 7.

almost forensic detail the circumstances of the death of their common acquaintance, Karl Wilhelm Jerusalem. Goethe, as we know, was to use material from that letter for the final pages of his novel. The 'intertextuality' between this letter and the novel could not be pursued in its day: the letter remained in the Kestner family and was not published until 1854 when all those involved in the 'real' circumstances of the novel were dead and gone. This letter, shorn of its beginning and its ending, remains an autograph. Where the author of *Werther* makes his own creation into a stylist who favours 'Inversionen' (24 December) and the periodic style in general, there is none of this in Goethe's own letter — and what bad grammar ('welches' as the relative after 'Teufel') and spelling and punctuation. We note that short broken statements ('Der unglückliche Jerusalem', 'Der unglückliche', 'Der arme iunge!') alternate with the period that arches over and takes in 'geniessen ', 'haben', 'predigen', 'hemmen', 'übertreiben' and 'verderben' before it unloads itself in the imprecation 'hohle sie der Teufel'. Notice the 'wenn' clauses, here a conditional followed by a temporal, something Werther does with far greater refinement. The biblical comparison (Jerusalem senior as Eli) and echoes ('Spreu der Eitelkeit', 'Götzen Lust in ihrem Herzen'), the immediacy of the response and the concern for Jerusalem's 'Gedencken', remembrance or even memorialisation, the sentimental association (wandering in the moonlight) remind us of *Werther* in tone and content, although the gap between actual reality and fiction has yet to be bridged. Above all, that phrase, 'Gott weis die Einsamkeit hat sein Herz untergraben', a reaction to what Kestner actually tells him and what he, Goethe, can bear out from memory, is a formulation found in other letters of Goethe from the period and, most famously, three times in the novel.[23] We know it especially from that letter of 18 August that begins 'Mir untergräbt das Herz die verzehrende Kraft, die im All der Natur verborgen liegt'. Thus both this letter and the novel have the destructive verb 'untergraben' in common. In the novel it is the spectacle of nature that kills all that Werther stands for, 'Herz' referring metonymically to 'self', 'body and soul'. The letter to Kestner sees the destructive force differently, attributing it to solitude, the avoidance of human society, the turning in on the inward self, the absence of friends.

23   1 July, 18 August, and 'Der Herausgeber an den Leser'.

There would be much that needs to be said about the relationship of fact and fiction in this novel, relating to the use by Goethe of material dealing with Jerusalem's suicide. I have set out my views elsewhere.[24] These are issues of tact, decorum, taste, and propriety. On balance, I would say: who are we to censure young genius? But you may think differently. The real point is that letters – Kestner to Goethe and Goethe to Kestner – generate further letters and then a novel in letters, which in its turn produces more letters about the alleged correspondence between events communicated in letters and the mental and physical processes set out in the novel. At the novel's publication, pens are put to paper that stress its proximity to real life and reduce it to a *roman à clé*. Goethe, aware of what he had unintentionally set in train, reacted angrily. Johann Georg Zimmermann, the author of the much-read *Von der Einsamkeit* (1773) , writing to Johann Caspar Lavater and setting out all the alleged parallels between 'real' events and the novel, ends his letter thus: 'Aber von diesem allem mußt du jedoch an *Göthe* nichts wieder sagen, damit er nicht Lust bekomme mich wie ein Löwe zerreißen zu wollen'.[25] The eighteenth-century cult of letters and the epistolary novel do not in this special case simply overlap and complement each other, and the essential parts of the novel will not respond to this kind of approach.

Still, perhaps there is a real link between that letter of Goethe's and the novel, one that extends beyond echoes and reminiscences: 'die Einsamkeit hat sein Herz untergraben'. The theme of solitude is one that runs through eighteenth-century literature and culture. The phrase 'lonely wisdom' is attributed to Dr Johnson:[26] we may revive our spirits and regain inner composure by being alone – with nature, with ourselves. All are, however, agreed that the one-sided avoidance of human society is unbalanced and as such conducive to melancholy, their shorthand for depressive states of mind. (Contemporaries commenting on Jerusalem's

---

24 *Die Leiden des jungen Werthers*, ed. by Roger Paulin (London, 1993), pp. xi–xv; Roger Paulin, *Der Fall Wilhelm Jerusalem. Zum Selbstmordproblem zwischen Aufklärung und Empfindsamkeit*, Kleine Schriften zur Aufklärung 6 (Göttingen, 1999), pp. 30–35.

25 *Der junge Goethe im zeitgenössischen Urteil*, ed. and with an introduction by Peter Müller, Deutsche Bibliothek 11 (Berlin, 1969), p. 208.

26 Quoted appropriately, if not necessarily accurately, in *Solitude, Written by J.G. Zimmermann* [...] (London, 1800), p. ix.

suicide used this argument.) It is, of course, a theme in *Werther*, but so
again is society, company. If only Werther could have Lotte's company,
presence, in the fullest sense, all would be well (perhaps). His madness
is revealed in the belief that he may have her company – 'in ewigen
Umarmungen' – in heaven, to which his voluntary death will be the
portal.

Above all, at some stage, we do not know when, Goethe decided
to make a radical break with the epistolary novel in the style of Rousseau
or even Sophie von La Roche. There, the letters are multi-perspectival;
they are exchanges between several correspondents and thus contribute
to that evocation of so-called 'authenticity' by which the century laid so
much store. Goethe breaks with this and prints only Werther's letters,
then at the end abandoning the epistolary framework altogether to
engage the reader in a dialogue with the 'editor' of Werther's papers
and of material relating to him ('mit Fleiß gesammlet'). I mentioned
before that this editor envisages two kinds of reader: those (pl.) capable
of 'Bewunderung', 'Liebe' and 'Thränen', and 'du gute Seele' (s.), the
individual who may empathise with Werther and feel drawn as he
was. 'laß das Büchlein deinen Freund seyn [...] wenn du [...] keinen
nähern finden kannst'. What does this mean? I think it is saying: read my
book, take it to heart, let it be your friend, but a real friend would be
better; only if your own misfortune ('Geschick') or your own choice
or behaviour ('Schuld') prevent you from having the 'real thing'. For
surely it is no coincidence that this admonition to 'du gute Seele' is
immediately followed by the first letter, of 4 May 1771.

Like all but a significant few at the end of the novel, this first letter
is addressed to Werther's friend, later identified by the name of Wilhelm.
If you read the novel carefully, you notice that a majority of these letters
contain a direct address to this absent friend, to whom he refers successively as 'Bester Freund', 'mein Freund', 'mein Schaz', 'mein Bester',
'Bruder', 'Lieber!', and their variants, all terms of endearment, in
increasing rhetorical intensity, ending with 'mein Theuerster'. In fact, so
many of the letters, especially in Part One, are an engagement with the
absent friend, a communication, a meeting of souls: 'Du fragst', 'Wenn
du fragst', 'Du kennst von Alters her meine Art', 'Ich schrieb Dir
neulich', 'ich weis, was du mir hierauf sagen möchtest', 'Unter uns',
'Du wirst mir also nicht übel nehmen', and one could go on. In this
way, we can almost reconstruct Wilhelm's responses, we can hear him

telling Werther to calm down, to see reason, to take hold of himself, to stop talking nonsense. Wilhelm is the absent voice of good sense, of moderation, of balance, but he is absent. Their correspondence begins with 'Dich zu verlassen' and it ends effectively in Part Two with (20 December) 'Auch ist mir's sehr lieb, daß Du kommen willst, mich abzuholen, verzieh nur noch vierzehn Tage' ('give me a fortnight's grace'; four days later, Werther is dead).

Whatever the reason for Werther's leaving home, his first letter (4 May) begins with 'Dich zu verlassen, den ich so liebe, von dem ich unzertrennlich war' and the resolution to put the past behind him ('Die arme Leonore!') and live for the present. Three paragraphs into the letter. and into the novel, we read 'Die Einsamkeit ist meinem Herzen köstlicher Balsam in dieser paradisischen Gegend, und diese Jahrszeit der Jugend wärmt mit aller Fülle mein schauderndes Herz'. It leads over to the passage with the garden, which we can identify as an English park landscape designed by one who, significantly, 'sein selbst hier genießen wollte'. Gardens in the novel are not places for company. If at all, we find Werther alienating himself from the company (1 July) or being left alone by it ('und es verschwand' 10 September). Thus garden and nature (one and the same thing, for the experience of 10 May takes place here) are places associated with retreat from society, 'Heiterkeit' (peace of mind) and the suspension of time. They become identified right at the beginning with states that are outside human expression and human calculation ('unausssprechliche Schönheit', 'ich erliege unter der Gewalt der Herrlichkeit dieser Erscheinungen', 'paradisisch'), all unqualified, all incapable of further articulation. Thus the absent friend, solitude, and extreme exaltation of mind and senses are the accompaniment of these opening letters. Indeed the letter of 10 May ends with 'Mein Freund' (twice), not with the address to some higher being as one might expect. It is as if he were wishing his friend were there to share his experience, or as if he could communicate to his closest and most intimate associate 'die Gegenwart des Allmächtigen'. I find it therefore interesting and significant that all of the great set-piece letters (including those quoted by Bergk), the ball scene, the scene at the vicarage (1 July), the conversation with Albert on suicide, the nature vision of 18 August, and the leave-taking (10 September) are accompanied by the address to Wilhelm, the last even with 'O daß ich nicht an Deinen Hals fliegen, Dir mit tausend Thränen und Entzükkungen ausdrükken kann, mein Bester, all die Empfindungen, die mein Herz bestürmen'. In Part One there is only one address or apostrophe that is not directed to Wilhelm, and that is to 'Edler!' (16 June), who is, of course, Klopstock, an authority even higher than friendship, 'der heilige Sänger', as his contemporaries called him. As Werther's state of mind deteriorates in Part Two, we notice significant appeals and direct addresses over the head and authority of Wilhelm to God Himself. They are part of Werther's identification with the Son of God that leads to the blasphemous and monstrous connotations of his 'sacrifice'. It is Werther's use of the words of Christ in his passion, 'Mein Gott! Mein Gott! warum hast du mich verlassen?', leading over (but reversing the sequence of Christ's words in the passion account) to 'den kalten schröcklichen Kelch' with similar echoes. As the addresses to his friend become uncertain, then sporadic, then die away altogether, Werther becomes the self-appointed son of God or his priest (the theology is at best confused and at worst perilous) extending his benediction to Wilhelm and then to Albert ('Und so wohne Gottes Seegen über dir'). He thrusts aside the intermediary function of the friend and spurns the offer by an alarmed Lotte of 'die Seligkeit einer wahren Freundschaft'. He no longer writes about Lotte; he writes spontaneously and directly to her, without intermediary and without inhibition, dropping formal modes of address (she has always been 'Sie'; now in those last terrible letters she is 'du'). The last letter ('nach eilfe') has him alone, 'still', 'ruhig', 'So sey's denn'. It is the end of the line that can be traced from 'weg' and 'verlassen' and 'die Einsamkeit ist meinem Herzen köstlicher Balsam'. 'Gott weis die Einsamkeit hat sein Herz untergraben'. Goethe's capacity to comprehend the mind of his hero has involved him in techniques of characterisation rarely, if ever, displayed in the European novel hitherto and certainly never employed by him again. It was the figure of Werther himself who ensured that this novel became a landmark of German literature, the first German novel of European stature and the harbinger of a new era in German letters.

RITCHIE ROBERTSON

Goethe, *Wilhelm Meisters Lehrjahre*

Goethe's *Wilhelm Meister* project, like *Faust*, accompanied him through much of his life. It originated as *Wilhelm Meisters theatralische Sendung*, written between 1777 and 1785, and lost until the discovery of the manuscript in 1910. Goethe returned to it, using it as the core of the *Lehrjahre*, in the early 1790s, and published *Wilhelm Meisters Lehrjahre* in 1795–96. Some differences between the *Sendung* and the *Lehrjahre* spring to the eye. The *Sendung* has much more obvious realism. For example, the domestic life of the Meister family is more fully portrayed than in the later text, with a painful depiction of the failed marriage between Wilhelm's parents. The misadventures of Madame de Retti's struggling theatrical troupe are reported in lively detail with knockabout comedy, representing a Fielding-like excursion into low life which was excised from the *Lehrjahre* for the sake of decorum. The action of the *Sendung* can be approximately dated, beginning in the 1740s, whereas in the *Lehrjahre* time is blurred: the actors on their travels are afraid of enemy troops, a surviving reference to the Seven Years' War;[1] Lothario has served on the American side in their War of Independence; yet at the end the 'Turm-Gesellschaft' is contemplating investing its money in various countries for fear of a 'Staatsrevolution', an allusion to the French Revolution (p. 945). The 'Turm-Gesellschaft' itself is an addition with no precedent in the *Sendung*; it turns out to have been watching over Wilhelm's development throughout the *Lehrjahre*, admits him to its community by an initiation ceremony, and prompts debates about fate, chance, and providence which are at most implicit in the *Sendung*.

1   Johann Wolfgang Goethe, *Sämtliche Werke: Briefe, Tagebücher und Gespräche*, Deutsche Klassiker-Ausgabe, 40 vols (Frankfurt a. M., 1986–2000), Vol. 9, p. 582. Future references are to this edition by page number only.

The *Lehrjahre*, then, move away from surface realism in order to address larger issues.[2] Prominent among these are questions about the pattern underlying an individual's life, and about how far an individual can shape his own development. The centrality of this issue justifies calling the *Lehrjahre* a *Bildungsroman*, even though the term was not used by Goethe, occurs only occasionally in his time, and owes its currency to the philosopher and critic Wilhelm Dilthey.[3] Long before the term was current, the *Lehrjahre* provided a model for emulation and criticism by subsequent novelists, particularly the Romantics, and may therefore qualify as a pre-eminent landmark in German fiction.[4]

The question of shaping one's own life is raised in a famous but problematic letter that Wilhelm writes to his friend Werner at a pivotal point in the text.[5] The *Sendung* ended with Wilhelm's decision, despite misgivings, to join the theatrical troupe run by 'Serlo' (based on the well-known actor-manager Friedrich Ludwig Schröder of Hamburg). In the *Lehrjahre*, Wilhelm is still trying to make up his mind when he receives a letter from Werner describing in glowing terms the life of a small-town businessman, yet unwittingly revealing how cramped, ungenerous and philistine such a life is. Wilhelm replies by disclaiming any aptitude or inclination for business. Instead of accepting such a narrow life, he says, he has always wanted to develop himself as a rounded personality – 'mich selbst, ganz wie ich da bin, auszubilden' (p. 657). But Wilhelm's conception of rounded self-development proves to be rather strange. It does not mean cultivating a wide range of interests and becoming a Renaissance man. Rather, it centres on public self-presentation, on acquiring a graceful manner, a dignified comportment,

2   The last book of the cycle, *Wilhelm Meisters Wanderjahre oder die Entsagenden* (published in 1821 and in an enlarged form in 1828), moves from realism towards the depiction of an ideal, utopian community, and has exerted some influence on later German fiction, notably on Stifter's *Der Nachsommer* and perhaps also on Hesse's *Das Glasperlenspiel*.

3   'Ich möchte die Romane, welche die Schule des Wilhelm Meister ausmachen (denn Rousseaus verwandte Kunstform wirkte auf sie nicht fort), Bildungsromane nennen.' Wilhelm Dilthey, *Das Leben Schleiermachers* (1870), quoted in Rolf Selbmann, *Der deutsche Bildungsroman* (Stuttgart, 1984), p. 18.

4   See Jürgen Jacobs, *Wilhelm Meister und seine Brüder* (Munich, 1972); A. Phelan, 'What *Wilhelm Meister* did next', *PEGS*, 75 (2006), 109–24.

5   For a detailed commentary on this letter, see Dieter Borchmeyer, *Höfische Gesellschaft und französische Revolution bei Goethe* (Kronberg/Ts., 1977).

an unshakable self-control, and a sonorous voice, all of which Wilhelm sums up in the word 'Persönlichkeit'. Only a nobleman can acquire personality in this sense, because his life is public, whereas a middle-class person can do good, can even cultivate his mind, but, because he is confined to private life, must always be unimpressive, even ridiculous, in his social manner. He cannot cultivate both his mind and his body, his inward and his outward selves, to achieve what Wilhelm calls '[harmonische] Ausbildung meiner Natur' (p. 659). The only way to do so is by going on the stage and training oneself in graceful manners.

How are we to interpret this letter? One might be tempted to regard it as mere snobbery, and as supporting Friedrich von Hardenberg's dismissal of the whole novel as an exercise in social climbing: 'Wilhelm Meisters Lehrjahre, oder die Wallfahrt nach dem Adelsdiplom'.[6] Or one might argue that the previous episode in which Wilhelm and the actors stay at the Count's castle has already shown the aristocracy in a negative light, and that the letter therefore must ironically illustrate how misguided Wilhelm's ideals are and how little he can learn from experience.[7] However, while the Count and his associates are certainly shown as trivial-minded, they receive a visit from a very different kind of aristocrat, a royal Prince who has a cultivated literary taste (shown in his appreciation of Racine) and perfect manners, in contrast to the egotism with which Wilhelm inflicts a boring monologue on him (p. 538). And Wilhelm's experiences really do improve his outward appearance and manner. Werner, visiting him late in the novel, 'behauptete, sein Freund sei größer, stärker, gerader, in seinem Wesen gebildeter und in seinem Betragen angenehmer geworden' (p. 877). His attraction to a different way of being may remind us of Proust's admiring analysis of the bodily comportment of aristocrats such as Saint-Loup, in whom the narrator discerns 'a personality more generalised than his own, that of the "nobleman," which like an indwelling spirit moved his limbs, ordered his gestures and his actions'.[8]

6   Novalis, *Werke und Briefe*, ed. by Alfred Kelletat (Munich, 1968), p. 466.
7   Ironic readings of this letter, and of Wilhelm's progress in general, are convincingly rebutted in Michael Beddow, *The Fiction of Humanity: Studies in the Bildungsroman from Wieland to Thomas Mann* (Cambridge, 1982), pp. 72, 108, 296–7.
8   Marcel Proust, *Remembrance of Things Past*, transl. by C.K. Scott-Moncrieff and Terence Kilmartin, 3 vols (London, 1983), Vol. 1, p. 791.

Besides expressing aspirations which are not necessarily absurd or contemptible, Wilhelm's letter supports the novel's bleak account of late eighteenth-century German society. Middle-class life is shown as increasingly narrow. Its fate is symbolised by that of the collection of paintings and sculptures brought back from Italy by Wilhelm's grandfather; after his death, Wilhelm's father sold the collection in order to invest the proceeds in a joint business venture with Werner's father, and now lives in an ostentatious style from which nobody derives any enjoyment (p. 392). Young Werner, who marries Wilhelm's sister, thinks it absurd to value mere works of art ('eine Anzahl unscheinbarer Kunstwerke', p. 654) which represent merely dead capital, and is devoted to accumulating money for its own sake. The culture of the aristocrats whom we meet in Book III is (apart from the Prince) scarcely wider. Their interest in the theatre is superficial; they accommodate the actors only in a tumble-down outbuilding; having displayed the actors to the Prince, they promptly show him their dogs and horses; and they amuse themselves with surreptitious sexual intrigues. The theatre as an institution receives equally unsparing treatment. Even during his youthful enthusiasm for the stage, Wilhelm notices how the actors are interested not in the poetic merit of a play but only in how large an audience it will attract and how long it will run for (p. 412). When he leaves Serlo's troupe, he is unaware that Serlo and his associate Melina are planning to increase their takings, at the expense of artistic standards, by putting on operas instead of plays (pp. 720–21). Since actual social conditions in Germany mean that aspirations such as Wilhelm's must be frustrated, Books VII and VIII, where Wilhelm meets and joins the 'Turm-Gesellschaft', move from a relatively realistic mode to a utopian one. Lothario's castle, the centre of the Society, represents the union of middle-class and upper-class endeavours, as is underlined by the three cross-class marriages with which the novel ends. A clinching piece of symbolism is that Wilhelm finds in Lothario's castle his grandfather's art collection, itself the relic of a period when members of the middle class could display the cultivated taste that is expected (though, as the novel has shown, rarely found) among the aristocracy.

The intervention of the 'Turm-Gesellschaft' in Wilhelm's life casts a further ironic light on his letter to Wilhelm. For in that letter he expressed the ambition to plan his own life by becoming an actor. The extent to which one can plan one's own life is among the key issues of the novel, and Wilhelm's ability to do so has already been disproved by a series of blunders, some of which he could not have avoided. During his passionate affair with the actress Mariane in Book I, he cannot know that she also has a relationship with a businessman called Norberg who is away on a journey, until he happens to pick up a note from Norberg announcing his return (p. 427). But if he had given way less impulsively to grief, he might have learnt that Mariane truly loves him, is already pregnant with his child, and wants to break with Norberg. Instead, Wilhelm learns all this from Mariane's attendant Barbara long after Mariane's miserable death (p. 850). Nor is this all the harm he has unwittingly done. While at the Count's castle, he was drawn into the atmosphere of sexual intrigue so far as to embrace the Countess passionately, and to play a trick in which, to surprise her, he put on the Count's clothes and sat at his dressing-table; the Count, arriving unexpectedly, thought he was seeing his own double. Long afterwards Wilhelm finds out that in embracing the Countess he inadvertently pressed a jewelled picture of the Count against her bosom, and that, though the mark soon vanished, the Countess (feeling guilty for desiring Wilhelm) persuaded herself that there was a cancerous lump there. Her resulting depression matched that of her husband, who imagined that the sight of his double was a portent of imminent death. Both are expected to join the Moravian Brethren and bequeath that sect the property which would otherwise have passed to their relatives (pp. 718–19). To make matters worse, Wilhelm discovers that his part in these misfortunes is known to Lothario, who is the Countess's brother – the same Lothario whom Wilhelm intended to rebuke for his unfaithfulness to Aurelie, Serlo's sister. The child Felix, whom Wilhelm has supposed to be Lothario's son by Aurelie, turns out to be his own by Mariane. By comparison, Wilhelm's other mistakes are harmless. As we have seen, he misjudges the theatre and the aristocracy. He thinks he has a talent for acting, when, as Jarno tells him, he can only play himself (p. 931). Generally, he is self-centred, imperceptive, and socially clumsy. On first meeting Aurelie, he delivers a long didactic disquisition on the meaning of *Hamlet* ('nach seiner Art weitläufig und lehrreich', p. 607), which understandably provokes Aurelie to say that, however eloquently he interprets Shakespeare, confronted with people he is as bewildered as a child with a set of toy animals (p. 621). And even near the end of the novel he nearly marries Therese, on the inappropriately rational grounds that she is impressively efficient, although Therese is much better suited as a partner for Lothario and Wilhelm fortunately ends up better matched with Lothario's sister Natalie.

Wilhelm's faults and errors, however, do not reduce the concerns of the 'Turm-Gesellschaft' for him. It sends emissaries to draw him into significant conversations about fate and chance (pp. 423–24, 473–76), to play the Ghost in Serlo's production of *Hamlet*, and to warn him, immediately afterwards, to flee the theatre. When he reaches Lothario's castle, he meets many people who have crossed his path and who turn out to be related. Lothario is the brother not only of the unfortunate Countess, but of Natalie, the 'schöne Amazone' (beautiful horsewoman) who has haunted Wilhelm's imagination since his first glimpse of her (p. 589), and of Friedrich, the harum-scarum lover of the actress Philine. All are cousins of the unnamed 'schöne Seele' whose memoirs form Book VI of the novel, and a friend of their recently deceased uncle, the Abbé, is the prime mover of the 'Gesellschaft'. Just as he is, to quote Voltaire, 'that mixed Being (not to be defin'd) who is neither of the clergy nor of the laity' in a word, the thing called Abbé in France',[9] so the 'Gesellschaft' is not religious but not quite secular either. Its conduct and ceremonies are loosely modelled on those of Freemasonry. In the Enlightenment, Masonic lodges provided an important forum for the free discussion of progressive ideas.[10] Goethe joined the Freemasons in 1780 and reached the grade of Master in 1782.[11] The novel treats the Masonic apparatus with some irony. The 'Gesellschaft' admits new members by an initiation ceremony, reading them a 'Lehrbrief' to show that they have completed their apprenticeship and are now able to live. Members write down their life-stories, which are called 'confessions'; and stored in an archive.

---

9   *Letters concerning the English Nation*, ed. by Nicholas Cronk, 2nd ed. (Oxford, 2005), p. 28. On the fluid identity of Goethe's Abbé, see Nicholas Boyle, *Goethe: The Poet and the Age*, Vol. 2: *Revolution and Renunciation, 1790–1803* (Oxford, 2000), p. 377.

10 See James Van Horn Melton, *The Rise of the Public in Enlightenment Europe* (Cambridge, 2001), pp. 252–72, with extensive references.

11 On the relation between Freemasonry and the *Lehrjahre*, see Hans-Jürgen Schings, '*Wilhelm Meister* und das Erbe der Illuminaten', in Walter Müller-Seidel and Wolfgang Riedel (eds), *Die Weimarer Klassik und ihre Geheimbünde* (Würzburg, 2002), pp. 177–203.

The principles underlying the activities of the 'Gesellschaft', however, are more serious. According to the Abbé's educational philosophy, one should not preserve young people from making mistakes, for it is only through making mistakes that they will learn. In his initiation ceremony he is told: 'Du wirst keine deiner Torheiten bereuen und keine zurück wünschen, kein glücklicheres Schicksal kann einem Menschen werden' (pp. 873–74). Not all the members of the 'Gesellschaft' agree with this philosophy. Jarno prefers to give people straight advice, while Natalie fears that by waiting for people's innate urges ('Triebe') to emerge, the Abbé has given insufficient direction to such frivolous people as her sister the Countess and her brother Friedrich (p. 901). But then, as Jarno also affirms, an ideal community should not be unanimous or homogeneous. People's diverse dispositions and talents must all be encouraged, so that the conflict among them will eventually produce harmony:

> Nur alle Menschen machen die Menschheit aus, nur alle Kräfte zusammengenommen die Welt. Diese sind unter sich oft im Widerstreit, und indem sie sich zu zerstören suchen, hält sie die Natur zusammen und bringt sie wieder hervor (pp. 932–3).

This conception of unity resting on productive conflicts corresponds closely to the model of human development proposed by Kant in *Idee zu einer allgemeinen Geschichte in weltbürgerlicher Absicht* (1784). Here Kant seeks an intelligible plan underlying the confusion of human history. As nature does nothing without a purpose, all the capacities implanted in humanity by nature must eventually be developed; not, however, in the life of the individual, but in that of the species. Human potential is developed through conflict, arising from the contradiction between man's desire for sociability and his desire for isolation. Without such conflict, humanity would have remained in a state of Arcadian lethargy. The goal of humanity is a justly regulated civil society permitting the maximum possible degree of freedom. Imagining such a goal, Kant introduces the concept of providence, saying that its attainment would represent the '*Rechtfertigung* der Natur – oder besser der *Vorsehung*'.[12] Providence is not a plan devised by God and

12   Immanuel Kant, *Werke*, ed. by Wilhelm Weischedel, 6 vols (Darmstadt, 1964), Vol. 6, p. 49.

imposed on humanity; it is a plan immanent in the natural constitution of humanity.

Applied to the story of Wilhelm, this concept of providentialism means that the 'Turm-Gesellschaft' only supervised his development, rather than directing it. Instead of making him conform to an external plan, it sought only to bring out the capacities already present in his character. In doing so, it relied on nature, a concept as prominent in the *Lehrjahre* as in Kant's essay. Having handed him his 'Lehrbrief', the Abbé declares: 'Heil Dir junger Mann! Deine Lehrjahre sind vorüber, die Natur hat Dich losgesprochen' (p. 876). A natural process has led Wilhelm to see through the limitations of the theatre, to become interested in the practical world, and, above all, to devote himself to Felix, who has been revealed as his child by Mariane. The self-centred notion of harmonious self-development formulated in his letter to Werner is quietly replaced by a concept of 'Bildung' through practical responsibilities. Accompanying Felix into Lothario's garden, and learning from the gardener about the names and uses of the plants, Wilhelm realises that he must learn in order to teach, and feels that his own 'Bildung' is just beginning (p. 877). The garden setting, where nature is cultivated, reinforces the narrator's summary of Wilhelm's development:

> Er sah die Welt nicht mehr wie ein Zugvogel an, ein Gebäude nicht mehr für eine geschwind zusammengestellte Laube, die vertrocknet, ehe man sie verläßt. Alles, was er anzulegen gedachte, sollte dem Knaben entgegen wachsen, und alles, was er herstellte, sollte eine Dauer auf einige Geschlechter haben. In diesem Sinne waren seine Lehrjahre geendigt, und mit dem Gefühl des Vaters hatte er auch alle Tugenden eines Bürgers erworben (p. 881).

The word 'Bürger' here implies 'citoyen', that is, somebody conscious of his civic duty within a larger unit. Wilhelm is a very different person from the narrow-minded Werner, who is concerned only with amassing money, or from the 'Bürger' earlier in the novel who, on seeing a young couple brought to court for eloping, thanks God that such events have either not occurred in their families or have not become known (p. 403). Although he confesses to Lothario that he has never thought about the state, Lothario hopes to make him a patriot and reveals his own plans for replacing the feudal structure of his estate with a system in which the peasants will share the profits. The utopian ending of the novel, like that of Schiller's *Wilhelm Tell* in which feudalism is likewise abolished, opens up possibilities of social reform without such violence as that of the French Revolution.

This providential scheme, however, may sound too smooth for the actual events of the *Lehrjahre*. For, as Kant admits in the same essay, the crooked timber of humanity cannot be made entirely straight: 'aus so krummem Holz, als woraus der Mensch gemacht ist, kann nichts ganz Gerades gezimmert werden' (Kant, Vol. 6, p. 41). Wilhelm is not an abstract subject of experience but an individual with his own complexities. In some respects he is a damaged person who needs to be healed. He comes in contact with areas of experience, represented by the mysterious figures of Mignon and the Harpist, that are alien to the 'Turm-Gesellschaft'. And what the Abbé mildly calls his follies ('Torheiten') have ruined the lives of three people — Mariane, the Count, and the Countess. These aspects of Wilhelm's life and character are expressed through a range of literary and mythic archetypes.

Wilhelm's psychic damage is suggested first by the narrative's insistent identification of him with the king's sick son depicted in one of his grandfather's paintings, which was Wilhelm's favourite painting in his boyhood: 'es stellte die Geschichte vor, wie der kranke Königssohn sich über die Braut seines Vaters in Liebe verzehrt' (p. 422). This story is much less familiar than Wilhelm here makes it sound. It comes from Plutarch's life of Demetrius, king of Macedonia (336–283 BC). Another king, Seleucus, marries Demetrius' daughter Stratonice. Seleucus already has a son, Antiochus, by a previous marriage. Antiochus falls passionately in love with the young queen Stratonice, and resolves to starve himself to death. His physician realises the cause of his sickness and persuades Antiochus by a trick to divorce Stratonice and allow Antiochus to marry her.[13] This sounds like a classical Oedipal constellation, in which the son is the sexual rival of the father, except that instead of attacking the father, the son transfers his aggression to himself.[14] Although Meister senior appeared in the *Sendung* as a harsh and intimidating man, he appears only indirectly in the *Lehrjahre,* and little is disclosed about his character. We learn that he disapproves of Wilhelm's

13 *Plutarch's Lives*, trans. by John Dryden, 3 vols (London, 1910), Vol. 3, pp. 255–6.
14 See David Roberts, *The Indirections of Desire: Hamlet in Goethe's Wilhelm Meister* (Heidelberg, 1980); Michael Minden, *The German Bildungsroman: Incest and Inheritance* (Cambridge, 1997), Ch. 1.

passion for the theatre and sends Wilhelm on a journey to find out about manufactures elsewhere in Germany; on this trip Wilhelm first falls in with actors, and satisfies his father by sending back fictitious reports. The puppet-theatre which first awakened Wilhelm's interest in the stage was given him by his father in the *Sendung*, but in the *Lehrjahre* by his mother, who is thus associated with his creative side (I 2). In the play enacted there, a tiny David overcame a huge Goliath and was rewarded with a beautiful princess – another Oedipal constellation.

Wilhelm's identification with a king's son is also a Freudian family romance in which Wilhelm imagines himself as the son of somebody much grander than his actual father.[15] While among the actors, he compares himself to Shakespeare's Prince Hal, who slums it among drunkards and whores in Eastcheap (p. 571). At the end of the novel (p. 992), Wilhelm is compared to the biblical figure of Saul, son of Kish, who went out to look for his father's strayed asses, and found himself being anointed king of Israel by the prophet Samuel (1 Samuel 9–10).

The most prominent archetype behind Wilhelm, however, is Shakespeare's Hamlet. Having been introduced to Shakespeare's works by Jarno, Wilhelm delivers an interpretation of Hamlet's character which was to influence a long series of Romantic critics.[16] For him, Hamlet is a damaged soul, thrown into depression by being denied the crown of Denmark and by his mother's remarriage. Curiously, Wilhelm does not think Hamlet regrets his father's death, but rather his loss of status in no longer being heir presumptive — in other words, the dissolution of the family romance which is so important to Wilhelm himself. Thus brought low, Hamlet is given a task, that of avenging his father, which is beyond his powers and casts him into gloom and bitterness (pp. 607–8). How far is this interpretation really a projection of Wilhelm's own character? He does seem to find in Hamlet, as in the king's sick son, his own propensity to punish himself for misfortunes. This propensity is clear from his reaction to Mariane's supposed infidelity, which brings on a breakdown lasting for months. Wilhelm takes his identification with Hamlet so far as to play this part in Serlo's production; the unknown person who plays the Ghost seems to speak in the voice of Wilhelm's

15   See Freud, 'Der Familienroman der Neurotiker' (1909), in *Studienausgabe*, ed. by Alexander Mitscherlich et al., 10 vols (Frankfurt a. M., 1970), Vol. 4, pp. 223–26.
16   See *The Romantics on Shakespeare*, ed. by Jonathan Bate (London, 1992).

father (p. 691). Playing Hamlet is thus a confrontation with paternal authority, except that the authority has passed from Wilhelm's father (whom he has long since disobeyed by joining the actors) to the 'Turm-Gesellschaft'.

A third model for Wilhelm is evoked early in the text when Wilhelm tells the sleepy Mariane about his youthful amateur dramatics. They included a dramatised version of Tasso's epic poem *Jerusalem Delivered (Gerusalemme Liberata)* — or would have done, if the absent-minded Wilhelm had remembered to write out parts for his actors. The poem had already taken hold of his imagination, particularly the character of Clorinda, the Saracen heroine who fights against the Crusaders in men's attire. He is moved especially by two episodes. In Book XII of Tasso's epic, Clorinda is unwittingly killed by her Christian lover Tancred in a combat at night. In Book XIII Tancred enters an enchanted forest and drives his word into a tree which then sheds blood and speaks, revealing that Clorinda is imprisoned within it. Although Wilhelm reports the voice from the tree is saying 'daß er auch hier Chlorinden verwunde, daß er vom Schicksal bestimmt sei, das, was er liebt, überall unwissend zu verletzen' (p. 378), the second, generalising clause is Wilhelm's addition, and it applies less to Tancred than to Wilhelm himself. He too seems destined to injure those whom he loves: first Mariane, then the Countess. Freud used this incident from Tasso to illustrate the 'Wiederholungszwang' (compulsion to repeat) that induces people to save psychic energy by re-enacting unpleasant experiences; but, as Catriona MacLeod points out, he seems to be 'reading Tasso via Goethe'.[17]

What especially appeals to Wilhelm about Clorinda is her 'Mann-weiblichkeit' (p. 378), her gender ambiguity. In this she anticipates the strange figure of Mignon, whom Wilhelm buys from the brutal manager of an acrobatic troupe for thirty Taler. At first he cannot tell whether Mignon is a girl or a boy; she is dressed in a waistcoat and trousers, and is referred to by the neuter words 'Kind' and 'Geschöpf' (pp. 443,

---

17   Catriona MacLeod, *Embodying Ambiguity: Androgyny and Aesthetics from Winckelmann to Keller* (Detroit, 1998), p. 89; see Freud, 'Jenseits des Lustprinzips', *Studienausgabe*, Vol. 3, p. 232. On Goethe's relation to Tasso, see Hans-Jürgen Schings, 'Wilhelm Meisters schöne Amazone', *Jahrbuch der Deutschen Schiller-Gesellschaft*, 29 (1985), 141–206.

444).[18] Her brown complexion and her broken German suggest an Italian origin, and she attends Mass every morning, but when asked who her father is she will only say 'Der große Teufel ist tot' (p. 451). The name she gives herself is masculine and has homosexual connotations: the pretty boys with whom Henri III of France surrounded himself were called his 'mignons'. She hints cryptically at her past in the song beginning 'Kennst du das Land? wo die Zitronen blühn', which we are told Wilhelm translates, presumably from Italian. It evokes a southern landscape, a Palladian mansion filled with marble statues, and a hazardous journey over the Alps. More sinisterly, the statues seem to gaze at the singer and to say: 'Was hat man dir, du armes Kind, getan?' (p. 503) The three stanzas are addressed successively to a lover, a protector, and a father: are they the same person? The poem sounds disturbingly like the utterance of an abused child, and conveys the need for love and security which makes a child vulnerable to abuse.

The three terms suggest also the complexity of Wilhelm's relation to Mignon. He protects her from violence and she serves him devotedly. But the defining moment in their relationship comes after an incident between Wilhelm and the carefree, promiscuous actress Philine. By caressing him in public, Philine has embarrassed him but also aroused his sexual passions (whose intensity was apparent in his love for Mariane). He heads for her bedroom, but is forestalled by the sudden arrival of Philine's lover Friedrich. His sexual frustration and jealousy are somewhat calmed by music, but his unease is reawakened by the need to decide whether to join the troupe of actors he has recently met. Mignon finds him in this troubled state; he caresses her ('Er spielte mit ihren Haaren und war freundlich', p. 497), and presently she quivers convulsively, utters a shriek, and collapses in his arms as though lifeless; she then trembles as though in agony, comes to life again, embraces him tightly, and bursts into a flood of tears, in which Wilhelm joins. To reassure her, he calls her his child, whereupon she responds: 'Mein Vater! [...] du willst mich nicht verlassen! willst mein Vater sein! — Ich bin dein Kind' (p. 498). The erotic undercurrents here are obvious: MacLeod calls it 'an orgasmic moment' (*Embodying Ambiguity*, p. 106), Roberts 'an orgasm of the heart' (*The Indirections of Desire*, p. 81).

18   On the gender ambiguity which pervades the *Lehrjahre*, see MacLeod, Ch. 2, and (more searchingly) Minden, Ch. 1.

Wilhelm becomes not only Mignon's protector but her surrogate father and, subliminally, her lover, and enjoys, we are told, pure and indescribable happiness ('des reinsten unbeschreiblichsten Glückes genoß', p. 499). His happiness may be 'pure' in the sense of unqualified, but Goethe has shown with great honesty how complex, and to that extent impure, its sources are. Not only has he anticipated Nietzsche and Freud in analysing what the former was to call 'the chemistry of emotions'[19]; he has also summed up a whole corpus of eighteenth-century domestic dramas by revealing the emotional brew that underlies such orgies of familial affection as the reunion between father and daughter at the end of Lenz's *Die Soldaten*.

Nor is this all. For Mignon's real father is present throughout this scene, on the other side of the door. He is the mild and venerable-looking Harpist who joins the actors and delights them by singing and playing. Much later, after Mignon's death, it emerges that she is the product of an incestuous union between Augustin, an Italian nobleman, and his sister Sperata. This story, presented as a manuscript given by Augustin's brother to the 'Turm-Gesellschaft', takes us into a Counter-Reformation atmosphere of priestly authority, visions, and miracles. Augustin entered a monastery and abandoned himself to religious ardours which the narrator rather drily calls 'Genuß einer heiligen Schwärmerei' (p. 962), alternating between ecstasy and depression.[20] Presently he seeks dispensation from his vows, claiming that the love of his neighbour Sperata has restored his peace; but when Sperata is revealed as his unacknowledged sister, Augustin transfers his 'Schwärmerei' from religion to love, claiming that she is his destined bride and that sibling incest is sanctioned by nature. Finally overcome by guilt, he returns to his monastery, while Sperata brings up the child, tormented by the conflict between her maternal affection and her guilt, assiduously nourished by her confessor, at having loved a monk.

19 'Chemie der [...] Empfindungen', *Menschliches, Allzumenschliches*, I, 1, in Nietzsche, *Werke*, ed. by Karl Schlechta (Munich, 1966), Vol. 1, p. 447.

20 On contemporary discussions of 'Schwärmerei', and its importance in this and similar novels, see Manfred Engel, 'Die Rehabilitation des Schwärmers. Theorie und Darstellung des Schwärmens in Spätaufklärung und früher Goethezeit', in Hans-Jürgen Schings (ed.), *Der ganze Mensch: Anthropologie und Literatur im 18. Jahrhundert* (Stuttgart and Weimar, 1994), pp. 469–98 (esp. p. 488 on the Harpist).

This extraordinary narrative evokes a world of unnatural emotional extremes which has left its mark on Augustin (the Harpist) and Mignon even after their escape. The Harpist is restored to sanity only by carrying a vial of poison with which he can commit suicide at any time. Mignon's helpless devotion to Wilhelm causes her to pine away when his attention is distracted by the 'Turm-Gesellschaft', and when Therese greets Wilhelm as her future husband, she utters a shriek and drops down dead. Their spiritual world is expressed in the Harpist's song ('Wer nie sein Brot mit Tränen aß') addressed to heavenly powers which cause man to incur guilt and then leave him to suffer (p. 491). These carefully unspecified powers may suggest the Greek gods who lead Oedipus into unwittingly committing incest (like Augustin) and then punish him. But they also suggest the difficult Christian doctrine that God gave man free will foreknowing that he would sin. The immanent teleology of nature appears in Goethe's novel as a surer guide than supposedly divine providence.

Mignon has, however, played an important part in Wilhelm's life by providing him with someone to love and care for, and, in their intense emotional scene, establishing a touchstone of genuine emotion. When Wilhelm embraces Therese after Mignon's death, his emotions do not reach this standard, implying that Therese is not right for him: 'in seinem Geiste war es öde und leer, nur die Bilder Mignons und Nataliens schwebten wie Schatten vor seiner Einbildungskraft' (p. 925). Natalie first appears after the troupe of actors have been attacked by robbers and Wilhelm, wounded in the fight, has been left for dead, accompanied only by Mignon and Philine. Wearing a man's coat, she strikes him as a 'schöne Amazone' (p. 589) of incomparable charm and dignity. That her party of travellers includes a surgeon, who attends to Wilhelm's wounds, reinforces the parallel with the story of the king's sick son Antiochus, who was healed through the artifice of a doctor. Wilhelm does not learn her identity, nor see her again, till he meets her in Lothario's castle, sitting under the picture of Antiochus (p. 892). After many complications, including the deaths of Mignon and the Harpist, a narrow escape from death by Felix, and his ill-judged engagement to Therese, Wilhelm falls into a state of nervous prostration, from which he is healed by Natalie: Therese, perceiving Wilhelm's attraction to Natalie, has promised to marry Lothario on condition that Natalie marries Wilhelm, and this solution – accompanied by Friedrich's engagement to

Philine – pleases everybody. Perplexingly, the implied equation of Natalie with Stratonice introduces a hint of incest and thus a parallel to Augustin's forbidden union with Sperata. Yet while in Augustin's gloomy Catholic world actual incest represented a rejection of society in favour of unmodified nature, the sunnier world of the 'Turm-Gesellschaft' acknowledges symbolically the natural tendency of sexual desires to overflow its boundaries and makes this tendency the foundation of a union sanctified by nature and society together, in which Wilhelm discovers in Natalie 'the ideal complement of his being, the feminine to his masculine, the moon to his sun'.[21]

Natalie would seem a crucial character in the novel. Yet she exists as an ideal rather than a person. As the fair Amazon, she belongs in a long series of cross-dressing women who appeal to Wilhelm, beginning with Tasso's Clorinda and including not only Mignon but Mariane, who dresses on stage as a young officer (p. 359), and Therese, who rides about her estate in male attire. Why is Wilhelm attracted to women in men's clothing? If all these women are approximations to his most suitable partner, Natalie, it may be that the 'masculine' aspect represented by men's clothing complements the 'feminine' aspect shown by Wilhelm's emotional volatility. Natalie's firmness of character, shown in ministering to the wounded Wilhelm, and Wilhelm's passionate sensibility, serve to complicate the simple antitheses between active, rational masculinity and passive, emotional femininity that were confidently asserted by such contemporaries as Wilhelm von Humboldt, who defines gender difference as follows: 'Alles Männliche zeigt mehr Selbstthätigkeit, alles Weibliche mehr leidende Empfänglichkeit.'[22]

While one might wish that Goethe had told Natalie's story as well as Wilhelm's, he has arguably come close to doing so by inserting into the novel, between Wilhelm's departure from Serlo's company and his arrival at Lothario's castle, a lengthy manuscript given to Wilhelm by a doctor who knows Lothario's family. The manuscript, which is the

21 Minden, op. cit., p. 45. On the sibling-incest motif in Goethe's works, and its connection with his own love for his sister Cornelia, see the chapter 'Goethes Geschwisterkomplex' in Otto Rank, *Das Inzest-Motiv in Dichtung und Sage*, 2nd, enlarged ed. (Leipzig and Vienna, 1926), pp. 476–94.

22 Wilhelm von Humboldt, 'Über den Geschlechtsunterschied und dessen Einfluß auf die organische Natur' (1794) in his *Werke*, ed. by Andreas Flitner and Klaus Giel, 5 vols (Stuttgart, 1960), Vol. 1, pp. 268–95 (p. 278).

autobiography/Lothario's and Natalie's aunt, is entitled 'Bekenntnisse einer schönen Seele'. A 'schöne Seele', in the language of Goethe's contemporaries, is a person who knows no conflict between duty and desire, but spontaneously and willingly does what is right, so that the harmony between morality and inclination renders the character beautiful.[23] Lothario affirms that Natalie is herself a beautiful soul who needs only to obey nature, the presiding deity of Goethe's novel: 'Unerreichbar wird immer die Handlungsweise bleiben, welche die Natur dieser schönen Seele vorgeschrieben hat' (p. 990). In reading the story of her aunt, therefore, we are reading a version of Natalie's own story. And the 'Bekenntnisse einer schönen Seele' are not only a rare example of a first-person female narrative written by a man (where the woman is not an extroverted quasi-male adventurer, like Defoe's Moll Flanders and Grimmelshausen's Courasche), but an exceptionally sensitive and accomplished piece of writing.

The unnamed 'schöne Seele' is modelled, as Goethe himself tells us in *Dichtung und Wahrheit*, on Susanna von Klettenberg (1723–74), a friend of Goethe's mother, a devout Pietist and 'Stiftsdame' (canoness: a member of a female religious community, a Protestant version of a convent).[24] Like Susanna, the 'schöne Seele' has poor health. At the age of eight she suffers the first of several haemorrhages. Her enforced inaction makes her meditative and initiates her religious experience, which consists not in self-examination but in cultivating a relationship with an invisible friend. In contrast to the futile and damaging self-obsession illustrated by the runaway monk Augustin, who contemplates the abyss of his 'hohles leeres Ich' (pp. 812–13), the religious experience of the 'schöne Seele' nurtures her emotional life. As an adult, she feels no need of the Pietist system of conversion, involving conviction of sin and fear of hell, to guide her to God and the good. Later, however, the confessions of a male friend make her sharply aware of her potential for sinfulness, which she overcomes by an intense attachment to the crucified Christ. Her inner faith enables her also to perceive God in nature.

---

23   See Schiller, 'Über Anmut und Würde' (1793), in *Sämtliche Werke*, ed. by Gerhard Fricke and Herbert G. Göpfert, 5 vols (Munich, 1958), Vol. 5, p. 468.

24   The key passages from *Dichtung und Wahrheit* are reproduced in the notes to the cited text of the *Lehrjahre*, and are quoted thence. On Susanna von Klettenberg's importance for Goethe, see Nicholas Boyle, *Goethe: The Poet and the Age*, Vol. 1: *The Poetry of Desire* (Oxford, 1991), pp. 75–6.

Religious language, ceremonies, and sermons cease to matter to her, since she has the essence of religion in her heart, not as an external commandment or law, but as an inner urge ('ein Trieb der mich leitet und mich immer recht führet', p. 793). The religious experience that began as friendship with an invisible being has been increasingly internalised and has become a second nature. While the life of the 'schöne Seele' does not contradict the novel's largely conservative view of women's role, her independence represents one among several valid ways of living.[25]

The outward life of the 'schöne Seele' has not been free from conflict. A strong, intelligent person, she was in childhood an insatiable reader, and so free from squeamishness that she enjoyed cutting up animals for cooking and would examine their intestines; her father called her his wayward son ('seinen mißratenen Sohn', p. 731). Disapproval of female learning frustrates her intellectual development, while the prospect of a trivial social life with her fiancé Narciss makes her feel suffocated. She therefore insists, defying her parents with masculine firmness ('mit männlichem Trotz', p. 750), on breaking off her engagement and on acting with complete freedom according to her convictions. In this she represents a counterpart to the Uncle with whom she has important discussions. A man of the Enlightenment who nevertheless respects her faith, he believes that most so-called evil results from people's not knowing how to achieve their goals, and thinks the most valuable qualities are decisiveness and consistency ('Entschiedenheit und Folge', p. 778). But neither her view nor his should be taken as the key to the novel. We may wonder how such strong characters negotiate their conflicts with other people. In withdrawing from marriage, the 'schöne Seele' did not withdraw from conflict; she does not tell us about her relations with other members of her 'Stift', but Goethe mentions that Susanna von Klettenberg got on badly with fellow-canonesses (p. 1451). She regrets the enlightened principles with the Uncle has followed in bringing up Lothario, Natalie, and their siblings. And the

---

25 I dissent from Barbara Becker-Cantarino's view that 'the deep structure of the novel eliminates her as a female role model, casting her as a barren, undomesticated and potentially castrating female': 'Goethe and gender' in *The Cambridge Companion to Goethe*, ed. by Lesley Sharpe (Cambridge, 2002), pp. 179–92 (p. 188).

Uncle's insistence on being clear about your goal and how to attain it is qualified by the whole course of the novel, which shows Wilhelm seeking a series of mistaken goals and attaining happiness by a combination of fortunate accidents and other people's generosity.

Although the 'Bekenntnisse einer schönen Seele' show that Goethe's utopia can accommodate the contemplative as well as the active life, the 'Turm-Gesellschaft' cannot be all-inclusive. It opposes morbid preoccupations with death and guilt by replacing the traditional motto 'Memento mori' with the more uplifting 'Gedenke zu leben!' (p. 920). The best penitence for misdeeds is practical action: thus Wilhelm cannot repair the wrong he has done to Mariane, but he can and does devote himself to rearing their child. The 'Turm-Gesellschaft' professes the 'religion of healthy-mindedness'[26] Instead of priests, it relies heavily on doctors, who, however, are unable to cure the psychic wounds inflicted on Mignon and the Harpist. Their fate, and that of Mariane, cast doubts on Goethe's utopia. Though more attractive than most, the 'Turm-Gesellschaft' shares the tendency of utopian schemes to amputate those parts of humanity's crooked timber that refuse to fit.

26   William James, *The Varieties of Religious Experience* ([1902] London, 1960), p. 92.

NICHOLAS BOYLE

Goethe, *Die Wahlverwandtschaften*

Die Wahlverwandtschaften[1] is set somewhere in south-central Germany, in a Protestant territory, probably Ansbach-Bayreuth, the homeland of Goethe's 'Urfreund' Carl Ludwig von Knebel, and in the early years of the nineteenth century, probably in 1806–7.[2] As in *Werther*, with which there are many more and less obvious similarities, the action stretches over a period of something under two years, from April in the first year to October in the second, and the novel is divided into two parts of which the second, as in *Werther*, retraces the trajectory of the first, but at

---

1   Page references are given to Volume 6 of the *Hamburger Ausgabe* (*HA*) ed. by Erich Trunz and Benno von Wiese (Munich, 1988).

2   I follow here the pioneer work of Stuart Atkins, '*Die Wahlverwandtschaften*: Novel of German Classicism' in Atkins, *Essays on Goethe*, ed. by Jane K. Brown and Thomas P. Saine (Columbia, SC, 1995), pp. 137–81, originally in *German Quarterly*, 53 (1980), 1, 1–45. Atkins recognises that the setting must be 'a Protestant region under Prussian suzerainty' (p. 139), since the reference to the size of the visiting guardsmen (*HA* 6, pp. 317f.) can only be intended to identify the Prussian origin of 'unsre höchsten Herrschaften' who have come to visit their 'Oheim' and stay 'auf dem weitläufigen Schlosse'. Franconia seems an obvious place to look for a model (because of its landscape, its formidable political and religious complexity, and its relative peacefulness during the campaigns of 1805–7 – this last factor rules out Weimar itself, which of course was anyway not 'under Prussian suzerainty'). Ansbach-Bayreuth was Prussian from 1791 until it was incorporated into Bavaria, Ansbach on 24 May 1806, Bayreuth in 1810. The visit of the royal couple is no doubt a fictional recombination of historical materials, but it is worth noting that both Friedrich Wilhelm III and Queen Luise had a relevant 'Oheim' (= uncle, or uncle by marriage, on the mother's side): for the King, Karl August of Weimar (the text does not require that the 'Schloss' is in the territory where the novel's action takes place, though before 1803 only courtesy could describe any of Karl August's residences as 'weitläufig'), and, for the Queen, the future Maximilian I of Bavaria, who lived in Ansbach from 1795 to 1799. I am particularly grateful to Peter F. Schwartz for drawing my attention to Atkins' dating of the events of the novel in 1806–7: for the conclusions I draw from this dating, which differ from those of Atkins, see below.

a higher level of intensity. It tells the story of Eduard – as the narrator chooses to call him – and Charlotte, who were once in love but forced to marry other partners who both subsequently died. Although they were both now free, Charlotte, thinking she was now too old to resume this bygone romance, had sought to interest Eduard in Ottilie, her niece. But Eduard would hear none of it and he and Charlotte were married.

So much for the pre-history. The novel starts shortly after this point. Eduard, a wealthy man of the lowest order of nobility, a baron, has decided that the newly-weds should retire to his country property. Here both set about improving the estates, though Eduard shows more flair in landscape gardening than his wife, who has an essentially tidy mind, which better expresses itself in sprucing up the graveyard of the village church than in Eduard's grand schemes. Eduard is already chafing under the constrictions of marriage, though he is hardly aware of it, and suggests that his childhood friend, regularly referred to as 'der Hauptmann', should come and join them, since he is now unemployed, probably after the reorganisation of the Empire in 1803,[3] when many smaller Franconian territories were incorporated into Bavaria and many local administrators lost their jobs. The Captain's name is Otto and so indeed is the real name of Eduard, Eduard being a name adopted early to avoid confusion. The element 'Otto' occurs in the names of all four principal characters, a fact in which it is open to us to see significance if we wish, but none is ever explicitly pointed out. Charlotte reluctantly agrees that the Captain may come provided her niece Ottilie may come too, for she fears she is not making good progress at her boarding-school.

One evening shortly after his arrival, but before Ottilie has arrived, the Captain, who is a man of technical and practical gifts, explains to Eduard and Charlotte the chemical principle which gives the novel its name. 'Verwandtschaft', affinity, is, we are told, a technical term of the chemistry[4] of some years before – the fashionable nomenclature, we are also told, may already have changed but Charlotte, for whose benefit the

---

3   See Atkins, '*Die Wahlverwandtschaften*', p. 141.
4   See Jeremy Adler, '*Eine fast magische Anziehungskraft*'. Goethes '*Wahlverwandtschaften*' und die Chemie seiner Zeit (Munich, 1987), pp. 86f. If we follow Atkins' chronology, the Hauptmann studied chemistry around 1796, well before the publication of C. L. Berthollet's attempt to present affinity in the terms of the new chemistry of Lavoisier (Adler, pp. 71f.), which explains his reliance on earlier authorities (p. 87).

explanation is given, is anyway interested only in the social and psychological analogies to this chemical phenomenon. 'Verwandtschaft' is the force which causes some substances to seek out and bind themselves to others, especially their opposites, as we see in the case of alkalis and acids. Charlotte sees parallels in the attractive and repulsive powers both of individuals and of social groups. In some cases the power of affinity is so strong that it has a divisive effect – in Eduard's words 'die Verwandtschaften werden erst interessant, wenn sie Scheidungen bewirken' (p. 273), 'Scheidung' being of course the word also for separation or divorce in a matrimonial context. When limestone – calcium carbonate as we would say – is introduced into dilute sulphuric acid, the acid combines with the lime to produce gypsum, calcium sulphate, while the gas, carbon dioxide, escapes and can be dissolved in water. In this case it appears that the lime has shown a preference for combination with the acid rather than for combination with the gas, and the gas shows a greater affinity for the water than for the lime. We are therefore justified in speaking of a 'Wahlverwandtschaft' – a substance chooses one partner in preference to another. Charlotte objects to this term: 'ich würde hier niemals eine Wahl, eher eine Naturnotwendigkeit erblicken' (p. 274). She makes a clear distinction, that is, between the human world, in which relations between people are in her view a matter of choice, and the natural world in which relations between substances are a matter of necessity. But, needless to say, this chemical analogy, which provides the novel with its title and which foreshadows the future relations between the four main characters, casts grave doubts on her clear-cut distinction between necessity and choice.

Ottilie arrives and a warmth of feeling between her and Eduard soon becomes apparent. Indeed it seems more than a matter of feeling, there seems to be a kind of natural harmony: Eduard cannot abide Charlotte looking over his shoulder when he is reading, but he is delighted when Ottilie does the same. Charlotte can by intelligence and effort accompany Eduard's halting flute playing, but Ottilie adapts herself naturally to Eduard's rhythms as if this were the only way to play the pieces. They have complementary headaches, he on the right side she on the left. Is there a 'Wahlverwandtschaft' at work? At a ceremony when the foundation stone of a pavilion is laid in the park, a glass thrown in the air miraculously fails to break. It is engraved with the letters E and O intertwined, which Eduard takes as a sign that his passion is favoured, if not by chemistry, then at least by fate. Meanwhile Charlotte and the Captain are themselves growing closer.

Nature seems to be taking a hand in other ways too. The landscape becomes a symbol or mirror of the passions at work, walks away from the house into uncultivated areas suggest and give the opportunity for a relaxation of social constraints, while Eduard's decision to link three medium-sized pools into one large lake can be seen as a symbol, or an unconscious expression, of his overflowing passion.

A visit from a notoriously adulterous couple, the Graf and the Baronesse, is the occasion for the climax of the first book of the novel: in the atmosphere of moral disorder introduced by the guests Eduard finds his way to Charlotte's room one night when he is preoccupied by thoughts of Ottilie and she by thoughts of the Captain. As they make love they both imagine they are embracing not their spouse but their lover. Almost immediately after this night of what Eduard will later call double adultery, a 'doppelten Ehbruch' (p. 455), Charlotte comes to her senses. A kiss from the Captain makes her realise the position, she resolves that the Captain should pursue the advantageous career that the Graf offers him and by separating they may hope to break the passionate bond between them. She now resolves also to send Ottilie away, but Eduard will not allow it. Claiming that he cannot bear to think of the fragile Ottilie alone in the world, Eduard decides to leave instead himself. In this way at least Ottilie will be able to stay at his home in the company of Charlotte. But Ottilie has no more given up Eduard than Eduard has given up her, despite their separation: 'Ottilie hatte Eduarden nicht entsagt' (p. 351).

It now turns out that Charlotte is pregnant as a result of Eduard's nocturnal visit and so their marriage seems to be rendered indissoluble. In despair Eduard decides to resume the military career in which he spent much of his youth, as hostilities have broken out again. He is deliberately seeking death, probably in the campaign which followed on Prussia's decision to abandon ten years of neutrality and to mobilise in August 1806. We have to assume that Eduard is fighting under Napoleon, if in the forces of Napoleon's ally Bavaria, since at this point there was no other military leader, and certainly no German leader, who could have given rise to the feelings attributed to Eduard by the narrator: 'Nun war es ihm eine herrliche Empfindung, mit einem Feldherrn zu ziehen, von dem er sich sagen konnte: unter seiner Anführung ist der Tod wahrscheinlich und der Sieg gewiß' (p. 359).[5] With this decision of Eduard's the first part of the novel ends.

The second part opens with a self-conscious pause in the narration: we have entered a period of latency, the winter of Charlotte's pregnancy and, with Eduard and the Captain both away, the plot seems not to advance. Instead time is filled during the winter months with the social turbulence of a visit from Luciane, Charlotte's daughter from her first marriage, and from a bevy of her young friends and admirers. There is frantic indoor and outdoor activity, with receptions, sledging trips, and party games, and Luciane's indulgence in the fashionable taste for *tableaux vivants* is described at length: participants dress up and position themselves so as to reproduce in life the impression of a famous painting. Luciane is assisted in these more cultural activities by the Architect, a young man who has been working for the family for some time but whose role becomes prominent once Eduard and the Captain have gone: he also assists Charlotte in restoring the village church in a medieval style and decorating the chapel with frescoes in which Ottilie's face recurs as the face of an angel, and he arranges for Ottilie to take the part of the Virgin Mary in a Christmas *tableau vivant* after Luciane and her swarm of camp-followers have left. Throughout these incidents we are given insight into Ottilie's thoughts by extracts from her diary.

The birth of Charlotte's child marks the end of this interlude, and it is accompanied by unsettling portents. First, the child proves to resemble neither of its natural parents but rather the two absent partners in the 'doppelten Ehbruch' of the night in which it was conceived: his features are those of the Captain, his eyes those of Ottilie. He is of course, like

5   Atkins thinks the commander may have been Prince Louis Ferdinand (p. 139, fn. 4), because he assumes Eduard must have served with the Prussians. But Ansbach became Bavarian in May 1806, the transfer of its troops from Prussia to Bavaria was immediate (Oskar Bezzel, *Die Haustruppen des letzten Markgrafen von Ansbach-Bayreuth unter preußischer Herrschaft* (Munich, 1939) pp. 46–51), and recruitment for any power other than Bavaria became illegal (Fritz Tarrasch, *Der Übergang des Fürstentums Ansbach an Bayern* (Munich and Berlin, 1912), p. 133). It is therefore unnecessary to assume that Eduard has a lower opinion of the victor of Austerlitz (by whom Goethe, while writing the novel, was admitted to the Legion of Honour) than of an ageing playboy who was, as Atkins notes, killed on 10 October in his first major engagement, or that the phrase 'Der Hauptzweck des Feldzugs war erreicht' (*HA* 6, p. 446) is ironical (p. 141).

everyone else, named Otto, but at his baptism the old village pastor, who has been frail for sometime, finally expires. An English Lord who has quite given up home life on his estate in England in favour of a travelling existence now visits the women. A companion of his recounts a novella inserted in the main narration which then turns out to be based on an event in the Captain's life, to everyone's embarrassment. Before leaving, the visitors arrange some experiments with magnetism which show that Ottilie has powers of divining the presence of minerals, which are associated with her headaches. These mysterious and ominous events introduce the last stages of the story.

We learn that the military campaign has been brought to a successful conclusion, presumably with the battle of Friedland in June 1807, and that Eduard has served in it with distinction. He seems to have taken part in the decisive defeat of Prussia at Jena on 14 October 1806 (and so perhaps in the sack of Weimar?), and to have gone on afterwards to face 'greater' dangers, probably in Russia.[6] The Captain too has been promoted to Major (Knebel's rank), and from now on he is referred to by that title. The two meet and Eduard asks the Major to go to Charlotte and ask her to consider a divorce, while encouraging the Major to envisage the resultant possibility of his marrying Charlotte. The Major agrees to take the message to Charlotte, but Eduard is so impatient that he follows him into the park. Here on the shore of the lake he meets Ottilie, carrying the child. Ottilie agrees to marry Eduard if Charlotte accepts the divorce and they embrace and part. Delayed by Eduard, Ottilie decides to return home across the lake in a rowing boat, but in her emotional confusion and in her haste she drops the child in the water and loses the oar. The child drowns and only slowly does she drift across the lake. Charlotte and Ottilie stay up all night with the dead child, but Ottilie seems to be in a swoon. The Major comes and to explain his presence tells of his

6   It seems unnecessary to identify the 'bedeutende Kriegsgelegenheit', of which Charlotte reads in the newspapers (p. 371), with the subsidiary engagement at Saalfeld (Atkins, p. 139). If the action of the book takes place in 1806–7, the only battle specifically mentioned is much more likely to be the central event of the campaign, a turning-point in German history, and in Goethe's life. It occurs around the time of Eduard's birthday (p. 374): in a novel built around significant coincidences, this is a coincidence which is likely to have a structural role. The love which for Eduard is more important than history and public affairs turns out to have a public and historical meaning.

mission. Charlotte agrees to the divorce and gives the Major grounds for hoping that the two of them may eventually be united. Ottilie, however, awakens from what turns out to have been a cataleptic trance in which, she reveals, she heard everything said. She asserts that she has had a flash of insight into her guilt and taken an irrevocable decision as a result: she will never marry Eduard and if Charlotte agrees to a divorce she will drown herself in the very lake in which the child has just died.

The possibility of a favourable resolution of the love intrigue is thus excluded. Ottilie decides to return to her boarding-school as a teacher and sets off. Eduard learns of her intention and intercepts her at a wayside inn. She refuses to speak to him but accepts being driven back to the house where a strange reprise of the situation at the start of Part One takes place, for the Major joins them and all four live together for some weeks. Ottilie maintains a complete silence, occasionally communicating by letter, and not taking part in meals, but otherwise joining in the communal life as before: a mysterious attractive power repeatedly draws her and Eduard together; Eduard reads aloud as before with Ottilie looking over his shoulder; and the couples play their duets again. On the day before Eduard's birthday – the birthdays of all the main figures being the occasion for festivities throughout the book – a visit comes from Mittler, an ex-clergyman who has given himself to social work and has played an important role as intermediary between the parties, hoping all the time to prevent a divorce. As Mittler is descanting on the undesirability of including in the catechism the biblical form of the commandment 'Thou shalt not commit adultery', Ottilie happens to enter. She appears thunderstruck and returns to her room where it becomes clear she is dying. She has, it turns out, been starving herself to death and this shock is fatal. With her last breath she finally speaks, saying to Eduard 'Versprich mir zu leben!'(p. 484), though it will not be long before Eduard follows her in the path of starvation and death. During Ottilie's funeral her chambermaid falls from a height and appears to be dead, but she is restored to life on touching Ottilie's corpse. Gradually other miracles are reported from visitors to her tomb in the chapel decorated by the architect, where Eduard's body eventually joins her.

Strange though this novel is – and it has never ceased to puzzle commentators[7] – Goethe claimed that every line in it was based on his own experience.[8] The work can perhaps be made a little less puzzling if we take Goethe at his word and read it in its biographical and historical context. We can best judge the significance of Ottilie's self-sacrifice if we first look at four areas of the subject-matter of the novel in which it draws on the world of Goethe's experience: (i) science; (ii) art; (iii) religion, fate, and the supernatural; (iv) marriage.

The scientific material in the novel is forced on our attention by the title, by the prominence given to the episode in which the concept of elective affinities is expounded, and by the analogy there insistently drawn by Charlotte between the behaviour of chemical substances and the behaviour of human beings.

An interpretation of the novel seems to be hinted at here: these events are the human equivalent of an experiment in a chemical retort. The movements of passion between Eduard, Ottilie, Charlotte, and the Captain are no different from the operations of 'Wahlverwandtschaft' between limestone, carbon dioxide, sulphuric acid and water. The human figures and events are but the manifestations of concealed natural forces, possibly not yet wholly understood by science – chemical or magnetic forces, such as those shown to be at work in the experiments of the English Lord. We can describe human behaviour in terms of magnetic attraction and chemical affinity, with quite as much justification as that with which we can apply the terms 'attraction', 'choice', or even 'love', to the behaviour of chemical elements, as scientists in Goethe's day frequently did.

Or rather: as a *certain* kind of scientist in Goethe's day frequently did. The interest in the applicability of human, emotional, terms to the fundamental forces of the natural world, and conversely in the application of magnetic, electrical or chemical terms to human phenomena, was not characteristic of the chemistry of Dalton in England, Lavoisier in

7   For a recent guide to the discussion, see Norbert Bolz, 'Die Wahlverwandt-
      schaften' in *Goethe-Handbuch*, Vol. 3, ed. by Bernd Witte, Peter Schmidt, and
      Gernot Böhme (Stuttgart and Weimar, 1997), pp. 152–86.
8   To Eckermann, 9 and 17 February 1830, confirmed by *Tag- und Jahreshefte* for
      1809 (*HA* 10, p. 505), and Wilhelm von Humboldt to his wife, 6 March 1810:
      'sehr viel Reminiszenzen in dem Roman aus dem wirklichen Leben'. See *HA* 6,
      pp. 642–44, 664.

France, or Lichtenberg or Rumford in Germany. This was an interest certainly widespread in the popular consciousness of Goethe's time, but peculiarly cultivated only by one group of quasi-scientists: the Romantic 'Naturphilosophen', the followers of Schelling. Indeed Goethe is said to have remarked that the inspiration for the novel was provided by Schelling,[9] though when he said this he probably did not have chemistry in mind. None the less, the experiments with Ottilie's magnetism and divining powers are closely modelled on experiments on an Italian water-diviner (Campetti by name) conducted in Munich by Schelling and two of his followers, F. X. Baader and J. Ritter, in the winter 1806–7.[10] Hegel reported on these experiments to Goethe and Goethe showed interest, but Hegel tells Schelling in a letter of 23 February 1807 that Goethe also 'einstweilen seine Späße dabei anbrachte':[11] Goethe did not take the matter wholly seriously – doubtless he found it too reminiscent of the occult and Masonic mumbo-jumbo of Cagliostro that he had once treated satirically in *Der Groß-Cophta*.

A few months earlier, on 22 August 1806, Goethe had written a lengthy exposé of his attitude to Romantic 'Naturphilosophie' in a letter to Wilhelm von Humboldt in which he informally reviewed one of the classic expressions of the doctrines of the movement: Henrik Steffens' *Grundzüge der philosophischen Naturwissenschaft*, published in Berlin in 1806. Goethe mentions elsewhere that this book put him in a bad humour,[12] and he told Humboldt 'es ist unangenehm, gerade diejenigen lassen zu müssen, die man so gerne begleitete'. Goethe certainly applauded the *intention* of Schelling and the 'Naturphilosophen' – the intention of reconciling the objective and the subjective, the natural and the spiritual, necessity and freedom, in philosophy and science. But he could not believe that this was the way to do it. Above all he objected to the language used, the symbolic application of terms outside their normal sphere of reference '[which] ...etwas höchst Wunderliches und zugleich etwas Gefährliches in sich hat. Die Formeln der Mathematik, der reinen und angewandten, der Astronomie, Kosmologie, Geologie,

9   Varnhagen von Ense, quoted in *HA* 6, p. 641.

10   Schelling to Hegel, 11 January 1807, in *Briefe von und an Hegel* ed. by Johannes Hoffmeister, 3rd edn (Hamburg, 1969) 1, pp. 134f., 466f.

11   Ibid. p. 151

12   In a draft of a letter to Steffens himself of September/October 1806 (*Weimarer Ausgabe* 4, 30, p. 91).

Physik, Chemie, Naturgeschichte, der Sittlichkeit, Religion und Mystik
werden alle durcheinander in die Masse der metaphysischen Sprache
eingeknetet, oft mit gutem und großem Sinne genutzt; aber das Ansehn
bleibt immer barbarisch'.[13]

The language of science in *Die Wahlverwandtschaften* is the language of Romantic 'Naturphilosophie', but that does not mean that *Die
Wahlverwandtschaften* is a Romantic, 'naturphilosophisch' novel. On
the contrary, Goethe did not believe that the language of Romantic
'Naturphilosophie' was remotely capable of dealing with the profoundest
issues in human life. But with the inscrutable, poker-faced irony which
we find in his other writings of this period, he is putting this quasi-
scientific interpretation before us as part of the way that his time might
understand what is going on. It is perhaps the way the Captain, or even
Charlotte, understands, at least part of the time, what is going on: Ottilie
and Eduard are seen as simply the victims of a mechanical, natural
necessity. It is an interpretation, or misinterpretation, that is bound to
offer itself because the story is set in the Romantic period, in Goethe's
own time. To present this possible interpretation, or misinterpretation, is
a part of Goethe's depiction of the intellectual milieu in which the events
occur. That it is a misinterpretation we know because Ottilie's self-
starvation and renunciation is an act of resistance, and successful
resistance, to compulsion of any sort, whether scientifically mechanical
or more simply emotional. She refuses to accept the logic of separation –
'Scheidung', divorce – and recombination, whether that logic is a logic
of chemistry or – as is intrinsically more probable – a logic of exped-
iency. The belief that her love affair with Eduard is a chemical necessity
is a temptation which she has to overcome if she is to rise to a clear
moral understanding of her situation, a temptation insidiously put by
some of the most prestigious intellectual developments of the Romantic
age.

The position is not fundamentally different with Art. In the parts of
the novel that treat of artistic or related matters we are presented with a
mass of material characteristic of the Romantic time in which it was
written, and Goethe's contemporaries registered this with enthusiasm. In
the detailed depiction of landscape gardening, of *tableaux vivants*, of the
collection of prehistoric antiquities, of medievalising architectural resto-

13   *WA* 4, 51, p. 200.

ration and of pre-Raphael frescoes they saw a realistic portrait of the habits of the time.[14] What they did not see is that Goethe's presentation of these tendencies is far from favourable, and we should not take their presence in *Die Wahlverwandtschaften* as evidence of Goethe's conversion to Romanticism in art. If we look closely at them we shall see that they all have in common a certain feature: they all involve a confusion of objective and subjective, or to put it less abstractly, of life and art. In *Die Wahlverwandtschaften*, art, like science, is always seeking to expand beyond its proper sphere into the sphere of emotion, society, morality or religion.

Take gardening, for example. The late F. J. Stopp drew attention to a note by Goethe for a section of an essay on 'Schaden des Dilettantismus in der Gartenkunst': 'Reales wird als ein Phantasiewerk betrachtet'.[15] Stopp showed in great detail how the alterations of the landscape around the house reflect Eduard's self-absorption and the gardening practised both by Eduard and Charlotte is a hermaphrodite, neither art nor nature, but a creation and reflection of their own desires and emotions.[16] The *tableaux vivants* are even more obviously a half-way stage between art and life – freezing the participants into unnatural stillness but vulgarising the great paintings they parody into a society game. Ottilie finds that they make her 'ängstlich'. The architect, who represents something like the serious and honest Romantic artist, genuinely devoted to his calling but with the limitations of his movement, persuades her to take part in only one – the Nativity scene – and we are significantly told that this *tableau vivant* had no audience other than the architect himself. The moment an audience appears, in the form of the teacher from her old school, Ottilie feels extremely ill at ease and changes her garments as soon as possible (there is a remarkable parallel

---

14   K. W. F. Solger, for example, praised 'die Einflechtung von allem, was jetzt Mode ist, als Gartenkunst, Liebhaberei an der Kunst des Mittelalters, Darstellung von Gemälden durch lebende Personen [...] nach einigen Jahrhunderten würde man sich hieraus ein vollkommenes Bild von unserm jetzigen täglichen Leben entwerfen können', quoted in *HA* 6, p. 655.

15   *WA* 1, 47, pp. 300f.

16   'Ein wahrer Narziß', *Publications of the English Goethe Society*, 29 (1960), 72–85.

here to a famous scene in Jane Austen's *Mansfield Park* and there are numerous other similarities between the two books).[17]

The *tableaux vivants* are art falsely transformed into life. Conversely the prehistoric artefacts excavated from burial mounds and displayed by the architect in lined cases and drawers are life falsely transformed into art. We are told that 'diese alten, ernsten Dinge durch seine Behandlung etwas Putzhaftes annahmen' (p. 367), and this treatment blurs the distinction between present and past so that the beholders do not know what age they are living in. A similar blurring of the boundaries, to the point of making it difficult to distinguish between existence and non-existence, is attributed by Ottilie to the effect on her of sitting in the chapel decorated by the architect: 'es schien ihr [...] als wenn sie wäre und nicht wäre, als wenn sie sich empfände und nicht empfände, als wenn dies alles vor ihr, sie vor sich selbst verschwinden sollte' (p. 374).

Even in literature such blurring of the distinction between art and life is possible: the 'Novelle' told by the companion of the English Lord is carefully marked off with a sub-title as if it were an insertion quite independent of the main story. Then it causes grave offence by its distortion, in the interests of literary effect, of an incident from the life of the Captain.

It is in fact a further common characteristic of all the manifestations of Romantic art in the novel that they put Ottilie in a false, embarrassing or uncomfortable position. Her very being is threatened by the architect's *Gesamtkunstwerk* in which she is represented among the angels. The treatment of the artefacts excavated from ancient graves – reminiscent of the vogue for the *Nibelungenlied* in 1807 – not only blurs historical boundaries, but also reveals to her, as we learn from her journal, the pointlessness of the human desire to immortalise the dead in works of art such as the reconstructed Chapel and graveyard (pp. 369f.). It is particularly important to remember that this is Ottilie's view of the relation between art and life after death when reading the book's closing description of her mausoleum, which makes it seem as if art *has* immortalised her. The *tableaux vivants* in particular seem to involve a playful attitude to serious things and cause Ottilie anxiety or a feeling of im-

17   See further my *Sacred and Secular Scriptures. A Catholic Approach to Literature* (Notre Dame, 2005), pp. 205–20.

propriety. And the landscaping in Part One of the novel is several times associated with morally doubtful acts, culminating in the death of the child by drowning in Eduard's artificial lake.

A third respect in which the novel seems to be impregnated with Romantic ideas is its concern with religion, fate, and the supernatural. The Catholicising turn of the conclusion, which was sufficiently powerful to inspire the Romantic playwright Zacharias Werner to think Goethe might be on the point of conversion, is fairly plainly a piece of added paraphernalia.[18] There has never been any suggestion that the architect believes in the religion that provides the motifs for his decoration of the chapel, nor does Ottilie believe in it. Not only does the concluding suggestion of a blessed afterlife, with Ottilie transformed into an angel, directly contradict what we know of Ottilie's expectations of mortality – after death there is a slow but eventually total forgetting (p. 370) – but none of the events that support this suggestion are presented as anything but subjective impressions – the resuscitated chambermaid merely *seems* to be dead, we are not told she is, and she alone has the vision of being forgiven and blessed by Ottilie, while all the other miracles are simply cures which people 'think' have happened.

More importantly, the same is true of the various allusions to fate made by the characters. By 1808, when Goethe started to write the novel (though it may have been first conceived in 1807), Fate was a popular motif in Romantic literature and Goethe was spending some time helping Werner with his fate tragedy *Der 24. Februar*. But the point of that play (produced in Weimar in 1810) is precisely that the only fate at work in it is *belief* in fate, the principal figures' belief that the 24th of February is a doom-laden day. Similarly in *Die Wahlverwandtschaften* numerous events are interpreted, particularly by Eduard, as indicating that his passion for Ottilie is approved, or even ineluctably decreed, by a super-

18   But it too is linked to the probable political context. About 10% of Prussia's direct subjects in Ansbach in 1792 were Catholic (Fritz Hartung, *Hardenberg und die preußische Verwaltung in Ansbach-Bayreuth von 1792 bis 1806* (Tübingen, 1906), p. 269): numbers increased significantly with the acquisition of Catholic spiritual territories after 1803 (p. 270), and with the absorption into Bavaria in 1806 Ansbach became part of a majority Catholic state. Thomas Mann's objection that in his last pages Goethe implausibly imputed Catholic credulity to a Lutheran population (quoted by Atkins, p. 140) overlooks that the novel is not, as Mann thinks, situated 'mitten in protestantischer Sphäre'.

natural force. Yet we are alerted, both by the narration and by Mittler, to the possibility that these supposed signs are merely reflections of Eduard's own wishes, and are either simply chance, such as the fact that a glass was not broken or that some plane trees were planted by Eduard on the day of Ottilie's birth, or have a purely natural explanation: that the glass was engraved with the letters E and O is hardly surprising since Eduard's two names are Eduard and Otto, that a door locked itself behind him in the inn so that he had to come face to face with Ottilie is explained either by his impetuosity, or by his unacknowledged desire to be so trapped. As for the plane trees, one might think they might more naturally stand as a reminder of the great difference of age between Eduard and Ottilie. Even the strange features of the mysterious child are not necessarily evidence of a supernatural intrusion – pre-modern medicine, not only among 'Naturphilosophen', held that the features of children were determined by the impressions received by the mother during pregnancy[19] – and there is even the possibility of an entirely natural explanation of its resemblance to the Captain, a possibility raised by Eduard when he first sees it and comments that, if he wanted to cast doubt on the fidelity of his wife and his friend, here is the evidence (p. 455).[20] More important still is that when Charlotte uses the term 'Schicksal', she does so to confirm her own wishes: she claims to agree to the divorce because fate clearly intends it: 'Es sind gewisse Dinge, die sich das Schicksal hartnäckig vornimmt. Vergebens, daß Vernunft und Tugend, Pflicht und alles Heilige sich ihm in den Weg stellen (p. 460).

It is not only Eduard, then, who makes use of a notion of fate that is really a piece of modish self-deception. Whenever any character, or for that matter the narrator, appeals to necessity, 'Verhängnis', 'Schicksal', or merely uses the verb 'müssen', the question has to arise: is this really justified? Or is there not a perfectly natural explanation of what is going on? H.B. Nisbet has done just such an investigation and come to the conclusion that for all the events in the novel there are good explanations in terms of psychology and character, and that none of the more grandiose supposed explanations, in terms of scientific causality or fate, is as

19   See e.g. Calvidius Letus [= Claude Quillet], *Callipaedia; seu De Pulchrae Prolis habendae ratione* (Paris, 1655), pp. 27, 30
20   Atkins points out that since Ottilie is Charlotte's niece it is not surprising that the child has her eyes (p. 153).

adequate as these.[21] We can go on to ask why there should be in the novel so many partial explanations that are really blind alleys. The answer, I would suggest, is that these partial explanations are all manifestations of the Romantic *Zeitgeist* which are being used by the characters to conceal from themselves the true nature of what they are doing. Eduard appeals to fate to conceal from himself that he is responsible for his feelings towards Ottilie, and that they are culpable feelings. Charlotte appeals to 'Schicksal' to conceal from herself that she wants to marry the Captain, and she never in the novel gives up the hope of doing so. The Captain – probably – suggests a scientific explanation of human behaviour for a similar reason. The one person who falls victim to none of these self-delusions, the one person who sees her actions in simple but profound moral terms, is Ottilie.

And so we come to the question of marriage, for Goethe himself said the theme of *Die Wahlverwandtschaften* was 'very simple': the words of Christ (Matthew 5:27) demanding the highest possible standard of fidelity in marriage, 'Wer ein Weib ansieht, ihrer zu begehren, der hat schon mit ihr die Ehe gebrochen in seinem Herzen'.[22] Simple or not, such a principle was directly opposed to the behaviour of the Romantic circle that in 1809 was dominating intellectual life in Germany. Caroline Schlegel already had in her past one marriage and an illegitimate child when she married A.W. Schlegel, and she soon deserted him for his good friend the philosopher Schelling. Fr. Schlegel in his collection of *Fragmente* in the *Athenäum* said there was nothing in principle objectionable about an 'Ehe à quatre',[23] and sang the praises of free love in *Lucinde*. The readiness of Eduard and Charlotte to contemplate a divorce reflects the great ease with which divorce could be obtained in the

---

21 '*Die Wahlverwandtschaften*: Explanation and its Limits', *Deutsche Vierteljahrs-schrift*, 43 (1969), 458–86.

22 Letter to J.S. Zauper, 7 September 1821, *WA* 4, 35, p.74. Zauper was an Augustinian canon (Atkins, p. 178), so no doubt Goethe was politely giving a Catholic turn to his reply. But he was not lying. And the Gospel quotation goes to the heart of the novel, for it warns that we are responsible for our thoughts, and corrupt thoughts lead to corrupt actions.

23 *Athenaeum 1798-1800. Herausgegeben von August Wilhelm Schlegel und Friedrich Schlegel. Mit einem Nachwort von Ernst Behler* (Stuttgart, 1960), 1, p. 187.

German Protestant states,[24] and the readiness of the Romantic generation to take advantage of the facility. The example of marriage shows us how we are to understand the other manifestations of the Romantic *Zeitgeist* in the novel: Romantic 'Naturphilosophie', Romantic attitudes to art, Romantic attitudes to religion and the supernatural are all ultimately self-delusions which tempt the individual to ignore his or her true state, and true obligations, and to slide into the moral anarchy manifest in the married lives of contemporary intellectuals. In the letter to W. von Humboldt in which he made clear his hostility to Steffens's 'Naturphilosophie', Goethe went on immediately to make mention of 'eines traurigen Falles [...] wie nämlich die idealen Ansichten [a sarcastic phrase meaning roughly 'Romantic ideas'] wahrscheinlich in Gesellschaft irdischer Leidenschaften, ein gar hübsches Gefäß zerstört haben'. He was referring to Caroline von Günderrode, a Romantic poet in Frankfurt, who stabbed herself to death out of unrequited love for a professor of mythology. An even closer parallel to the events of the novel can be found in the tragic turn taken by the Schellings' marriage: Caroline's legitimate daughter by her first husband, a lively girl of whom all the circle was fond, fell ill and died, reportedly (though the report was certainly malicious) as a result of Schelling's insistence on treating her in accordance with the theories of 'Naturphilosophie'.[25] Dorothea Veit thought the death 'a sacrificial offering for sin'.[26] In these examples of an association of high ideas and low passions that leads to disaster and death Goethe may actually have found the kernel of his work. Far from being a Romantic novel, in fact, *Die Wahlverwandtschaften* is an anti-Romantic novel.

So let us turn finally to consider Ottilie's renunciation of Eduard. Once we have seen the enormous weight of Romantic ideology in the story, that renunciation is not difficult to interpret. Goethe remarked to Eckermann that tragic fear, or 'Bangigkeit', is a feeling that 'wird in uns rege, wenn wir ein moralisches Übel auf die handelnden Personen und

---

24   In Ansbach matrimonial jurisdiction over Lutherans (but not Calvinists or Catholics) was transferred to a secular body in 1796 (Hartung, *Hardenberg*, p. 268).

25   See the recent account in Robert J. Richards, *The Romantic Conception of Life. Science and Philosophy in the Age of Goethe* (Chicago and London, 2002), pp. 166–76.

26   Ibid. p. 172.

sich über sie verbreiten sehen, wie zum Beispiel in den Wahlverwandtschaften' (21 July 1827, quoted *HA*, Vol. 6, p. 644). Spiritual evil
does indeed engulf the characters, but it is not an evil that comes from a
supernatural world outside. 'Die ungeheuren zudringenden Mächte' (p.
468) against which Ottilie seeks by her sacrifice to protect those around
her are simply the forces in society and in her time that are making for
the destruction of Eduard and Charlotte's marriage. It is only gradually
that she realises what is happening.

For the whole of the first part of the novel Ottilie is carried away by
her feelings for Eduard – she does not attempt to justify them to herself,
as Eduard does by invoking Fate, she simply sees the good that there
always is in love, and closes her eyes to its moral implications. In the
first chapters of Part Two she starts to come to herself as she becomes
aware of a distance between herself and the society around her: the
behaviour of Luciane and the attitudes to art and life represented by the
Graf and Baronesse, the Lord, and even in his own way the Architect.
But the crucial moment, the moment, in her own words, when her eyes
are opened and she realises the criminal nature of her entanglement with
Eduard, is the death of the child. Because that death opens the way for an
easy divorce of Eduard and Charlotte it makes it clear that to accept the
divorce would be to accept the death of the child – retrospectively to
murder it, so to speak, by wishing it dead. For that reason, once Ottilie
has heard the conversation between Charlotte and the Major, in which
the full squalor of what is proposed is apparent to anyone who can read
between the narrator's decorous lines, she threatens to commit suicide by
drowning in the same lake in which the child died. The child is the
embodiment of the guilt in which all four are involved. They will bring
that guilt on themselves if they accept the divorce and remarriage, and it
is only by renouncing the fulfilment of love that guilt can be kept at bay.
Ottilie, we are told 'hatte sich in der Tiefe ihres Herzens nur unter der
Bedingung des völligen Entsagens verziehen' (p. 464). Ottilie is the *only*
character in the entire book who understands what guilt is, and therefore
what atonement is. All the others are blinded by their succumbing to one
or other of the alluring Romantic self-deceptions. By her vow of silence
and refusal of food Ottilie withdraws all moral approval from the world,
the society, surrounding her. She has to live in it for a while, and her
love for Eduard is intrinsically a good thing, but it is not possible for that
love to find any realisation at all in the corrupt milieu we have been

shown in such detail. Her final request of Eduard that he should live is a request that he too should accept renunciation – that is, parting from her – as she has accepted parting from him. But his will is too weak for that and he follows her into death – the final saccharine, Romantic, quasi-Catholic, crypto-erotic hopes of a joint resurrection, voiced by the narrator, are doubtless the hopes with which he dies. But Ottilie is made of sterner stuff: even the moment of her death is a moment of protest against the morally degraded world in which she finds herself. Mittler's milk and water paraphrase of the sixth commandment recalls Schleiermacher's *Idee zu einem Katechismus der Vernunft für edle Frauen*, published in the *Athenäum*.[27] There Schleiermacher – whose early theology, incidentally, gives a special significance to the concept of a 'Mittler' – substitutes for 'Du sollst nicht ehebrechen' the commandment 'Du sollst keine Ehe schließen, die gebrochen werden müßte'. Faced with the assertion that the words of God are 'grob' and 'unanständig' to the ears of modern Romantic man, Ottilie may well retire to her room and die. If the reconstruction of the chronology of the novel offered here is correct, its catastrophe occurs in the autumn of 1807, perhaps on the precise anniversary of the battles of Jena and Auerstädt.[28] We are thus reminded at its end that, thanks to the decision which concluded its first part, Eduard has been an active agent in the greatest public disaster Goethe personally experienced, the historical moment which, in every sense, brought home to him the new, revolutionary, era. Napoleon's victory destroyed the Germany which had both permitted the intellectual flowering of the previous twenty years and allowed it to fester into Romanticism. It is to that landmark event in German culture that *Die Wahlverwandtschaften* is the literary monument.

27   F. D. E. Schleiermacher, *Schriften aus der Berliner Zeit 1796-1799*, ed. by Günter
       Meckenstock (Berlin and New York, 1984), pp. 153f., originally in A.W. and F.
       Schlegel, *Athenaeum* I, 2, pp. 109–11 ['Fragmente', No. 364].
28   Ottilie dies on the eve of Eduard's birthday (p. 481) (as Werther on the eve of
       Christmas), the anniversary of her experience of being and non-being in the
       redecorated chapel (p. 374), which took place at the time of Eduard's involvement
       in the 'bedeutende Kriegsgelegenheit' (p. 371). For Goethe's concealed symbolic
       representations of the battle of Jena, both in his drawing and in his writing
       (especially the sonnet 'Mächtiges Überraschen'), see my 'Goethe's Later Cycles of
       Drawings', in *Goethe und das Zeitalter der Romantik* (Stiftung für Romantik-
       forschung, Vol. 21), ed. by W. Hinderer (Würzburg, 2002), pp. 281–306.

MARTIN SWALES

Keller, *Der grüne Heinrich*

This essay, and the lecture from which it derives, belongs to a series entitled 'Landmarks in the German Novel'. I want to begin by commenting on the three concepts which are named in this title – and to indicate ways in which the text that concerns me engages with them.

The novel is, by common consent, and has been over the past two centuries or so, the dominant literary genre within modern literature. It is a narrative form which derives its particular urgency from an all-pervasive sense of the dynamic interaction of the individual self and the corporate social world. That dynamic is provided by the perception that both entities in the equation – individual selfhood on the one hand and the social world on the other – are not givens but are made in the multiple processes of their interaction. The self is not a predetermined entity; it is, rather, to be discovered and defined experientially. Similarly, the practical outward world is not ordained by God or destiny – it is to be explored, to be challenged, fought for, and fought over. Keller's great novel manifestly partakes of this narrative project. So much for the novel, then. But what of its German-ness? It is a novel written in German and it is set in the German-speaking lands, in Switzerland and in Germany. But it is not merely – and certainly not narrowly – a German novel, if for no other reason than that its creator was Swiss. A number of matters could be explored under this heading, although this is not the occasion to do so. But what I do want to suggest is that *Der grüne Heinrich* engages with and interrogates a number of features of the German novel tradition. One issue is salient here. It is often said that much of the finest German novel writing stands apart from the broadly speaking realistic narrative and thematic thrust of European fiction (Stendhal, Balzac, Dickens, George Eliot, Flaubert) by virtue of its inwardness and reflectivity. The German tradition has world enough and time for a thoughtful, patient, and circumstantial investigation of the inner life – of emotion, imagination, thought as constitutive of the evolving self – but has relatively little time for the outer world. The so-called *Bildungsroman* is one key expression of this concern. It is a tradition, I shall want to suggest, that animates Keller's novel; but there is also at work in Keller's fictional universe a lively interest in the outer world, in, to borrow a phrase from Henry James, the world of anger and telegrams. And on this account *Der grüne Heinrich* bridges the gap between the German and European traditions. And finally, to comment on the third key concept in this series, *Der grüne Heinrich* is a 'landmark' because it engages with many possibilities of the novel genre in the nineteenth century; it takes stock of the inherent structural, stylistic, and thematic possibilities, and opens perspectives for further development. Like all good landmarks, it has many directions built in to it.

What is the story that *Der grüne Heinrich* tells? Heinrich Lee loses his vital and charismatic father young. In consequence he lives in somewhat joyless and straitened circumstances with his mother. His experience of school is fraught; he is an awkward and quirky boy and he finds it difficult to make headway. He is expelled for a group misdemeanour of which he is only tentatively part. Visits to relatives who live in the country bring him much consolation. Above all his erotic life is awakened by his meetings with the ethereal Anna and the robustly sensuous Judith. He tries to pursue a career as a painter and his ambition takes him to Munich. But he is unsuccessful, and he returns home with his tail between his legs. The local boy has, alas, failed to make good; and the closing phase of his life is characterised by melancholy and emotional deprivation. In the first version of the novel he dies, a broken man. In the second version he becomes a somewhat withdrawn, austere, and monosyllabic civil servant.

Let me at this point say something about the two versions of the novel. The first appeared in 1854–55, the second in 1879–80. The first version begins in the third person at the point where Heinrich is leaving his native Switzerland for Munich. As he is assembling his possessions in a rented room, he takes out the story of his youth up to the point of his departure for Germany. That story – which is incorporated into the novel – is in the first person and it tells us, in flashback, of Heinrich's years before the departure for Munich. When we get to the end of the 'Jugendgeschichte', we resume the story, in the third person, of his adventures in Munich, his return home and death. The second version of the novel – and this is the one that concern me in this essay – is told in the first person throughout, and it respects chronology: that is to say, it begins with Heinrich's childhood and youth and takes us to Munich and then back to Switzerland where the melancholy civil servant completes the account of his life. Scholars who have discussed *Der grüne Heinrich* have, of course, referred to and explored the differences between the two versions of the novel. But on the whole, the matter of these two versions has been related to Keller's own temperament, his notorious inability to meet deadlines, to complete work and get it in on time. When he publishes the first volume of the first edition, he attaches a preface in which he reflects on the artistic untidiness of what he has written. The result, he says, is not really a 'streng gegliedertes Kunstwerk' (X1, 14).[1] Rather, the text is more akin to a letter which has come about in fits and starts and whose truth, therefore, is to be found more in the mode of personal confession than in any artistic integrity. In writing this preface, Keller is looking back on a lengthy process of genesis – he began writing in 1847 and only in 1855 was the first version completed. Yet the interval between the first and second versions is much longer than that – it amounts to something like a quarter of a century. The point that I am after is that *Der grüne Heinrich* is the product of lengthy writing and re-writing that accompanied Keller throughout his creative life. I have no wish to deny that this protracted genesis had intimately to do with Keller's creative personality.[2] But in my view it is important to stress that these prevarications produce a corpus of texts which is profoundly expressive of the various modes available to the novel-writer in the second half of the nineteenth century. Keller's irresolution – his oscillation between first and third person, for example – is, in other words, not only psychologically, biographically significant. It is also novelistically so; it is what makes his great project a 'landmark novel'.

---

1   Sources for quotations, from the second edition of *Der grüne Heinrich*, appear in brackets after the text. In each case the part of the novel is given (in roman), then the number of the chapter (in arabic), followed by the title of the chapter. Page references follow, giving the volume number (in roman), then the page number (in arabic); they are to Gottfried Keller, *Sämtliche Werke*, ed. by Walter Morgenthaler (Basel, Frankfurt a. M., Zurich, 2006).

2   For a discussion of that creative personality see, for example, Adolf Muschg, *Gottfried Keller* (Munich, 1977); Gerhard Kaiser, *Gottfried Keller: Das gedichtete Leben* (Frankfurt a. M., 1981); Silvia Menke, *Schreiben als Daseinsbewältigung: die Bedeutung literarischer Produktivität für Hans Fallada und Gottfried Keller* (Aachen, 2000).

What, then, are the various modes that jostle in Keller's *Der grüne Heinrich*? One is the confessional register, the rhetoric of the auto-biographical, the account of the self that explicates the chronological and epistemological coming-into-being of its own individual identity. In one sense, of course, there is nothing new under the sun and the confessional mode goes back at least as far as St Augustine. But in another, we would do well to remember that the eighteenth century sees a profusion of (in the broadest sense) confessional texts. Rousseau is a key witness here, as is the epistolary novel in all its forms (*La Nouvelle Héloise*, *Les Liaisons dangereuses*, *Pamela*, *Werther*). Such texts derive from the need in bourgeois culture for keeping a record of the inner life (diary, letter-writing, and so on). Such seemingly private, intimate documents are frequently made public (letters are sent and received and read aloud); editor figures abound who, at the risk of seeming indiscreet (or of pandering to prurience), disseminate, publish, make available the confessions of the troubled and complex soul. *Der grüne Heinrich*, as an autobiographical novel, partakes of this culture. It has to do with Keller's need constantly to write and to re-write the self. Keller's text is con-fessional, then, not just in the sense that there are obvious parallels between Heinrich Lee's life and Gottfried Keller's (the involvement in painting, the stay in Munich, the climate of sexual frustration, the work as bureaucrat); it is also confessional in that it feels open, questing, it constantly worries at and about the self. There is very little feel of the cut and dried, very little sense of the experiencing self and the narrating self being reconciled – and this is something that we register regardless of whether we know anything about Keller's life or not. Take the motif of 'greenness'. The novel begins with a naïve young man, a greenhorn. He is also green in the sense that his mother constantly makes clothes for him from the dead father's wardrobe – and green was his favourite colour. In this sense, Heinrich is 'reach me down' man. And this proves true of much of his experience; it is somehow re-cycled, re-packaged. Yet at the end of the second version, which leaves us with a somewhat arid, tired old man, reference is made to 'die alten grünen Pfade der Erinnerung' (IV, 16, 'Der Tisch Gottes', III, p. 281). And here the adjective 'green' vibrates with life, with vitality sustained and intensified by its articulate distillation in the autobiographical mode. Paradoxically, even the life-story of a life-denying man may have life-affirming force.

So much, then, for the rhetoric of the confessional or autobiographical novel – although I shall want to come back to these issues later.

The second generic possibility of the nineteenth-century European novel which *Der grüne Heinrich* enshrines is that of the realistic account of the interplay between the individual self and the social world, and I want to dwell on this aspect because it has all too often been underplayed by critics. I have already had occasion to mention that nineteenth-century German fiction is often criticised for its lack of thoroughgoing narrative realism. *Der grüne Heinrich* can be exempted from this stricture because it is so acute in its understanding of society not just as a set of facts and concrete circumstances but also as a world made of certain attitudes, values, and beliefs. Keller is unforgettable on the mentality of social life. It is important to register at the outset that *Der grüne Heinrich* centrally concerns the multiple processes by which the individual is defeated by social pressures and expectations. We would do well to remember that failure is a key theme of the realistic novel. One could think of Effi Briest's verdict on her life, a verdict that speaks of half-heartedness, inauthenticity, insufficiency: 'Es ist komisch, aber ich eigentllich kann von vielem in meinem Leben sagen "beinahe"'.[3] It is worth recalling Lionel Trilling's diagnosis of half-heartedness as a central proccupation of the European realistic novel:

> *Little Dorrit*, Dickens's great portrayal of what he regards as the inauthenticity of England, has for its hero a man who says of himself 'I have no will'. Balzac and Stendhal passionately demonstrated the social inauthenticity which baffles and defeats the will of their young protagonists. By the time Flaubert wrote *L'Education sentimentale* the defeat could be taken for granted – the will of Frédéric Moreau was infected by the culture virtually at his birth and his existence is nothing but the experience of the duplicity of every human enterprise. Love, friendship, art, and politics – all are hollow.[4]

Trilling only gives us part of the picture, of course. The nineteenth-century realistic novel does also have its protagonists of moral integrity (Dorothea in *Middlemarch*), of ferocious will-power (Becky Sharp in *Vanity Fair*), of hard social ambition (Rastignac in *Le Père Goriot*) and

3   Theodor Fontane, *Effi Briest*, in *Sämtliche Werke*, ed. by Edgar Groß (Munich, 1959), Vol. 7, p. 413
4   *Sincerity and Authenticity* (London, 1974), p. 132.

tragic grandeur (Goriot himself). But Trilling reminds us of how often, in realistic fiction, the social world triumphs over and erodes the individual self. Heinrich Lee is one such victim. The depiction of his years at school is superb – fully equal to anything in Dickens. He is aware of, and ashamed of, his poverty. He is an imaginative child, but soon learns that imagination is not welcomed within the literal-minded ethos of the institution. Yet he also learns to exploit the gullibility of his teachers; at one point he fabricates a story to the effect that bigger boys have taught him to use swear words. He is believed, and the boys in question get into trouble. Above all, Heinrich's relationship to the communality of the school is finely portrayed. He is both proud of, and resents, the fact that he never quite belongs. And when he does seek to join the group, as in the victimisation of an unpopular teacher, he is blamed and punished for behaviour with which he is only marginally involved. Somehow he is guilty on both counts – guilty of being and doing too much and too little.

   Der grüne Heinrich abounds in memorable and extended instances of social portraiture. One thinks of the depiction of Frau Margret, of the lodgers, of Hulda, the tough, unsentimental working-class girl in Munich, and of the mother whose emotional deprivation and poverty becomes a curiously comforting way of life. The depiction of her delight in her own manic frugality is unforgettable:

> Das weiße Stadtbrot, das bislang in ihrem Hause gegolten, hatte sie auch abgeschafft und bezog alle acht Tage ein billigeres rauhes Brot, welches sie so sparsam aß, daß es zuletzt steinhart wurde; aber zufrieden dasselbe bewältigend, schwelgte sie ordentlich in ihrer freiwilligen Askese. (IV, 3, 'Lebensarten', III, p. 31)

To recall a point I made earlier about German realism: what is remarkable about this description is not just its attention to outward detail but its ability to capture the inwardness, the mentality that sustains this particular instance of socialised living – almost an orgy of self-denial.

   This issue of the mentality of social life connects with an aspect of Heinrich Lee's psychology – his lively imagination. *Der grüne Heinrich* is profoundly impressive in its understanding of the manifold, complex, and shifting interplay between imagination and materiality, between inner energy and outward affairs. Not least because of his difficulties at school, Heinrich tends to oscillate between what a moment ago I called too much and too little, between all or nothing in his imaginative relationship to the world about him. Above all, he tends to separate inagination from material reality, to devalue material things as mere matter and to make imaginative things ethereal. This propensity blights his erotic life. He can only love the insubstantial, sickly Anna; he cannot find beauty and nobility in Judith's splendid physicality. On two occasions in the novel he witnesses a festival, a pageant in which a community endeavours to give imaginative and symbolic expression to the values by which it lives. The first is a performance of *Wilhelm Tell* in the Swiss countryside. Heinrich is very critical, mistaking the awkwardness and clumsiness of what goes on for philistinism. Of course the pageant is imperfect judged by demanding aesthetic standards. But, for all its limitations, it does genuinely and touchingly express the allegiances within which and by which the villagers live. By contrast, the carnival in Munich, which seeks to recreate medieval Nürnberg, secures Heinrich's approval. But we are left in no doubt that the whole spectacle is pretentious in the extreme.

A particularly impressive instance of Keller's ability to probe the commerce between imagination and practical reality is to be found in the 'revalenta arabica' episode.[5] Capitalism, Heinrich reflects, is amazingly vigorous in its ability to live from and off fictions. Once fictions are in circulation, once they are negotiable, they become an operative force within the prevailing political and economic reality. He refers to an innovation that goes by the name of 'revalenta arabica', a kind of bran that is falsely claimed to have all manner of beneficial medical properties:

> Ein Spekulant gerät auf die Idee der Revalenta arabica (so nennt er es wenigstens) und bebaut dieselbe mit aller Umsicht und Ausdauer; sie gewinnt eine ungeheure Ausdehnung und gelingt glänzend; tausend Menschen werden in Bewegung gesetzt und Hunderttausende vielleicht Millionen gewonnen, obgleich jedermann sagt: Es ist ein Schwindel! Und doch nennt man sonst Schwindel und Betrug was ohne Arbeit und Mühe Gewinn schaffen soll. Niemand wird aber sagen können, daß das Revelentageschäft ohne Arbeit betrieben werde, es herrschen da gewiß so gute Ordnung, Fleiß und Betriebsamkeit, Um- und Übersicht, wie in dem ehrbarsten

5   See Gerhard Kaiser, Friedrich Kittler, *Dichtung als Sozialisationsspiel. Studien zu Goethe und Keller* (Göttingen, 1978).

Handelshause oder Staatsgeschäfte; auf den Einfall des Spekulanten gegründet ist eine umfassende Tätigkeit, eine wirkliche Arbeit entstanden. (IV, 3, 'Lebensarten', III, pp. 39–40)

There then follows a passage which itemises the various forms of work that are generated by the 'revalenta arabica' industry; and they are indistinguishable from other forms of institutional and mercantile activity. Heinrich comments:

So wird Revalenta arabica gemacht in noch vielen Dingen, nur mit dem Unterschiede, daß es nicht immer unschädliches Bohnenmehl ist, aber mit der nämlichen rästelhaften Vermischung von Arbeit und Täuschung, innerer Hohlheit und äußerem Erfolg, Unsinn und weisem Betrieb. (IV, 3, 'Lebensarten', III, pp. 41–2)

The point at issue here is not simply a denunciatory one – to the effect that all business depends ultimately on confidence tricks. Rather, Heinrich as commenting, reflecting narrator argues that it is impossible to draw reassuring dividing lines between the solidity of honest labour on the one hand and the volatility of imaginative speculation on the other.

The theme of the interplay of imagination and reality also informs the many sections of the novel that explore Heinrich's chosen profession as artist, specifically as a painter. The novel is perceptive about the place of art as a social product. The text makes clear that, as a creative artist, Heinrich is largely ungifted. But on occasion he has his uses. One manifests itself when the fiancée of the heir to the throne is due to visit Munich and in consequence the city has a great need to put on a show. One feature of the pomp and circumstance is coloured flagpoles – and Heinrich is invited to produce them. The original design is marked out; the real skill lies in the painter's being able to follow the spiral line in one go. The boss gives a demonstration:

Der Alte legte eine der grundierten Stangen in die Schießscharte, hielt sie mit der linken Hand wagrecht, und indem er, den Pinsel eintauchend, mich aufmerksam machte, wie dieser weder zu voll noch zu leer sein durfte, damit eine sichere und saubere Linie in einem Zuge entstände, begann er, die Stange langsam zu drehen und von oben an die himmelblaue Spirale zu ziehen, womöglich ohne zu zittern oder eine unvollkommene Stelle nachholen zu müssen. (IV, 5, 'Die Geheimnisse der Arbeit', III, pp. 77–8)

The second exemplification of the relationship between art and social commodification is to be found when Heinrich comes to work for one Habersaat, an immensely successsful artistic entrepreneur who rents the refectory of a nunnery and transforms it into a factory that mass-produces Swiss landscapes 'in einer verschollenen Manier' (II, 5, 'Beginn der Arbeit; Habersaat und seine Schule', I, p. 265). The cultural diagnosis looks forward to Walter Benjamin's analysis of what happens when the 'auratic', unique work of art is replaced by the interchangeable objects of technical reproducibility. The assembly line is described as follows:

> Das Haupttreffen dieser Armee bildeten vier bis sechs junge Leute, teils Knaben, welche die Schweizerlandschaften blühend kolorierten; dann kam ein kränklicher, hustender Bursche, der mit Harz und Scheidewasser auf kleinen Kupferplatten herumschmierte und bedenkliche Löcher hineinfressen ließ, auch wohl mit der Radiernadel dazwischen stach und der Kupferstecher genannt wurde. Auf diesen fogte der Lithograph, ein froher und unbefangener Geist, der verhältnismäßig das weiteste Gebiet umfaßte, nächst dem Meister, da er stets gewärtig und bereit sein mußte, das Bildnis eines Staatsmannes oder eine Weinkarte, den Plan einer Dreschmaschine, wie das Titelblatt für eine Erbauungsschrift junger Töchter auf den Stein zu bringen mit Kreide, Feder graviert oder getuscht. (II, 5, 'Beginn der Arbeit; Habersaat und seine Schule', I, p. 266)

The breathlessness of the description ('dann kam', 'auf diesen folgte', 'im Hintergrund arbeiteten') seems to capture the conveyor-belt ethos of Habersaat's domain. At the centre of this Nibelheim (to invoke Wagner's *Ring*, a work contemporary with *Der güne Heinrich*) is not dwarf labour but child labour, a workforce of nimble fingers accurately colouring all-purpose landscapes. Heinrich the narrator bitterly reflects:

> So begriff er [Habersaat] vollständig das Wesen heutiger Industrie, deren Erzeugnisse um so wertvoller und begehrenswerter zu sein scheinen für die Käufer, je mehr schlau entwendetes Kinderleben darin aufgegangen ist. (II, 5, 'Beginn der Arbeit; Habersaat und seine Schule', I, p. 269)

This is a magnificent passage; and, in our age, when so much that we buy is outsourced to China or India, its diagnostic force is in my view undiminished.

One final reflection on Keller's exploration of the relationship between art and reality; and this time it concerns a moment when

Heinrich seeks to check and correct his propensity to sunder imagination from material reality. He decides to capture the physical world in a work of scrupulous mimetic accuracy. The drawing in question is not a mass-produced artefact in Habersaat's spirit; it is not pretty-picturedom any more. On the contrary, this, Heinrich resolves, is to be the real thing, real nature rendered the more vibrantly real by the mediation of art. Heinrich sits, sketch pad and pencil in hand, before a mighty beech tree:

> Endlich wagte ich, von unten anfangend, einige Striche und suchte den schön gegeliederten Fuß des mächtigen Stammes festzuhalten; aber was ich machte, war leben- und bedeutungslos. [...] Aber hastig und blindlings zeichnete ich weiter, mich selbst betrügend, baute Lage auf Lage, mich ängstlich nur an die Partie haltend, welche ich gerade zeichnete, und gänzlich unfähig, sie in ein Verhältnis zum Ganzen zu bringen, abgesehen von der Formlosigkeit der einzelnen Striche. Die Gestalt auf meinem Papiere wuchs ins Ungeheurliche, besonders in die Breite, und als ich an die Krone kam, fand ich keinen Raum mehr für sie. (I, 20, 'Berufsahnungen', I, p. 201)

This is a memorable passage – not least because of the scrupulous intelligence with which it reflects and reflects upon the mediations between material (in this case, natural) reality and aesthetic expression. Heinrich's grotesque attempt at mimesis in – and of – detail leads to something monstrous – a labyrinthine travesty of the physical world.

Let me bring this phase of my argument to a close – reluctantly, I have to admit, because the temptation to go on quoting and discussing instances of the ways in which *Der grüne Heinrich* engages with the project of literary realism is great.

I have been suggesting that *Der grüne Heinrich* is a confessional novel and a realistic novel. I want now to return to my generic starting point – the confessional-cum-autobiographical novel – and to suggest that there is a German novel tradition that interlocks very intimately and suggestively with the confessional novel – the *Bildungsroman*. The *Bildungsroman* puts before us the story of a young person's movement through adolescenece to early maturity, and it does so by according much space to inward things, to gradual, subtle, indeterminate processes of inner growth and spiritual unfolding. The protagonist tends to be a thoughtful, reflective person and the narrative context in which he or she has his or her being is similarly thoughtful and reflective. There are moments when unmistakably *Der grüne Heinrich* partakes of this philosophical charge that quickens this form of the novel. One example is to be found in the passage I have just quoted where Heinrich tries, and fails, to draw a tree. Take a section such as the following:

> Endlich trat ein gewaltiger Buchbaum mit reichem Stamme und prächtigem Mantel und Krone herausfordernd vor die verschränkten Reihen, wie ein König aus alter Zeit, der den Feind zum Einzelkampfe aufruft. Dieser Recke war in jedem Aste und jeder Laubmasse so fest und klar, so lebens- und gottesfreudig, daß seine Sicherheit mich blendete [...] Die lebendige Buche aber strahlte noch einen Augenblick in noch größerer Majestät als vorher, wie um meine Ohnmacht zu verspotten. (I, 20, 'Berufsahnungen', I, pp. 200, 202)

The rhetoric here takes us beyond a simple constation of Heinrich's failure to achieve an adequate visual representation of a tree. Rather, the passage in question is full of metaphors ('Mantel', 'Krone', 'König', 'Feind', 'Einzelkampf', 'Sicherheit', 'Majestät') and thereby raises the whole cognitive issue of the relationship between human beings and the natural world, of the ways in which natural entities can speak as metaphors to the human onlooker. Here the tree is an instance of ontological splendour; it is both innocent and authoritative, both at one with itself yet constantly changing its aspect; it is both physically and metaphysically integral. (Rilke will later find unforgettable lyric expression for such perceptions.) My point simply is that this confrontation between the human subject and the (in this case, natural) world around it partakes of the thoughtfulness and reflectivity of the *Bildungsroman* tradition. Similar instances of reflectivity are in evidence in the description of Heinrch's language-acquisition at school, of his enchantment with its literal and metaphorical possibilities. Or one could think of Heinrich's encounter with the 'borghesischer Fechter', with Feurbach's and Goethe's works, or the frequent discussions of philosophy, art, religion as mental activities that can endow human life with meaning. Or there are his erotic experiences, caught as he is between the ethereal Anna and the sensuous Judith (that compartmentalisation of Eros is a recurrent feature of the *Bildungsroman*). I do not want to belabour the point; I merely wish to suggest that intertextually *Der grüne Heinrich* is connected with Wieland's *Agathon*, Goethe's *Wilhelm Meisters Lehrjahre*, Stifter's *Der Nachsommer*, Thomas Mann's *Der Zauberberg* and Hesse's *Das Glasperlenspiel*. Yet in Keller's narrative universe these connections coexist with a robustly realistic narrative project. In *Der grüne Heinrich* the protagonist is harried by social pressures, is worsted by his own lack of talent. The complex, questing self also has to worry where the next meal is going to come from (a fate which the protagonists of Wieland's, Goethe's, Stifter's, Thomas Mann's and Hesse's novels are spared). Moreover, the polarisation of the erotic life leads to scenes of excruciating sexual embarassment. And providential moments (of which the *Bildungsroman* tends to have more than its fair share) turn out on the whole not to hold out the redemptive possibility of a second bite at the experiential cherry (an opportunity which is often vouchsafed to the *Bildungsroman* protagonists). One incident is particularly telling in this context. As Heinrich returns to Switzerland, he meets up with the count and his niece, one Dortchen Schönfund. He has met them many years before; now he finds himself again in their company. The count is an admirer of – and has bought several examples of – his work. Moreover, Dortchen manifestly loves Heinrich. Yet he remains the 'gefrorner Christ', the figure who is blighted by his experience, blighted by his need always to sever things that are material and real from things that are imaginatively, inwardly valuable. There is no comforting afterglow in *Der grüne Heinrich*. The clock cannot be turned back – not even with the return of Judith from America at the end of the novel. What is lost is forfeited, once and for all.

I want to bring my argument about the generic pluralism of *Der grüne Heinrich*, partaking as it does of the confessional autobiography, of the realistic novel, and of the *Bildungsroman* to a close. And I would like to return to a point that I made at the beginning of this essay – to the effect that Keller's is a novel that has centrally to do with the writing and re-writing process.[6] The first version of *Der grune Heinrich*, we have already noted, is in both the first and third person. The second version – and it is the one that I am concened with here – is in the first person throughout. The Heinrich we know at the end of the novel is a somewhat disillusioned and monosyllabic civil servant. He it is who, on the literal level, writes his own life-story in the pages before us. And yet somehow we do not receive the text in this way. What we read is neither disillusioned nor monsyllabic. Rather, in narrative terms, we hear a dual voice – on the one hand, one that is close to the disenchantments and

6   For further details, see Dominik Müller, *Wiederlesen und Weiterschreiben: Gottfried Kellers Neugestaltung des 'grünen Heinrich'* (Bern, 1988).

failures of Heinrich's life as lived, to the 'beinahe' of Effi Briest's verdict on herself; and, on the other, one that looks back on and transforms the life into instances of artistic and cognitive delight. Let me give a few examples. Here is the narrator (manifestly the older, sadder Heinrich) commenting on the letter of bitter reproach which Römer sends him after he (Heinrich) insists on the repayment of a debt:

> Den unheimlichen Brief wagte ich nicht zu verbrennen und fürchtete mich, ihn aufzubewahren; bald begab ich ihn unter entlegenem Gerümpel, bald zog ich ihn hervor und legte ihn zu meinen liebsten Papieren, und noch jetzt, so oft ich ihn finde, verändere ich seinen Ort und bringe ihn anderswo hin, so daß er auf steter Wanderschaft ist. (III, 5, 'Torheit des Meisters und des Schülers', II, p. 60)

Or take the description of his attempt as a young boy to do what many of his fellows do, to make a butterfly collection. Yet he finds that all his specimens so fight for life that when he finally puts them on display, they are merely 'eine zerfetzte Gesellschaft erbarmungswürdiger Märtyrer' (I, 10, 'Das spielende Kind', I, p. 99). One can think of the night that he spends in the theatre together with the actress who has played Gretchen in Goethe's 'Faust'; he sleeps at her feet and the two of them look like 'jenen alten Grabmälern, auf welchen ein steinerner Ritter ausgestreckt liegt mit seinem treuen Hunde zu Füßen' (I, 11, 'Theatergeschichte; Gretchen und die Meerkatze', I, p. 117). Mention should also be made of the description of his going to sleep at the end of the first day he has spent with his relatives in the country: 'und die kühle erfrischende Luft atmend, schlief ich sozusagen an der Brust der gewaltigen Natur ein' (I, 17, 'Flucht zur Mutter Natur', I, p. 178). The 'sozusagen' relativises the presence of the great post-Romantic topos of Mother Nature. There is also the description of the first kiss he exchanges with Anna: 'Ich hatte mich schon zu ihr geneigt, und wir küßten uns ebenso feierlich als ungeschickt' (II, 4, 'Totentanz', I, p. 260). Or, finally, let me recall the description of the mother, which I have already quoted, resolutely chewing her way through the hard, cheap bread, finding an eerie voluptuousness in the sense of her own deprivation: 'zufrieden dasselbe bewältigend, schwelgte sie ordentlich in ihrer freiwilligen Askese' (IV, 3, 'Lebensarten', III, p. 31). All of these passages seem to me to have a sophistication, a writerly delight that takes us beyond the psychological particularity of the disenchanted Heinrich. What we hear is a narrative performance that does not simply write but also re-writes the life. In that narrative performance we detect a kind of meta-voice, one that points us forward to some of the major achievements of twentieth-century fiction (Proust, Joyce, Woolf, Thomas Mann).

Let me, by way of conclusion, try to sharpen and take further the point that I am after. Frequently first-person novel narratives operate with a measure of discrepancy between the demands of lively, interesting narration on the one hand and, on the other, the less-than-writerly persona of the narrator as a psychologically specified figure. Heinrich Lee is, in other words, not the only first-person protagonist to be a better writer than his actual character would lead us to expect from him. But in *Der grüne Heinrich* the issue is more complex than simple poetic licence. And it is so because Keller's text constantly reflects on processes of representation, of mediation between self and world, on what is entailed in the adequate human depiction of and reponse to the surrounding world. In a sense, it is about little else; constantly it alerts us to the project of transforming the given material world into its humanly perceived and represented medium.[7] To return to a point I made at the beginning of this essay: Keller's *Der grüne Heinrich* is somehow still in quest of the self because the experiencing self and the writing self have not come into secure and conciliatory congruence. I invoked the two meanings of 'green' in the text. 'Green' refers to the protagonist's clothes; Heinrich is reach-me-down man. Yet at another level 'green' implies vitality and energy, and that vitality can be sensed in the act of narrative recall, in the process of walking 'die alten grünen Pfade der Erinnerung'. Hence, there is at the heart of Keller's novel a dialectic between experiencing and writing. As an experiencing instance Heinrich Lee is blighted and blighting. The separation of imagination and reality takes its toll – his inner life becomes unfocused, his outer life becomes devalued to a sequence of reach-me-down experiences. One could think of his formulation of the growing attraction between Anna and himself: 'Ich war am Ende der Einzige, welcher heimlich ihr den Namen Liebe gab, weil mir einmal alles sich zum Romane gestaltete' (II, 4, 'Toten-

---

7   See Gail K. Hart, *Readers and their Fictions in the Novels and Novellas of Gottfried Keller* (Chapel Hill and London, 1989); Anne Brenner, *Leseräume. Untersuchungen zu Lektüre-verfahren und -funktionen in Gottfried Kellers Roman 'Der grüne Heinrich'* (Würzburg, 2000).

tanz', I, p. 251). The self-consciousness here is intriguing; it devalues the experience being invoked but energises the written account being offered. Whole tracts of Heinrich's experience – the fraught schooldays, the relationships with Anna and Judith, the painting, the bohemian life in Munich, the joyless return home are curiously arid, lived as ready-made, off-the-peg experience. Yet the written account is enthralling – witty, ironic, penetrating, intelligent, touching. The narrating self knows better, knows more richly than does the experiencing self. Writing is, it would seem, closer to liveliness than is life itself.

At this point it is pertinent to recall that Nietzsche, that matchless disgnostician of the spiritual barrenness of the modern world, could only hold out hope for a redemption of the world through art. It seems to be no accident that Nietzsche admired Keller's work – perhaps for its ability, and here I envoke a memorable phrase of Baudelaire's, to turn mud into gold. Nietzsche also admired Stifter; and the latter's novel *Der Nachsommer* (1857) is perhaps the most single-minded justification of the world as aesthetic phenomenon that we possess. Keller the realist acknowledges the resistant experiential world that stands in need of transformation; Stifter, by contrast, by-passes all that refractory wordliness by writing a novel that is, apart from a few renegade pages of retrospective agony, the monument to a transformed world. Flaubert, we remember, wanted to write 'un livre sur rien'. Presumably such a thing cannot be achieved; nor indeed even be imagined – although Stifter helps us to start those imaginings. In any event, that strangely aestheticising voice, one that is a meta-voice to the anger and telegrams of the unregenerate world, runs parallel to the great achievements of literary realism in the European nineteenth century. We have heard it in Keller. And it points us forward to the twentieth century, to classic works of High Modernism (as I have already suggested). But it also points forward to texts that are unmistakably close to our world. I am thinking of Günter Grass, Thomas Bernhard, Christoph Ransmayr, W. G. Sebald (himself a great admirer of Keller), of the strange concatenation of catastrophic suject matter and virtuosic linguistic mode that is so characteristic of their work. But all this is another story; or, perhaps more accurately, it is another version of the story that is told by Keller's *Der grüne Heinrich*.

CHARLOTTE WOODFORD

Fontane, *Effi Briest*

Effi Briest (1895), Fontane's most successful work, is the best example of German social and political fiction of the nineteenth century. Works in this category were commercially successful and were very widely read, but the tradition of the 'social novel' has now faded slightly from view. Other figures from Fontane's generation, once exceptionally well-known, no longer command the attention they once did: Marie von Ebner-Eschenbach (1830–1916), for example, Gustav Freytag (1816–1895), Louise von François (1817–1893) or Wilhelm Raabe (1831–1910). The impact of these figures on their period was considerable, and this essay will attempt to draw on some of the themes of their fiction in order to show how *Effi Briest* is indebted to it. Part of the strength of Fontane's work is that it responds critically to the novelistic discourses of its time and the thought which underpins them. As such, it can be seen as the high-point of the bourgeois novel and, simultaneously, an important stage in that genre's decline and the transition to Modernism.

A masterpiece of nineteenth-century fiction, *Effi Briest* is one of very few German novels generally seen as participating in the great tradition of nineteenth-century European Realism.[1] As Martin Swales outlines in his essay on Keller's *Der grüne Heinrich* in this volume and elsewhere, realism also had a different character in German than in other European traditions. So to compare Fontane – still less his predecessors – with French or Russian novels, for example, is not to compare like with like.[2] Fontane writes of Realism: 'Vor allen Dingen vestehen wir nicht darunter das nackte Wiedergeben alltäglichen Lebens, am

1   See Martin Swales, 'Half Truths: Theodor Fontane', in *Studies of German Prose Fiction in the Age of European Realism* (Lewiston, 1995), pp. 65–79 (p. 65), or Alan Bance, 'The Novel in Wilhelmine Germany: from realism to satire', in *The Cambridge Companion to the Modern German Novel*, ed. by Graham Bartram (Cambridge, 2004), pp. 31–45 (p. 31).

2   Martin Swales, '"Neglecting the weight of the Elephant...": German Prose Fiction and European Realism', *Modern Language Review*, 83 (1988), 882–94.

wenigsten seines Elends und seiner Schattenseiten'.[3] Rather, the aim of German 'realism' of the mid-nineteenth century was poetically to transfigure the material world. It has been described as an attempt to depict the 'wholeness and harmony' that was the 'true' nature of the world, drawing on German idealist philosophy. German 'realism' of the mid-nineteenth century aimed not to represent but to *transfigure* the material world.[4] Such a consciously poetic representation of life necessitated the repression of certain topics. Russell Bermann, for instance, in a recent article on *Effi Briest*, highlights how Effi's father's pet phrase, 'das ist ein zu weites Feld', draws attention the function of realism as 'the literary language that proscribes treatment of ultimate questions, even in the face of death'.[5] However, in drawing attention to realism's repression of such questions there is in Fontane also an implicit engagement with them. Martin Swales convincingly argues that Keller in *Der grune Heinrich* offers an aesthetic redemption of the world through the poetic metanarrative, in compensation for the absence of redemptive possibilities in the real world and in line with Nietzsche's idea that only one kind of redemption is possible – redemption through art.[6] This is a theme which is also pertinent to *Effi Briest* and this essay will argue that Effi's death *is* in fact a treatment of ultimate questions, even in its rendering of them as 'poetic'.

Fontane, the son of a pharmacist and lacking a university education, made his living from journalism until the publication of his first novel, *Vor dem Sturm* (1878), when he was nearly sixty. He depended for his living on the fees which bourgeois periodicals would pay for serialisation of a novel before publication. The income of the periodicals came from regular subscriptions, so editors could not risk publishing material that would offend its largely bourgeois audience. As David Jackson points out, authors needed to be alert to 'the effect of works on impressionable young ladies'; it was important for sales that a reader could

3   'Unsere Lyrische und Epische Poesie seit 1848' [1853] in *Werke*, Vol 21.1, *Literarische Essays und Studien. Erster Teil*, ed. by Kurt Schreinert (Munich, 1963), pp. 7–33 (p. 12).
4   David Jackson, 'Taboos in Poetic-Realist Writers', in *Taboos in German Literature*, ed. by David Jackson (Oxford, 1996), pp. 59–78 (p. 64).
5   'Effi Briest and the end of Realism', in *A Companion to German Realism*, ed. by Todd Kontje (Rochester, NY, 2002), pp. 339–64 (p. 340).
6   See Swales's essay on *Der grune Heinrich* earlier in this volume.

comfortably leave a work 'lying about in the drawing room' without risking a scandal.[7] For this reason opposition to *Irrungen Wirrungen* (1888) had briefly threatened Fontane's commercial viability. That novel's sympathetic treatment of the extra-marital sexual relationship between the aristocratic officer Botho von Rienäcker and the seamstress Lene Nimptsch aroused widespread indignation. *Effi Briest* is more cautious in its treatment of female sexuality, one of the many taboo subjects in realist fiction.[8]

But while the literary codes which govern *Effi Briest* are indebted to poetic realism, the text also points forward to twentieth-century writing. It draws our attention to the largely unspoken psychological reality of characters' inner lives, a layer of reality corresponding to the romantic imagination which realism had repressed. It has been read by Bermann, for example, as a work in which we can see the realist tradition disintegrate.[9] Fontane's narrator largely withholds comment on the psychological reality of the characters, a discretion which has been interpreted as a sign of the narrator's complicity in the social world of the characters and one that undermines the novel's ability to criticise its society.[10] Yet as Martin Swales has argued, the narrative reticence also marks Fontane's recognition of the complexity of subjectivity.[11] It is an inferential means of conveying that the self eludes adequate representation. The authenticity of the self has been compromised by social discourses which, according to Swales, 'penetrate deep into the recesses of the individual mind' and show us how 'human beings feel, think, and understand themselves and their experience'.[12] But in addition to that, you could say that Fontane's works also reveal the *limited* nature of characters' under-

7   'Taboos', p. 72.
8   *Effi Briest*'s connection with the tradition of the European novel of adultery is explored by Felicia Gordon, 'Legitimation and Irony in Tolstoy and Fontane', in *Scarlet Letters: Fictions of Adultery from Antiquity to the 1990s*, ed. by Nicholas White and Naomi Segal (Basingstoke, 1997), pp. 85–97 and in Bill Overton, 'Children and Childlessness in the Novel of Female Adultery', *Modern Language Review*, 94 (1999), pp. 314–27 (pp. 324–5).
9   'Effi Briest and the End of Realism'.
10   Michael Minden, 'Realism versus Poetry: Theodor Fontane, *Effi Briest*', in *The German Novel in the Twentieth Century*, ed. by David Midgley (Edinburgh, 1993), pp. 18–29 (p. 25).
11   *Studies of German Prose Fiction*, p. 74.
12   '"Neglecting the weight"', p. 894.

standing of themselves. Michael Bell argues that nineteenth-century novelists show us, well before psychologists had developed a discourse to explain it, that 'the imperatives of feeling may come in large measure from unconscious sources'.[13] *Effi Briest* thus participates in the philosophical developments which make Fontane a 'precursor' of Freud.[14]

Far from being a 'Naturkind' in the pre-lapsarian idyll of Hohen-Cremmen, Effi simply knows of no other way of experiencing reality than through social discourse.[15] Her incorporation of society's role for her is clear from the beginning, but it is in tension with a longing that alienates her from herself and results in the deep anxiety that marks her years in Kessin. When Luise von Briest informs Effi of Innstetten's proposal of marriage and appeals to Effi's social ambition, Effi fails to find a socially appropriate answer and trembles nervously as Innstetten comes into view. Her body betrays emotion which she is neither able – nor permitted – consciously to formulate. Later, she tells her friends that Innstetten is of course the right man for her, for so would any aristocrat be who has a suitable social position and good looks: 'Gewiß ist es der Richtige. [...] Jeder ist der Richtige. Natürlich muß er von Adel sein und eine Stellung haben und gut aussehen' (p. 182).[16] This passage is often read as an example of Effi's 'insouciant' internalisation of the bourgeois code.[17] However, Hertha's shocked reaction to this suggests that one could interpret it as performative language through which Effi reassures herself that her acceptance of the proposal is correct and displays pride at becoming the first friend to be engaged. Hertha comments: 'Gott, Effi, wie du nur sprichst. Sonst sprachst du doch ganz anders' (p. 182).

---

13   *Sentimentalism, Ethics and the Culture of Feeling* (Basingstoke, 2000), p. 142. Bell is particularly illuminating on nineteenth-century sentimental fiction and the depiction of unconscious behaviour.

14   See Renate Böschenstein, 'Fontane's Writing and the Problem of "Reality" in Philosophy and Literature', in *Theodor Fontane and the European Context*, ed. by Patricia Howe and Helen Chambers (Amsterdam, 2001), pp. 15–32 (p. 21).

15   The idea of women in Fontane being 'poetic' and hence set apart from society is put forward, amongst others, by Alan Bance, *Theodor Fontane: The Major Novels* (Cambridge, 1982) and criticised by Martin Swales, *Studies in German Prose Fiction*, p. 73.

16   All quotations from the novel refer to *Effi Briest, Sämtliche Werke*, ed. by Edgar Gross (Munich, 1959), Vol. 7, pp. 171–427.

17   See, for example, Patricia Howe, "A Visibly-appointed Stopping-place", in *Theodor Fontane and the European Context*, p. 143.

'Ja, sonst', says Effi. *Then* it was different. *Now* she has a new role to play in the 'Gesellschaftskomödie' of life, a role which comes conveniently with its own discourse. Effi knows exactly how she *should* behave as a newly-engaged woman. The ready-made nature of the discourse avoids her or the narrator having to probe her emotional state more deeply. However, by foregrounding the discrepancy between the emotion described and the unacknowledged emotional confusion which lies behind it, this is a step towards the more self-consciously ironic narrative style of Thomas Mann.

Although the metaphor of 'Komödie' recurs frequently in the text and Effi engages in play-acting, both literally and figuratively, in general the category of conscious hypocrisy seems to have been superseded by the idea of self-deception. Truth of feeling is compromised by the subject's internalisation of social discourses, though it can perhaps sometimes be inferred though Freudian slips. Effi's mother, when talking of her fears that Effi does not love Innstetten, places the greatest importance on the information which Effi had not been conscious of confiding: 'gerade weil es so ungewollt und wie von ungefähr aus ihrer Seele kam, deshalb war es mir so wichtig' (p. 198). Luise comments anxiously on Effi's ability seemingly to repress her feelings and deal with them on her own: 'Sie hat nicht das Bedürfnis, sich so recht von Herzen auszusprechen' (p. 198). Luise has little appreciation of the irony of her remark, since for her too 'spontaneity' is carefully contrived.[18] Most likely she is projecting onto Effi an unacknowledged emotion of her own. She has hit, however, on a moment of truth, for to speak from the heart could be seen in the text as an impossibility. Effi is unaware of what she truly feels. She is 'mitteilsam und verschlossen zugleich' (*ibid.*). She talks a lot but much of it is in keeping with Botho's definition of social chit-chat in *Irrungen Wirrungen*: 'yes' is much the same as 'no'; there is little authenticity to her words. On the other hand, Effi's indifference to Innstetten is worryingly clear to Luise when Effi puts a letter from him straight in her pocket without reading it (p. 199). And the way Effi dismisses as laughable her mother's idea that she might marry 'Vetter Briest', is interpreted by Luise as implying that Effi has only married Innstetten out of social ambition. Though there is some truth in

18   Minden, 'Realism versus Poetry', pp. 26–7.

this statement, ironically, Luise does not reflect on the fact that Effi only married Innstetten because her mother told her to do so.

When Effi has moved to Berlin, she reflects in an internal mono- logue that she is weighed down not by *guilt* but by *fear* that her adultery will come to light retrospectively and by *guilt* at her lack of true guilt. She possesses neither proper remorse nor proper shame ('die rechte Reue'; 'die rechte Scham'):

> Aber Scham über meine Schuld, die hab ich nicht oder doch nicht so recht oder doch nicht genug, und das bringt mich um, daß ich sie nicht habe. Wenn alle Weiber so sind, dann ist es schrecklich, und wenn sie nicht so sind, wie ich hoffe, dann steht es schlecht um mich, dann ist etwas nicht in Ordnung in meiner Seele, dann fehlt mir das richtige Gefühl (p. 359).

This passage highlights Effi's self-condemnation, linked to her un- conscious reluctance to burn the letters which would prevent the adultery coming to light. Her self-condemnation contrasts with the narrator's sympathetic treatment of her and intensifies the reader's sympathy. In *Effi Briest*, there is ample indication that Effi is not an exception; many women transgress, but most destroy the evidence. The syntax of this passage indicates that even such an interior monologue can not be interpreted as Effi's *authentic* emotion. Effi does not know her real feelings; she can only keep trying to reformulate them, scrutinising them and interpreting them through the moral discourses of her childhood. Her reflections revolve around the issue of sincerity, of true feeling, a key theme of the nineteenth-century sentimental novel.[19] Niemeyer has told Effi that the most important thing to possess is 'ein richtiges Gefühl'; but the adjectives 'recht' or 'richtig' cannot be used to describe Effi's emo- tions. Truth of feeling is problematic; it is no longer possible to separate an authentic self and social conditioning.[20]

Social conditioning is evident in the way Effi narrates to her three female companions the story of Geert von Innstetten's unrequited love for Effi's mother, Luise. She comments: 'Eine Geschichte mit Entsagung ist nie schlimm' (p. 174). This echoes the discourses of popular fiction, where renunciation *is* never 'schlimm'; it is what makes the story excit-

19   Bell, 'Victorian Sentimentality: the Dialectic of Sentiment and Truth of Feeling', in *Sentimentalism*, pp. 118–49.
20   See Swales, *Studies of German Prose Fiction*, pp. 68–9.

ing and leads to spiritual growth and moral validation of the hero or, more usually, heroine. Effi calls Innstetten's story 'beinahe romantisch'; 'beinahe', perhaps, because its ending is not the poetic death in battle which Innstetten might have preferred, but a successful career in the prosaic world of Prussian administration.[21] Innstetten and Luise were forced to separate when both were barely twenty, so that Luise could marry the older and more successful Herr von Briest. The story ends, Effi tells us, as such stories always end and Effi herself, the product of the arranged marriage, is regarded by the girls as adequate compensation for Luise's lost love. As far as they are concerned, the story is closed. The girls accept unquestioningly that renunciation is inevitable, for social duty is more important than personal inclination.

Yet the failure of Innstetten's love for Luise looms large over the novel in a way which the reader can only infer. During the twenty years since losing her, Innstetten has sublimated his sexual energy successfully into his cigars and his career; when married to Effi he is unable to resurrect it and he remains 'ohne rechte Liebe', in the words of Effi on her death bed, which shift the reader's attention back to Luise, the cause of Innstetten's sadness.[22] Innstetten appears anxious to avoid Luise, refusing without adequate explanation to renovate the upper floor of their Kessin home so that Luise and Briest can stay with the young couple. He fails to visit Effi and the infant Annie when they return for an extended visit to Hohen-Cremmen, incurring criticism from Effi's father. Even at the start of their marriage, Effi describes him as 'frostig wie ein Schnee-mann' (p. 224), while also telling her mother that she felt afraid of Innstetten's physical caresses: 'er hatte so was Fremdes. Und fremd war er auch in seiner Zärtlichkeit. Ja, dann am meisten; es hat Zeiten gegeben, wo ich mich davor fürchtete' (p. 356). Innstetten retreats into his study in the evenings to work, before returning with the newspaper to bore Effi with stories about Bismarck. The statesman is symbolically the cause of the couple's first parting, for all of twelve hours, when Innstetten is invited to dine with Bismarck and his wife, and Effi scares

21   Valerie D. Greenberg, 'The Resistance of Effi Briest: An (Un)told Tale', *Publications of the Modern Language Association of America*, 103(5), 770-82 (p. 771).

22   Renate Böschenstein, 'Die Ehre als Instrument des Masochismus in der deutschen Literatur des 18. und 19. Jahrhunderts', in *Masochismus in der Literatur*, ed. by Johannes Cremerius and others (Würzburg, 1988), pp. 34–55 (p. 49).

herself with thoughts about the ghost of the Chinese man, another symbol of a failed relationship.

Pleasanter evenings, as far as Innstetten is concerned, would be for them to go through his writings about their honeymoon trip to Italy in order that they might learn more about what they saw. Roswitha would stand near them holding their child and Effi would knit him a woollen cap for winter (pp. 291–92). This is how Innstetten conceives of a model bourgeois marriage, but Effi had tired of his discussions of art on the trip itself. His enthusiasm for the plans makes him insensitive to her feelings; she is delighted when they fall through and are replaced by amateur dramatics, a performance of the play aptly entitled *Ein Schritt vom Wege*, one of a series of references in the text to illegitimate sexuality which symbolically prefigure the events of the novel.[23] Innstetten's vision of domestic harmony is reminiscent of the images from family magazines. Rather than experiencing authentic emotion for her ('rechte Liebe') and permitting that to guide their behaviour, he fashions their relationship second-hand to conform to a social norm. Effi recognised before her marriage that she would not be fulfilled by such conformity: 'ich bin nicht so sehr für das, was man eine Musterehe nennt' (p. 192). Bourgeois marriage requires the subordination of women's interests to those of their husband or family. Renate Böschenstein regards such voluntary submission as a form of masochism,[24] but the example of Innstetten makes clear that it is a universal condition and not one restricted to women. Innstetten's principal act of masochism is his subordination to the 'Gesellschafts-Etwas' when he divorces Effi, a decision which ultimately destroys any hope he has of happiness.[25] Martin Swales points out that when deliberating whether to challenge Crampas to a duel, Innstetten takes solace in the rhetoric of the cult of honour.[26] Again, this is for him a ready-made discourse, and it enables him to avoid confronting his true emotions.

---

23   Others are, for example, Effi's reference to the punishment of adulteresses in Islam and Roswitha's story of the social stigma of her illegitimate pregnancy.

24   See Böschenstein, 'Die Ehre als Instrument des Masochismus'.

25   'Die Ehre als Instrument des Masochismus', p. 50.

26   *Studies of German Prose Fiction*, pp. 70–72.

Michael Minden suggests that *Effi Briest* can be read on the one hand as a poetic tale and on the other as a story of 'pure waste'.[27] As he points out, the futility of Effi's suffering is made very clear in the novel: divorced for adultery which took place six years previously with a man whom she did not love, and because of the accidental discovery of letters which should have been destroyed. The real-life story from which Fontane drew his subject material concerns Elisabeth Freiin von Plotho (b. 1853), who was married to the army officer Armand Léon von Ardenne. She fell in love and had a long-standing affair, which continued even after a move from the Rheinland to Berlin. Ardenne uncovered the affair by discovering her letters. He killed the lover, Emil Hartwich, in a duel and went on to become a general in the German army. His wife prosaically survived being divorced for adultery and she died in 1952, aged ninety-nine, after devoting her life to charitable works.[28] Fontane's changes diverted attention away from the real-life forbears.[29] But they also underline the idea of waste. Effi is far younger than Elisabeth von Ardenne. Her involvement with Crampas is devoid of any love and gratefully terminated as soon as she has the strength to do so. Her early death may be 'poetic' and rework the traditional death of the fictional adulteress, but it is not poetic justice in the sense that it so often is in adultery novels: the punishment of a male author for female transgression of the patriarchal institution of marriage.[30]

The narrator's uncharacteristic interjection in her final illness – 'arme Effi' – puts paid to any negative judgment *on* the protagonist. While the chair on which Effi's mother Luise sits at Effi's deathbed can be interpreted as a judge's seat and Luise's words as a cruel judgment of her daughter, they are, as Patricia Howe points out, a condemnation to which the reader cannot assent.[31] Luise's words, informing Effi that she has brought her fate on herself, 'miss the point', according to Howe; for Böschenstein they instead pass judgement on Luise's behaviour.[32] They

27   'Poetry versus Realism', p. 23. See also Minden, '"Effi Briest" and "die historische Stunde des Takts', *Modern Language Review*, 76 (1981), 871–79.

28   See Walter Müller-Seidel, *Theodor Fontane: Soziale Romankunst in Deutschland* (Stuttgart, 1975), pp. 352–54.

29   Minden, 'Realism versus Poetry', p. 18.

30   Gordon, 'Legitimation and Irony', p. 85.

31   '"A Visibly-appointed Stopping-place"', p. 146.

32   'Fontane's Writing', p. 29

might also be read as a psychological projection of Luise's own feelings of guilt, feelings to which she cannot bring herself to admit. Even at the end of the novel, she is incapable of and ultimately prevented from fully exploring those feelings. Her first and only attempt to broach the subject is when she wonders tentatively to Briest whether Effi was, perhaps, still too young for marriage. Again, though, Luise misses the point; Effi's youth is surely less significant than Luise's choice of husband for her. Any discussion of that, however, would threaten to reveal the latent tensions in Effi's parents' relationship. Luise, as Briest previously acknowledged, would have made Innstetten a far better wife than Effi.

Fontane draws so much attention to the 'waste' of Effi's life that I would argue it is possible to read it as a response to the way in which religious discourses were employed in this period to attribute spiritual value to suffering. In sentimental fiction of the nineteenth century, religious consolation strategies are frequently employed to validate suffering and provide models of religious faith for the reader to emulate. They provide a moral education which parallels the religious education of girls in the period.[33] Such fiction may have provided women readers with the comfort that the hardships they suffered in the domestic sphere would be remembered in the afterlife, but it was also instrumental in women's subordination to patriarchy's limited roles for them. Some of the archetypal models for religious-sentimental deaths in nineteenth-century fiction come from the English tradition, which Fontane so admired. One thinks, for example, of the sentimental death of Little Nell in Dickens' *The Old Curiosity Shop* (1841), while one of Fontane's favourite English novels was Charlotte Brontë's *Jane Eyre* (1847). There, Jane's best friend from Lowood school, Helen Burns, dies a beautiful death from consumption, strengthened by the sincere belief that she is about to enter the kingdom of heaven. She instructs Jane: 'We must all die one day. [...] By dying young, I shall escape great sufferings. I had not qualities or talents to make my way very well in the world: I should have been continually at fault' (Ch. 9). Helen gently proclaims that she is going to meet her maker; she is calm and composed and dies a peaceful death in Jane's arms.

---

33   See, for example, Eda Sagarra, 'Marie von Ebner-Eschenbach and the Tradition of the Catholic Enlightenment', in *The Austrian Enlightenment and its Aftermath*, ed. by Ritchie Robertson and Edward Timms (Edinburgh, 1991), pp. 117–31 (p. 121).

Finding meaning in suffering is a basic human need. For Nietzsche, the human race practically invented the Gods, 'damit das verborgene, unentdeckte, zeugenlose Leiden aus der Welt geschafft und ehrlich negirt werden konnte' (1887).[34] Yet Effi, in keeping with the increasing religious scepticism of the late nineteenth century, finds it hard to take solace in religion, as earlier literary heroines had done (such as Emilia Galotti or Marie in *Woyzeck*). Compensatory beliefs are outlined for Effi by Frau von Padden in the chapter which follows Effi's seduction by Crampas. She discusses marriage with Effi, while watching the dancing at her second New Year's Ball in Kessin. Effi has taken her place with the 'old ladies', despite being only eighteen years old. Frau von Padden is rather unconventional ('ein Original') and possesses attractive high cheek bones, but she has been inured against their likely effect on men by a Christian faith strong enough to withstand temptation. With ironic timing, three days *after* Effi submits to Crampas' adulterous advances, the older woman enquires cheerfully about Effi's romantic attachments, asking if Effi is ever tempted to stray from her marriage vows. The old woman takes for it granted that a pretty young girl like Effi will answer in the affirmative and Effi is relieved to encounter someone who tacitly acknowledges the difficulties of marriage. Effi's hesitant answer, 'Ach, gnädigste Frau...', confirms the pious old woman's suspicions. Consequently, Frau von Padden reiterates the religious discourse outlined above: virtue consists of the successful struggle against temptation, a struggle against the natural, fallen state of mankind, a struggle of the spirit against the body: 'Man muß immer ringen mit dem natürlichen Menschen. Und wenn man sich dann so unter hat und beinah schreien möchte, weils weh tut, dann jubeln die lieben Engel!' (p. 311). The angels delight in the purifying nature of suffering. Effi replies poignantly that it is so *difficult* to resist temptation. The old woman recommends Effi to take pleasure in the difficulty: 'je schwerer, desto besser' (p. 312) and refers to Luther, alluding to the Lutheran tradition of passive obedience. Submission through faith leads to redemption.

For Nietzsche, however, 'the compensatory belief in heaven [...] reduces the value and dignity of human existence' (in the words of

---

34 'Zur Genealogie der Moral', *Kritische Studienausgabe*, Vol. 5, ed. by Giorgio Colli and Mazzino Montinari, p. 304.

J. P. Stern).[35] Such beliefs reinforce the political and the social status quo; they make the subject complicit in its own subordination. This is inherent in von Padden's response: 'Im Glauben sich unterkriegen, meine liebe Frau, darauf kommt es an, das ist das Wahre' (p. 312). Such a response fails to acknowledge the damaging effect of these beliefs on the individual subject. One of Fontane's contemporaries, the Austrian writer Marie von Ebner-Eschenbach, herself a Roman Catholic, repeatedly challenges compensatory beliefs in her own fiction for this same reason. In *Unsühnbar* (1892), Ebner's novel of female adultery, the protagonist Maria Dornach commits adultery on a single occasion with a man, Felix Tessin, who turns out to be unworthy of her love. His attraction to her is partly an act of revenge on her father, who overlooked him as a suitor for Maria. As the complexity of adult sexuality and its consequences is revealed to the sheltered aristocratic girl, Maria loses faith in human nature. She also rejects God, for she is unable to regard as good a being who finds merit in suffering. She proclaims her lack of faith on her death-bed, making her the antithesis of the sentimental heroine such as Helen Burns.

In *Effi Briest*, Effi's wasteful death also undermines such compensatory beliefs. Yet on her deathbed, Effi clutches at them, leading to a division in perspective between that of the protagonist and the meta-voice of the narrator. Effi's own religious education has been a failure. She cannot initially identify with von Padden's submission through faith. Innstetten refers to her lack of constancy or 'Festigkeit', the language of neo-stoicism (p. 310). She has 'keine starke Natur' (p. 315). She stands therefore in stark contrast to the conventional fictional heroine, who resists temptation through virtue in the Christian stoic tradition. But Effi fails to resist because she cannot see the value in resistance. She knows the language: in response to Crampas' flirtatious discussions of romantic poetry by Heine, she tells him of a poem which she learnt at school, called 'Gottesmauer', about a widow besieged by the enemy who prayed to God to build a wall around her to protect her (p. 299). In the moment of seduction, Effi recalls that widow's religious faith and prays the same words, but all at once she realises they are meaningless for her: 'daß es tote Worte waren' (p. 308). When Fontane writes that Effi is as if enchanted, he is upholding the realist taboo on the depiction of female

35   *Nietzsche* (London, 1978), p. 93.

sexuality. Effi does not *want* to free herself, for at the end of the day she has no particular reason to do so. While the conventional literary heroine resists seduction through virtue,[36] Effi lacks such a heroine's doctrinal certainty and sense of self-worth.

Indeed, Effi is branded an atheist by Sidonie von Grasenabb. This is clearly not the whole story – Sidonie is a bitter old maid and an uncharitable witness. Effi is attracted to the idea of God and believes in a form of transcendence – but she admits that she has always been a poor Christian (p. 423). Luise says Effi thinks of God as like a kindly old gentleman who will not judge her too severely on how she has behaved: 'Sie hat einen Zug, den lieben Gott einen guten Mann sein zu lassen und sich zu trösten, er werde wohl nicht allzu streng mit ihr sein' (p. 355). It is a sign of her daughter Annie's subordination to Innstetten's will that the subject in which Annie performs best at school is religion (p. 407). Sound religious teaching will ensure there is no repetition by the daughter of Effi's 'Fehltritt'. Effi's best subject was mythology, which emphasises the hold of the imagination over her psychological development. But mythology stands in opposition to the Christian tradition and contains an abundance of stories unsuitable for virgins. In the last scene of the book, Luise von Briest attempts to blame Pastor Niemeyer for Effi's fate because of the ambiguity of his religious teaching (p. 427), again another case of Luise sidestepping her own guilt by projecting it onto others. Niemeyer's own moral relativism is linked to Effi's adultery, not just because of his influence over her but because both are typical of the late nineteenth-century decline in religious certainty, to which the works of Nietzsche and Freud are a response. Niemeyer points out in apparent respect and admiration that Innstetten is a man of *character*, a man of principles, something which always engendered fear in Effi (p. 195). Pastor Niemeyer has no such moral certainty, neither is he able to impart any to Effi, but on the other hand his ambivalence is contrasted sympathetically with his wife's hypocritical and uncharitable high moral stance.

At the end of Effi's life, Effi searches for consolation from religious discourses, worrying about the Last Judgement. Whether or not there is a heaven – and she says on another occasion that she does not want to

---

36   Christine Lehmann, *Das Modell Clarissa: Liebe, Verführung. Sexualität und Tod der Romanheldinnen des 18. und 19. Jahrhunderts* (Stuttgart, 1991), p. 11.

know – she is anxious to fulfil the criteria for admission. She has no other way of finding meaning in her early death. Niemeyer quietly re-assures her that she will be redeemed (p. 414). On her deathbed, she is thus able to adopt the Christian stoicism of the sentimental heroine. Like Helen Burns, she is 'ganz ruhig' in the face of death (p. 424) and offers comfort to her mother, by narrating a moral tale which comes second hand from Innstetten. It concerns a person called away early from a dinner party, who is afterwards told he missed nothing by leaving before everyone else (p. 425). Effi uses it to reassure her mother that an early death is no worse than death in old age. This is reminiscent of Helen Burns' comments to Jane Eyre that she will miss nothing by dying young. However, in the poetry of this sentimental scene we are uncom-fortably reminded of Innstetten's role as 'Erzieher', even while Effi is able to refer to him for the first time with composure.

Effi has come to terms with the wrongs which Innstetten has done to her and ends her life with a moment of reconciliation: 'ich sterbe mit Gott und Menschen versöhnt, auch versöhnt mit *ihm*' (p. 425). Effi is concerned 'to do a righteous deed before dying'.[37] In the stoical tradi-tion, still influential in Catholic and Lutheran religious teaching of girls in this period, imparting forgiveness of those who have wronged you is an important aspect of dying a good death. Effi follows the script, saying that her forgiveness of Innstetten 'wird ihn trösten, aufrichten, vielleicht versöhnen' (p. 425). But in her confessions to her mother, Effi reminds us of the wrongs committed against her. She refers also to her earlier anger against Innstetten. Michael Minden calls it a Brechtian '"short anger", not the long anger through which objective circumstances might be challenged'.[38] Short it may be, and Effi has overcome it, but for the reader her poetic death is interrupted by the recollection of the injustice done to Effi. The reader is surely inclined to disagree with Effi's senti-ment that Innstetten's calculated punishment of her through the child was just (p. 425). Perhaps in the meta-voice of the narrator there are still resonances of that anger, resonances which enable the reader to chal-lenge the society whose codes have produced such resignation.

Although Peter Klaus Schuster interprets the ending of *Effi Briest* rather traditionally in the Christian context of Marian symbolism (with

---

37   Greenberg, 'The Resistance of Effi Briest', p. 777.
38   'Realism versus Poetry', p. 28.

Effi representing both Eve and Mary and the narrative one of fall and redemption), Patricia Howe's argument that the ending of the novel should be read as 'a site of resistance' seems more persuasive.[39] Effi's death, according to Howe, offers resistance to 'the discourses available to the society that produced Effi Briest and her story, to the moral design of Victorian fiction'(p. 148). Effi's behaviour at the end of her life is a further sign of the social conditioning which led her to marry Innstetten in the first place. Her death is not individualistic, but staged – though she is not conscious of it being a performance. To use a term employed by Martin Swales, it may be considered 'pre-packaged'.[40] The meta-voice of the narrator surrounds the conventional heroine's death with too many indications of the meaningless of her suffering for the reader to assent to the moral design in the way that Effi does. Even in her last illness, the beauty of Effi's teeth is brought to our attention as a way of indicating the long and healthy life which might have been (p. 423). The only redemption possible is the redemption of Effi through the poetic patterning of her death, redemption through art. The consolatory discourses in which Effi tries too hard to attain redemption are called into question, surely precisely because they rob Effi of her anger and prevent all resistance except the mental resistance of the sympathetic reader.

Effi Briest is a threshold novel, indebted to realist and sentimental novels of the nineteenth century, but in other ways anticipating Modernism. It does so particularly in its secularism and in its lack of moral certainty. Furthermore, there is no clear division between subject and world in this novel; society is carried within the protagonists and they are incapable of distinguishing between genuine emotion and social conditioning. By depicting its protagonists' subjectivity from a distance, through conversations and body-language – as well as through internal monologues – Fontane's restrained narrator is able to convey the complexity of subjectivity and to highlight the element of performance involved in social interaction. The novel draws attention to the discourses of bourgeois society and as such to the formation of the modern subject. It does so by its very participation in the discourses, and as such its resistance is rendered ultimately problematic. Even by withdrawing to

---

39   Schuster, *Ein Leben nach christlichen Bildern* (Tubingen, 1978), p. 130, quoted by
     Howe, '"A Visibly-appointed Stopping-place"', p. 147.
40   *Studies of German Prose Fiction*, p. 68.

Hohen-Cremmen, Effi cannot escape society, for it is a part of her. Similarly, the resistance of the author to those same social discourses is also only partial. But that is perhaps not merely a feature of realist fiction. Perhaps it also truer of Modernist writers than we might sometimes care to admit.

ELIZABETH BOA

Mann, *Buddenbrooks*

Buddenbrooks was published in 1901 in a two-volume edition of only 1000 copies. But sales took off from 1903 with the publication of a cheaper, single-volume edition, and in the following year the novel jumped to near the top of the lending library lists.[1] Sales grew steadily and by 1918 had reached 100,000 copies. But the mass, popular success began in 1929 when Mann was awarded the Nobel Prize – with the citation not for *Der Zauberberg*, published so much more recently in 1924, but for his first novel. A special edition launched a few days earlier became an immediate bestseller, and sales quickly passed the million mark. In 1936 Mann's work was banned in Germany, and in the postwar period attention initially centred on later works such as *Doktor Faustus*; but a paperback edition, published in 1960 alongside a new collected edition of Mann's works, relaunched *Buddenbrooks* as a bestseller. Current estimates suggest sales of German-language editions of over six million copies. Opinions differ over which of Thomas Mann's novels is the landmark work in the canon. After all, three of his novels feature in the present publication. But who better to settle the matter than Marcel Reich-Ranicki? In a *Spiegel* article of 2001 celebrating the publication centenary, Reich-Ranicki hailed *Buddenbrooks* as *the* work by Thomas Mann which had won a place in his Noah's Arc of essential reading.[2]

The Shorter Oxford English Dictionary defines figurative uses of 'landmark' as 'a conspicuous object in a landscape' and as 'an object which is associated with some event or stage in a process; *esp.* an event which marks a period or turning point in history.' So, bestsellerdom

1   See Gero von Wilpert, 'Editionsgeschichte', in *Buddenbrooks-Handbuch*, ed. by Ken Moulden and Gero von Wilpert (Stuttgart, 1988), pp. 319–21; for a recent estimate of sales see Boris Prem, *Buddenbrooks Thomas Mann. Inhalt, Hintergrund Interpretation* (Munich, 2005), p. 38; on lending library figures see http://www.karlheinz-everts.de/meistgelesen.htm; visited on 18.04.2005.
2   'Arche Noah der Bücher', *Der Spiegel 25,* 18 June 2001, pp. 206–233 (p. 216).

apart, what has made *Buddenbrooks* conspicuous? In what landscapes does it stand out? And does it mark a period or turning point in a process?

The landscapes of literature might better be called timescapes. I shall return eventually to the timescape around 1900, but want to start with nowadays. Is *Buddenbrooks* still a landmark on today's horizon? In a recent study of the concept of generation, Sigrid Weigel looks back to *Buddenbrooks* as simultaneously the 'Höhe- und Endpunkt' of the family novel as a nineteenth-century genre.[3] Weigel is writing about the post-*Wende* revival 'einer totgeglaubten Gattung', for the *Generationenroman* is in fashion again at a time when the surviving eye-witnesses of National Socialism are the grandparental generation and unification has intensified the struggle over competing national narratives.[4] Recent family novels are sometimes cast in allegorical parallel to a national narrative, but some explore the tension or gap between subjective experience and large-scale political history. One irritating ambiguity which hooks the reader of *Buddenbrooks* is whether the family is typical or not typical, or whether the historical truth of *Buddenbrooks* lies precisely in the gap which makes the family significantly untypical? I lean to the third view. But the question is hard to answer because the richly complex world *Buddenbrooks* conjures up resists easy answers. In its wealth of observed detail and subtle representation of historical change, *Buddenbrooks* is arguably the greatest realist work in the German canon.

As Weigel notes, the concept of generation may follow a diachronic, genealogical time-line. Or it may be synchronic, drawing horizontal connections to age cohorts defined relative to current events or social trends: 'die Generation nämlich als Titel – wenn nicht Label – einer Jahrgangsgruppe, deren Name den spezifischen politisch-kulturellen Habitus einer Gruppierung bezeichnet, für die eine bestimmte historische Erfahrung oder Situation mentalitäts- und stilbildend ist.' Weigel cites 'Generation Berlin' or 'Single-Generation' as examples.[5] The different emphases produce two kinds of explanation: where does something come from or where is something located? History versus

---

3   *Genea-Logik. Generation, Tradition und Evolution zwischen Kultur- und Natur-wissenschaften* (Munich, 2006), p. 88.
4   Op. cit., p. 88.
5   Op. cit., p. 93.

sociology, if you like, or process versus structure. Genetic inheritance adds a further complication, of course: the subtitle 'Verfall einer Familie' flags up the theme of decadence intensifying down through the generations of a family. But many elements besides biology intertwine in the family history, and family history is only one strand in the histories unfolding in the novel: the local and regional history of Lübeck, North Germany, and the Hanseatic ports; German national history; *Mentalitätsgeschichte*; modernisation; globalisation. Complex mixings of these vertical time lines and unevenly paced processes produce, along with current events as catalyst, the horizontal sense of a new generation. Today's generational novels centre on questions of identity: competing historical narratives serve competing versions of national or post-national identity in recently unified Germany: where has the 'Generation Berlin' come from, where is it going? The different histories intertwining in *Buddenbrooks* construct but also hollow out pre-national identities, leaving the reader to puzzle over what the novel may signify about the recently unified German Reich. The novel closes in Autumn 1877, a few months after the death of Hanno, but the questions stretch forwards to 1900 and beyond. No one has ever thought *Buddenbrooks* is simply progressive, but neither is it simply conservative or reactionary. There is instead a double direction of critique – of the new as measured by the old and of the old as measured by the new. Social and political changes are evaluated and criticised against persisting family and local traditions; but conversely too, tradition is measured against new experiences and ways of thinking. This goes on throughout, leaving scope for readers to reach different views on the ethical stance or political position implicit in the novel, scope too for the same reader to reach different views at different times. Such readability and re-readability generated by ethical complexity and political ambiguity are another landmark feature.

Put as a diagram: the vertical line of familial and local tradition constantly intersects with the synchronic horizontal line of current affairs, and the locus of intersection is the psyche. Intensely affecting and memorable characters make *Buddenbrooks* a landmark in German literary history. The main characters all face at some point or other, and ever more consciously, the double question: where have I come from; where am I now? These are surely the questions old Johann asks when, close to death, he repeats: 'Kurios! Kurios!'[6] The third question, of course, is where am I going? In his untimely reflections on history, 'Vom Nutzen und Nachtheil der Historie für das Leben' Nietzsche distinguished three kinds of history. Monumental history looks at past greatness to encourage present pursuit of future aims; antiquarian history preserves and honours ancestral tradition. Critical history passes judgement: 'Denn da wir nun einmal die Resultate früherer Geschlechter sind, sind wir auch die Resultate ihrer Verirrungen, Leidenschaften und Irrthümer, ja Verbrechen.'[7] *Buddenbrooks* is short on monumental history. If the Napoleonic Wars mark the conception of German political nationalism, then Madame Antoinette's spoons, rescued from marauding French soldiers, seem to be the main monument. Johann Buddenbrook as corn merchant to the Prussian army was a war profiteer, but not a German nationalist: his manner of speech at the start of the novel combines local patriotism – 'Je, den Dübel ook' – with cosmopolitan civility – 'c'est la question, ma très chère demoiselle' (p. 9). Another historical landmark, 1848, appears as a storm in a beer mug. Martina Lauster notes the prevalence in *Vormärz* journalism of cartoon stereotypes based on political geography. Thus the journalist Eduard Beurmann, a Lübecker by birth, sets beer-drinking Lübeck, 'das schwerfällige alte Haupt der seligen Hansa' against the modern tempo of Frankfurt and the Rhine/Main 'Schoppenland': 'diese [...] jähe Übersiedelung aus dem Phlegma des Nordens in den heiteren Weinhumor des Südens verdankte ich [...] dem Eilwagen.'[8] Another journalist, August Lewald, alludes to the latest technology, English microscopy, when examining the unchanging landscape of a Munich beer drinker's face, 'Was ist der Schimmelwald, was sind Wasserschlangen und Essigdrachen, was ist die

---

6   *Buddenbrooks. Verfall einer Familie*, ed. by Eckhard Heftrich in collaboration with Stephan Stachorski and Herbert Lehnert (*Große kommentierte Frankfurter Ausgabe*, Vol 1.1 (Frankfurt a. M., 2002)), p. 77. Subsequent page numbers to this edition.

7   'Unzeitgemässe Betrachtungen. Zweites Stück: Vom Nutzen und Nachtheil der Historie für das Leben', in *Sämtliche Werke. Kritische Studienausgabe in 15 Bänden*, ed. by Giorgio Colli and Mazzino Montinari, Vol. 1 (Munich, 1980), p. 270.

8   *Frankfurter Bilder* (Mainz, 1835), p. 3, cited in Martina Lauster, *Sketches of the Nineteenth Century. European Journalism and its 'Physiologies'* (Basingstoke, 2007), p. 77, note 32.

Welt im Käse [...] gegen meine Entdeckungen mit Hülfe einer vortrefflichen englischen Lupe auf dem Gesichte eines vier und zwanzig Maaßers?'[9] It speaks for Alois Permaneder that he preferred a bottle of red wine for breakfast over the beer Thomas Buddenbrook initially offered. The invisible 'die in Frankfurt' may be the liberal branch of the Buddenbrook family living in the German city most associated with liberalism, but we hear nothing much about them other than bankruptcy. The birth passage of the German Reich was the Franco-Prussian War, but this is passed over virtually in silence; half a sentence, an odd phrase or so. Not much monumental history, then, to signpost where Germany as emerging world power is, or should be, going. Measured by the dominant ideology of the time, the Buddenbrooks are untypical. Whatever else it is, Mann's novel is not a monument to German nationalism.

A much stronger case can be made for allocating *Buddenbrooks* to the realm of antiquarian history, which, so Nietzsche argues, serves to link people to their *Heimat*, so strengthening their sense of identity and belonging. 'Urväter-Hausrath' cements the attachment:

> Das Kleine, das Beschränkte, das Morsche und Veraltete erhält seine eigene Würde und Unantastbarkeit dadurch, dass die bewahrende und verehrende Seele des antiquarischen Menschen in diese Dinge übersiedelt und sich darin ein heimisches Nest bereitet. Die Geschichte seiner Stadt wird ihm zur Geschichte seiner selbst.[10]

Much of the popularity of *Buddenbrooks* comes from reading it as a *Heimat* novel. We savour its evocative sense of place. We luxuriate in 'Urväter-Hausrath': the furniture, the landscape room, Madame Antoinette's spoons, the family book and Bible. Nietzsche's antiquarian man finds himself in the architecture of his town: 'die Mauer, das gethürmte Thor, die Rathsverordnung'.[11] So too in *Buddenbrooks* we visit the Mengstrasse, the Breite Strasse, the Bürgerschaft, or the splendid Kröger mansion beyond the town gate. But Nietzsche also warns that the past may become the 'Todtengräber des Gegenwärtigen'.[12] For a danger

---

9   *Panorama von München* (Stuttgart, 1835), Vol. 1, p. 51, cited in Lauster, op. cit., p. 82, note 44.
10   'Vom Nutzen und Nachtheil der Historie', p. 265.
11   Op. cit., p. 265.
12   Op. cit., p. 251.

lurks in antiquarian history: 'endlich wird einmal alles Alte und Ver-
gangene [...] einfach als gleich ehrwürdig hingenommen, alles was aber
diesem Alten nicht mit Ehrfurcht entgegen kommt, also das Neue und
Werdende, abgelehnt und angefeindet.'[13] Two recent exhibitions in
Germany explored the loss of *Heimat* through flight and expulsion, but
also urged the need to move on and make a new *Heimat*.[14] *Buddenbrooks*
too shows this loss, but as a loss from within, a loss of belief or an inner
flight, a psychic catastrophe, as in the case of Hanno. *Buddenbrooks* is
arguably the ultimate *Heimat* novel in German literature, but it deci-
sively rejects this mode by showing the deadly effects when *Heimat*
becomes a cult. The whole novel is imbued with the resulting tension
between nostalgic love or *Heimweh*, and *Fernweh* – an anguished longing to escape the narrow confines of the old city.[15] 'Das Neue und
Werdende' are not simply 'abgelehnt und angefeindet' as Nietzsche puts
it. It is rather that the psyche becomes an arena where the old and the
new fight it out and the body shows forth the wounds of battle.

   In my diagram of *Buddenbrooks*, the vertical line of tradition,
Nietzsche's antiquarian history, intersects with the horizontal connections to the current age group: the weight of the past, especially upon
Tony, Christian and Thomas, prevents them from engaging fully with
their own generation even though they deeply desire to make such horizontal connections. This is one way in which *Buddenbrooks* fulfils
Nietzsche's programme for a critical history. The novel explores sins of
the fathers which weigh down upon later generations. The Buddenbrook
family secrets are full of 'Verirrungen, Leidenschaften und Irrthümer',
perhaps even 'Verbrechen'. Critics often write of old Johann as a man of
the Enlightenment; maybe so, but below the urbane, sceptical exterior,
he is driven by irrational passions. Patriarchal legitimacy rests upon the
law of primogeniture, yet the patriarch has the power to observe or to
break the line of descent from which his authority supposedly flows. His

13   Op. cit., p. 267.
14   'Flucht, Vertreibung, Integration' (Bonn, Berlin, Leipzig, November 2005–April
     2007); the word *Heimat* cuts vertically through the title words. 'Erzwungene
     Wege. Flucht und Vertreibung im Europa des 20. Jahrhunderts' (August–October,
     2006).
15   On this tension within *Heimat* discourse see Elizabeth Boa and Rachel Palfreyman,
     *Heimat – A German Dream: Regional Loyalties and National Identity in German
     Culture 1890–1990* (Oxford, 2000), pp. 27–29.

power is thus ultimately arbitrary. Whereas the Biblical patriarch Isaac was tricked into disinheriting his hairy son Esau, Johann Buddenbrook knowingly chooses that smoothie, Konsul Jean. Father and younger son then collude in robbing first-born Gotthold of his birthright. Old Johann himself married Gotthold's mother for love, but cast off Gotthold when *he* married for love. Ostensibly Gotthold's crime was disobedience in marrying 'einen Laden', a shop. But the father's rejection long predated the son's mésalliance. In Johann's irrational imagination, Gotthold was the infant murderer of a beloved first wife who died in childbirth. The role of head of the firm provides an alibi masking a vengeful father's secret hatred and behind Konsul Jean's commercial common sense lurks a younger son's and stepbrother's envy.

Conflict is built into the very structure of bourgeois patriarchy. The role of father and that of head of the firm constantly conflict, notably in the familial duty owed to women whose dowry is a loss to the firm and the converse duty demanded from women to marry well, as is required of sons too, especially the eldest. This is most brilliantly played out in the comic yet horrific portrait of Konsul Jean, the loving father who bullies a beloved daughter into a miserable marriage. That the daughter herself eventually accedes merely increases the horror of the marriage market. Current generational novels explore far greater horrors. They probe the mentality of people who committed or acceded to terrible crimes: *wie aus ganz normalen Menschen Massenmörder werden*, as the subtitle of a recent study puts it. Writing of such people Harald Welzer argues that in their own perception at least, they were not 'Ungeheuer', but acted 'im Rahmen zeitgenössischer normativer Standards, wissenschaftlicher Lehrmeinungen, militärischer Pflichtauffassungen und kanonisierter Ehrendefinitionen [...].'[16] A few amendments – 'religiöser Lehrmeinungen', 'kaufmännischer Pflichtauffassung' – and one could say the same of the Konsul. Without wanting to overstate the case, I would argue that *Buddenbrooks* remains a landmark for its representation of historically infused mentalities which produce behaviour that seems incomprehensible, even monstrous, to later generations, but which from the perspective of the times seemed normal. Grünlich is a comic monster in Dickensian mode, a creep and a hypocrite. But the Konsul is not a creep, not even a

---

16 *Täter. Wie uas ganz normalen Menschen Massenmörder werden* (Frankfurt a. M., 2005), p. 30.

hypocrite, and is harder to understand. In his mentality religious senti-
ment, paternal affection, and duty to the business co-exist in parallel,
each seeming to provide an ethical basis for actions which ruin his
deeply beloved daughter's life. To the Konsul, the ethical imperatives
point in the same direction, but they blind him to Tony's perspective and
to the ruthless business practices of the times. The strange expression on
the Konsul's face when Tony tells him of her true feelings of disgust for
Grünlich signals a momentary glimpse into an abysmal truth.

In Tony herself the criss-crossing lines of past and present are especially clear and disastrous in effect: faced with the chance to reach out to
her own generation, to be an 1848er, to learn new ideas, to marry
Morten, she eventually accedes less to family pressure so much as to her
own ingrained sense of herself as a patrician Buddenbrook. The narrator
and, following him, most critics, see Tony as child-like, perennially
Johann Buddenbrook's granddaughter. But she also exemplifies a widespread cultural infantilisation of middle-class women whose energies, at
a time of rising individualism, were reined in to making a good match
and bearing an heir. Yet Tony is perhaps not as childish as the narrator
keeps insisting. In the moment of truth it is the daughter who opens the
father's eyes to a grim insight: 'Ach… was fragst du, Papa!… Ich habe
ihn [Grünlich] niemals geliebt… er war mir immer widerlich… weißt du
das denn nicht…?' (p. 237) Here Tony speaks with a patient, grown-up
voice to her childish, deceived and self-deceiving father. She lets slip a
mask she has worn to hide her true feelings of disgust for the man whose
bed she shares in order to serve her equally true sense of family pride
stretching back deep into the past. Tony knows more than her father does
of unbridgeable conflict between incompatible desires and principles.
Then there is big brother Thomas urging a common sense view of
Permaneder's peccadilloes: 'Aber das ist es ja Tony: du nimmst die
Sache nicht komisch genug, und daran ist natürlich dein Magen schuld.'
(p. 418) Here Thomas echoes the narrator who has pervasively presented
Tony in a comic light. The narrator in turn, of course, follows the loving
but condescending perspective of the men in the family as established in
the opening page of the novel. Why can't the silly goose see the funny
side? But then Tony reveals that it was not just that awful word we have
all laughed at. The wound to her self-esteem goes deeper: 'Wie? ist nur
das Schande und Skandal im Leben, was laut wird und unter die Leute
kommt? Ach nein! Der heimliche Skandal, der im stillen an einem zehrt

und die Selbstachtung wegfrisst, der ist viel schlimmer!' (p. 422) Here the author's voice surely sounds through.[17] Tony speaks prophetically, for secret humiliation will eat away also at Thomas. The Konsul and Tony brilliantly exemplify that mixing of modes – comedy with tragedy, horror with farce, sometimes too the sense of a pit of meaningless absurdity opening under our feet – which makes *Buddenbrooks* so intriguing. Tony's confrontations with the patriarchs, her father and her brother, strikingly convey the tension between past and present and her stomach is the arena of psychosomatic battle. As a divorcée, the second time emphatically by her own choice, Tony is a modern woman: she no longer passively accepts the position allocated her under bourgeois patriarchy of object of exchange; unlike Madame Antoinette who let Pastor Wunderlich tell the spoon story for her, Tony speaks for herself – 'Jetzt sei still, Thomas! Jetzt bin ich an der Reihe! Jetzt höre zu!' (p. 422) Yet she still hankers after the imagined world of her grandfather. Measured by the incipient new freedoms which even women might hope for, Tony is at once a modern woman and a victim of the past, Nietzsche's 'Todtengräber des Gegenwärtigen'.

For a while Christian seems to be the Buddenbrook who leaves the past behind for a globalising future in great cities like Hamburg, London, and Valparaiso.[18] But as he keeps turning up again like a bad penny, the global intimations Christian carries merely intensify the sense of a local identity which has become suffocating and is now falling apart. *Buddenbrooks* has a great range of comic effects. Farce, however, is the most threatening in showing human beings caught up in automatic machinery; this is what Christian portends. With his great nose, Christian is like Mr Punch, a clownish parody of a patriarch who enters a parody of a marriage to Aline Puvogel. Christian is a brilliant mimic who imitates in exaggeration the mannerisms of honest citizens in clownish mockery of the puppet-like automatism of social life. To his brother, Christian is an

17 In *Das Blaubartszimmer: Thomas Mann und die Schuld* (Frankfurt a. M., 2000) Michael Maar argues that from early on Mann was plagued to the extent of contemplating suicide by fear that a shameful secret – *not* his homosexuality, but something else – might come out.

18 In 1900 Germany passed Britain to become the second trading nation after the USA. Estimates for global trade around 1914 were only matched again in the 1970s; see Philippe Legrain, *Open World: The Truth About Globalisation* (London, 2002), p. 108.

uncanny emanation, a *Doppelgänger* showing forth all that Thomas fears
he too might become without the sustaining family ethos. Thomas comes
to suffer too from the 'heimlicher Skandal' of Gerda's musical adultery.
By the 1890s adultery was long established as a novelistic motif signalling fear of the modernising processes eating away at the foundations
of traditional authority and social order; Goethe's *Die Wahlverwandtschaften* or Fontane's *Effi Briest* are classic German examples.[19] That
and the terrible fraternal quarrels with Christian leave Thomas crucified,
so to speak, on the criss-crossing lines of tradition and modernity. As
head of the firm Thomas drags with him an ever heavier weight of tradition and civic representation across lengthening decades; as head of the
family in an age of growing individualism he bears his own burdens as
brother, son, husband and father and those of increasingly unbiddable
family members. In a bitter quarrel with his mother over his sister
Clara's inheritance, for example, Thomas claims a power he cannot in
practice exercise when he asserts, 'daß aber meine Eigenschaft als Sohn
zu Null wird, sobald ich dir in Sachen der Firma und der Familie als
männliches Oberhaupt und an der Stelle meines Vaters gegenüberstehe!'
(p. 475) But Thomas cannot cease to be his mother's son. In making the
demands of patriarchal law so harshly explicit, Thomas merely uncovers,
in an age which had seen the rise of Biedermeier family sentiment, the
impossibility of their fulfilment. As his father never quite did, Thomas
becomes aware that old law and new feeling are out of kilter. Such
awareness makes the subject position he seeks to hold, as man and businessman, untenable, though Thomas keeps trying as his son will not.
So far then, if the old order is criticised in the name of new freedoms
and sentiments, then conversely, the new world of globally expanding
business and sharp financial practice is criticised in the name of old
decencies: the business ethic the Buddenbrooks believe they live by
seems to be overwhelmed by modern ruthlessness. Yet the perceived
ethical decline may largely flow from the heightened awareness of the
younger generation. Christian threatens to undo the difference when he
suggests along with Proudhon that property is, and always was, theft. In

---

19   See Tony Tanner, *Adultery in the Novel* (Baltimore, 1979); also Elizabeth Boa,
      'Aping and Parroting: Imitative Peformance in Goethe's *Die Wahlverwandt-
      schaften*', in *Peformance and Performativity in German Cultural Studies*, ed. by
      Carolin Duttlinger, Lucia Ruprecht and Andrew Webber (Berne, 2003), pp. 21–40.

their different ways the brothers convey a sense of absurdity and loss of self-identity once belief in the sustaining frameworks of family ethos and local community crumbles.

Buddenbrooks differs in one respect from today's family novels. The *Generationenroman* is now generally narrated retrospectively from the perspective of the youngest generation and overtly explores the processes of memory. The Buddenbrooks do remember, of course; there are communal family stories, like the rescued spoons, which get transmitted through what is now called communicative memory; there is the family album of archival memories; Proustian triggers such as honey as 'reiner Naturprodukt' (pp. 132, 319, etc.), prompt memories in Tony of breakfast in Travemünde and Morten Schwarzkopf.[20] But the main remembering instance is the unseen, disembodied narrator; the whole novel is an extended exercise in remembering. Does this mean, then, that for the narrator, indeed for Thomas Mann, '[d]ie Geschichte seiner Stadt wird ihm zur Geschichte seiner selbst'? This is more or less what Yahya Elsaghe argues:

> Der 'Verfall' der 'Familie' verläuft zwar gegenläufig zur nationalen, aber parallel zur Geschichte der 'Vater*stadt*', welcher der Autor im hierfür berühmten Roman ein Denkmal gesetzt hat, nicht eigentlich der Stadt schlechthin, sondern vorwiegend eben der noch wahrhaft 'Freien Stadt [...].

Such a historical narrative, Elsaghe concludes, is an expression of its author's 'hanseatischen Identität'.[21] In two studies of Mann's work Elsaghe argues roughly as follows: around 1900 Thomas Mann was not a political nationalist, but did believe in a version of German-ness of Nordic and Protestant hue; politically he identified as a 'lübisch-norddeutscher Bürger'.[22] Characteristic of a Nordic tendency, Elsaghe suggests, is 'die Stilisierung Bayerns zum eigentlichen Ausland'.[23] But this is surely to misread a comic highpoint in the novel. The southern

---

20   On the terminolgy of memory culture, see Aleida Assmann, 'Die Schlagworte der Debatte', in Aleida Assmann and Ute Frevert, *Geschichtsvergessenheit. Geschichtsversessenheit. Vom Umgang mit deutschen Vergangenheiten nach 1945* (Stuttgart, 1999), pp. 53–96.

21   *Die imaginäre Nation. Thomas Mann und das 'Deutsche'* (Munich, 2000), p. 173.

22   *Thomas Mann und die kleinen Unterschiede. Zur erzählerischen Imagination des Anderen* (Cologne, 2004), p. 103.

23   *Die imaginäre Nation*, p. 157; also pp. 20–2.

manners, dialect, and cuisine of Munich are a magic mirror sharpening perception of the redolently local peculiarities of the northern *Heimat*. Announcing the arrival of a visitor, the maidservant warns her mistress: 'Je, Fru Kunsel, [...] doar wier 'n Herr, öäwer hei red' nich dütsch un is ook goar tau snaksch...' (p. 355). Thus the Platt speaker accuses the Bavarian of not speaking proper *Hochdeutsch*! As Permander enters the drawing room clutching his 'grünes Tirolerhütchen, geschmückt mit einem Gemsbart' (p. 357) to meet Konsulin Bethsy in her red wig, it is hard to say which of the two is more comical; each heightens the comic effect of the other. Ludicrously different, Lübeck and Munich are in a deeper sense alike in amusing an author who, being at home in both cities, can see the familiar in each mirrored in the other in comic estrangement. Bavaria is not the 'eigentliches Ausland', but a potential other *Heimat*, as her author, if not poor Tony, recognised.

If a certain competitive spirit between North and South marked *Heimat* discourse around 1900, the *Heimat* ideologues also often infused an anti-liberal critique of modernisation with antisemitism. Elsaghe discerns such a tendency in *Buddenbooks* in 'die "jüdische" Assoziation ganz bestimmter deutscher Städte und Staaten.'[24] Frankfurt is a case in point. In the 1830s Eduard Beurmann wrote about the Judengasse in Frankfurt which the Rothschild sons left to go out in 'alle Welt', but where Madame Rothschild 'die alte betagte fromme Mutter' still lives and means to die.[25] Here the Jews figure simultaneously as the acme of modernity and of deepest tradition, both sympathetic traits in the eyes of the liberal journalist. But in *Buddenbrooks* Hinrich Hagenström's marriage to a young woman from Frankfurt aroused 'einiges Befremden' (p. 67), a motif intended to signal, so Elsaghe argues, the danger to the Lübeck patriciate of Jewish infiltration which will transform the enrooted *Bürger* into the rootless cosmopolitan bourgeois. Elsaghe picks up too on physiognomic signals: Hermann Hagenström has a flattish nose pressing down on his upper lip, stereotypically a Jewish nose, while his sister Jülchen has coal black eyes and, like her mother, wears big earrings from an early age, a signal of nouveau-riche vulgarity. The very avoidance of explicit mention of Jewishness combined with such

24   Op. cit., p. 157.
25   Beurmann, *Frankfurter Bilder*, p. 27; cited in Lauster, *Sketches of the Nineteenth Century*, p. 78, note 36.

well-recognised markers, so Elsaghe argues, tacitly appeals to a racist readership.[26] Not all early critics got the message, however, one article seeing in the author of *Buddenbrooks* 'ein Vorkämpfer für jüdische Rassenpolitik'.[27] So how is Jewishness represented? Is Elsaghe's suspicion justified? Accepting that the discourse linking modernisation and Jewish emancipation is obliquely present in *Buddenbrooks*, evaluative judgements on modernity and on Jewish participation in social life are liable to impact on one another. Many critics have suggested that *Buddenbrooks* portrays a shift from 'Gemeinschaft' to 'Gesellschaft', or from the mercantile Bürger rooted in a local community to the disembedded, cosmopolitan bourgeois. Put crudely: the Buddenbrooks represent the *Bürger* and the Hagenströms, 'diese hergelaufene Familie' (p. 127), the rising bourgeoisie. Or more subtly: Thomas is broken on the tension he himself lives out between older ethical ties and new freedoms or new amoralism. To borrow from analysis of the bourgeoisie in *The Communist Manifesto*, 'die heiligen Schauer der frommen Schwärmerei' which the Konsul still feels have given way to 'eine gewissenslose Handelsfreiheit' which Thomas cannot, however, quite exercise.[28] One character, marked as Jewish through his nasal manner of speech, is the banker Kesselmeyer who, without conscience, is intent on screwing profit from human misery. But the whole Hamburg business community seems to have colluded in deceiving the Buddenbrooks in the hope of saving their investment in Grünlich, the pastor's son. Readers are left wrestling with the problem of how to distinguish ethically between Grünlich's performance of piety and the Konsul's 'fromme Schwärmerei', which blinded him to the evil he was doing, in accord with Christian conscience, to his daughter. Nor, Hermann's nose and Jülchen's earrings apart, is there any substantial difference between the Buddenbrooks and the Hagenströms. At most, as Martin Swales concedes in arguing a powerful case for the shift from *Bürger* to bourgeois, it may be a matter of perception, of the 'felt, value-heavy symbolisations

---

26 *Thomas Mann und die kleinen Unterschiede*, p. 194.
27 Otto Schmidt-Gibichenfels, 'Ein Vorkämpfer für jüdische Rassenpolitik', in *Thomas Mann im Urteil seiner Zeit*, ed. by Klaus Schröter (Hamburg, 1969), pp. 50–52. The argument rests, however, on grotesque misreading.
28 Karl Marx and Friedrich Engels, *Manifest der Kommunistischen Partei* (Stuttgart, 1969), p. 26.

of social life'.[29] The Buddenbrooks and other townsfolk think they see a difference, but urbane, elegant Thomas who smokes Russian cigarettes and reads poetry and philosophy, is not so different from urbane, open-minded Hermann or his intellectual brother Moritz. The townspeople see Hinrich Hagenström's marriage as dubious but they also come to admire the son's open, generous spirit. A Jewish nose does not seem to have made much difference. Hermann's nose and Jülchen's earrings are largely seen through Tony's eyes. Her way of seeing the Hagenströms is part of the snobbish family pride which drives her into a series of self-destructive life choices. Tony's judgements, whether of the Hagenström family or the city of Munich, cannot be simply transferred to the author, but they are a key aspect in a critique less of the new or of Jewish infiltration, than of the old to which Tony herself falls victim. In sum, the *Bürger*/bourgeois contrast does not hold up all that well, and this greatly weakens the charge of anti-Semitism. Jews and gentiles alike share the positive and negative features associated with modernisation, nor do business ethics change substantially with modernisation. For all the brilliance in representing historical change, a dilemma haunting the literature on *Buddenbrooks* is the nagging doubt over whether under-neath the surface all that much has changed. Schopenhauer's anti-historicist vision which so affects Thomas threatens in turn to subvert *Buddenbrooks* as landmark *Zeitroman*: perhaps nothing changes; his-torical progress is mere illusion.[30] Christian's great beaky nose and urbane Hermann's more squashy organ signify collapsing differences: Christian between business ethics old or new and Hermann between business men, Jew or gentile. Christian is the mimic, not half-Jewish Hermann; were mimicry attributed to assimilating Hermann, that would be in line with anti-Semitic discourse.[31] Having said that, for readers who see the Hagenströms as intended to embody a more ruthless and rootless modern world, the recourse to racial physiognomic markers may

29   *Buddenbrooks; Family Life as the Mirror of Social Change* (Boston, 1991), p. 93.
30   On historicism and the *Zeitroman* see Dirk Göttsche, *Zeit im Roman. Literarische Zeitreflexion und die Geschichte des Zeitromans im späten 18. und im 19. Jahrhundert* (Munich, 2001).
31   Elsaghe sees in Grünlich a Jew passing as Christian on the grounds that Bendix was a common Jewish name (*Die imaginäre Nation*, pp. 118, 188). But the text points more strongly towards the Molièresque or Dickensian stereotype of the Christian hypocrite.

well appear as a disturbing symptom, in the author and not just in his characters, of a vulgar prejudice that would later assume deadly virulence under a regime which Thomas Mann, of course, opposed

The discussion so far has considered affinities and differences between *Buddenbrooks* and today's generational discourse and looked with hindsight at the representation of Jewishness. But an absolutely key feature of *Buddenbrooks* is its eminence as a landmark in the literary landscape around 1900. This comes in large measure from its rich inter-mixing of aesthetic and intellectual tendencies of the time. I have allo-cated the novel to a genre: the family or generational novel. But other-wise it resists easy definition. *Buddenbrooks* is a Realist masterpiece, but also echoes Romanticism and Poetic Realism, as in the *Doppelgänger* motif which adds an uncanny undertone to the psychology of fraternal relations between Thomas and Christian. Alternatively, *Buddenbrooks* is a *Heimat* novel. Or we recognise scientistic Naturalism tending towards a more mystic decadence in the inheritance of attributes across the gen-erations and the Buddenbrooks' declining vitality. Hanno's epicene body belongs in the ambit of *Jugendstil* eroticism around 1900.[32] Or we discern incipient Modernist reflection upon the processes of modernisa-tion, changing beliefs systems, values and sensibility, changing psycho-sexual feeling, changing consciousness and self-understanding. The notorious leitmotifs may be Wagnerian devices transmitting resonances of the past into the present; they signify both continuing homogeneity yet heterogeneity, what Ernst Bloch called 'die Gleichzeitigkeit des Un-gleichzeitigen' resulting from the differing pace of different processes of change. Or they may belong in the ambit of eugenics or Lamarckian theories of inherited characteristics which informed much Naturalist writing. Or they may be post-Naturalist emblematic motifs: emancipated from their immediate metonymic meaning they take on diffuse or her-metic metaphoric resonance. Thomas mentions Gerda's shining white teeth for special praise. This grotesque fixation on a facial detail by a man destined to die after a visit to the dentist does not draw us into the world represented in the story, but highlights repetitious patterning in the text; it evokes not an actual woman but demons haunting the male imagination in the gender discourse of the times. Gerda's teeth as a

32 See Elizabeth Boa, '*Buddenbrooks*: Bourgeois Patriarchy and fin-se-siècle Eros', in *Thomas Mann*, ed. by Michael Minden (London, 1995), pp. 125–42.

symbol of vitality anticipate the panther's powerful teeth in Kafka's *Ein Hungerkünstler* or the hyper-real detail in surrealist art. A landmark, the dictionary says, may be a stage in a process, especially an event marking a period or turning point. Teeth and a myriad other motifs in *Buddenbrooks* signify a turning point between Realism and Modernism, they evince too the crucial role of Naturalism and the emancipation of the seemingly random detail in that cultural and aesthetic sea-change. Most miraculous of all is how the turning point between Realism and a Modernist aesthetic comes in the actual course of the novel as the narration shifts towards increasing inwardness in exploring the psychic tensions to which Thomas and Hanno fall prey, then moves beyond psychology towards a montage of philosophical, scientific and mythic discourses which disrupt Realist representation, notably with the death of Hanno.

   Buddenbrooks may not offer political signposts to the future, but it is certainly full of literary omens. As a last landmark I would like to return to the tension between *Heimweh* and *Fernweh*. *Buddenbrooks* is a lament for a dying world, but pulsing through it is also a kind of *Fernweh*, an urgent desire for something else that is not here and is neither the past nor the present, an unfocused energy underlying the surface of this story of decline. The author himself often uses the metaphor of surface and depth, for example à propos James Möllendorpf, the diabetic who secretly stuffed himself with tarts and in consequence died a horrible death: 'Die widerlichen Einzelheiten dieses Todesfalles wurden von der Familie nach Möglichkeit geheimgehalten, aber sie verbreiteten sich rasch in der Stadt.' (pp. 447-8) And who will follow James Möllendorpf as Senator? – 'Welche Spannung und welche unterirdische Geschäftigkeit! […] Aber welch Treiben unter der Oberfläche!' (p. 448). Such phrases as 'Widerliche Einzelheiten' and 'Treiben unter der Oberfläche' reflexively hint at indecent events beneath the Realist surface, as lust and disgust ambiguously intertwine. Marital sex in *Buddenbrooks* is decently veiled, not something we want to think about, dutiful rather than exciting, stressful perhaps. With poor Tony, however, marital sex becomes thoroughly disgusting. Paradoxically the more disgusting Grünlich is, the more he offers a kind of perverse negative pleasure: if this is bourgeois marriage, licit sex, then it's revolting. Eroticism is displaced from 'normal' sex to death. Like the townsfolk, we enjoy the 'widerliche Einzelheiten' of a whole sequence of deaths, which become ever more spectacular. Bethsy's and Thomas's deaths are orgasmic breakthroughs in female and male mode in bodies hitherto held in strict check: Bethsy drowns in fluid rising in the lungs, but the text evokes the throes of a passion diffusely spreading throughout her body, until she lies, arms flung wide, in a supine posture of abandon. Her son by contrast is thrown to the ground by a concentrated, explosive cerebral orgasm, blood spurting from facial orifices. As realistic episodes the deaths are touching; in a symbolic or Dionysian subtext, they convey the iconoclastic overthrow of matriarchal and patriarchal order. Something quite other breaks through in the revoltingly pleasurable details of bodies in revolt against a lifetime of control and restraint. The affliction visited upon Hanno of scurf and black pustules is a nauseous rejection, erupting in a still youthful, girlish body, of the manhood his father has urged upon him. Winfried Menninghaus places the discovery at the turn of the nineteenth to the twentieth century of 'die (verbotenen) Reize des Ekelhaften' in a history of the shifting meanings of disgust in different discourses.[33] Evolutionary theory sees disgust as protecting the body from harm and for psychologists disgust is a boundary marker between self and other, body and world, marking what is allowed to penetrate and what is kept out. According to cultural anthropologists, the disgust provoked by tabooed persons, objects, and feelings serves to police the social order. To take pleasure in the disgusting is therefore to subvert, or undermine, or iconoclastically overthrow the boundaries and taboos which sustain individual identity and social order. Thus my last landmark feature in *Buddenbrooks* is the intensely pleasurable disgust underlying the mourning for a lost world. This extreme tension makes *Buddenbrooks* indeed a landmark of its time and a portent.

33   *Ekel. Theorie und Geschichte einer starken Empfindung* (Frankfurt a. M., 1999), p. 27.

RONALD SPEIRS

Mann, *Der Zauberberg*

It is hard to think of another German novel with which the idea of a
'landmark' has greater natural affinity than with Thomas Mann's *Der
Zauberberg*. The very title suggests singularity, a mountain of numinous
reputation that stands out from its surroundings, inspiring awe in passing
travellers and inviting only the more intrepid to attempt its ascent and
exploration, either simply because it's there or in the hope of gaining a
better view of the landscape behind and beyond. How many students of
German can have contemplated tackling this mountain of words without
fearing that they might not be up to the challenge? The more determined
generally report that the adventure fully repaid the effort.

Oddly enough, its author originally had the idea (in 1912) of making something more like a molehill than a mountain, intending to write
'ein humoristisches Gegenstück zum *Tod in Venedig*'[1] as light relief after
completing that highly wrought, artistically and personally demanding,
tragic *Novelle* of dignity hard won and quickly lost. The initial aim was
to take a luxurious Swiss sanatorium as the setting for a comical (self-
mocking) exploration of the decadent fascination with death and disease.
In the course of its twelve year-long gestation, however, both the dimensions and the character of the new project changed radically.[2] By the
time he had completed the novel in 1924, Thomas Mann had come to
regard it as a major landmark both in his own development and in that of
his fellow countrymen. In the prelude to the novel he invoked another,
rather different topographical trope to express this notion, the image of
a deep abyss, a 'Leben und Bewußtsein tief zerklüftende(n) Wende
und Grenze' (p.7),[3] which had opened up during those twelve years to

---

1   'Einführung in den *Zauberberg*'. *Rede und Antwort*. Thomas Mann, *Gesammelte
    Werke in Einzelbänden*, ed. by P. de Mendelssohn (Frankfurt a. M., 1981), p. 71.
2   For an account of the novel's complicated genesis, see T. J. Reed, *Thomas Mann:
    The Uses of Tradition* (Oxford, 1974).
3   All references to *Der Zauberberg* are taken from Thomas Mann, *Gesammelte
    Werke in Einzelbänden*, ed. by P. de Mendelssohn (Frankfurt a. M., 1981).

change utterly the intellectual and moral landscape of Europe, dividing the historical world described in the novel from the world inhabited by its narrator and his audience.

The abyss in question was of course the one created by the First World War which began before Mann could complete the intended narrative, obliging him to set it aside in favour of a series of ever-longer essays explaining and justifying Germany's readiness to wage war as a consequence of the cultural mission in Europe it was fated to carry out.[4] In those essays Mann had advanced anti-democratic arguments similar to those attributed to Naphta in *Der Zauberberg,* one of the self-appointed mentors acquired by Hans Castorp, the young hero of the novel, during his seven-year sojourn at the 'Sanatorium Berghof' in Davos. By invoking the image of the deep gulf in life and consciousness opened by the war, Mann, who had become a defender of the new republican order in Germany by 1922–23, clearly intended to suggest that his own path and that of his compatriots had crossed an important border ('Grenze') and taken a radically new turn ('Wende') as a result of the war.

The trope of the abyss becomes oddly confused, however, as the narrator goes on to speak of the war 'mit dessen Beginn so vieles begann, was zu beginnen wohl kaum schon aufgehört hat' (p. 7). If things that began in the war are still unfolding at the point of narration, the war seems less like an unbridgeable abyss and more like a terrain through which a path leads from the past into the present. The mixed metaphor is revealing. Whereas Mann plainly wanted the *Zauberberg* to be seen as a landmark at the far side of a great divide separating one historical and intellectual or moral epoch from another, he may have feared that no such divide existed, and that he, his countrymen, and the rest of Europe could not in truth regard life on the magic mountain as belonging to a far distant world, inaccessible thanks to its degree of 'pastness' ('hochgradige Verflossenheit', p. 7). In fact he confessed precisely this fear to a correspondent as late as December 1921:

> Dieser wunderliche Bildungsroman führt doch eigentlich auch wieder aus dem 'Verfall' nicht heraus, er wird das, was den guten Hans Castorp vor der Bergverzauberung geschützt hätte, wenn es ihm eben nicht gefehlt hätte, kaum noch

4   The most important of these essays were 'Gedanken im Kriege' (1914), 'Friedrich und die große Koalition' (1915) and *Betrachtungen eines Unpolitischen*, first published serially and then as a separate volume in 1919.

aufnehmen, und zwar weil mein eigenes Leben es wahrscheinlich nicht mehr aufnimmt.[5]

The shape Mann eventually decided to give to the evolving fiction was inspired not by the image of the abyss but by the search for a new beginning, by the wish to imagine some way of progressing out of the pre-war world and into new forms of life and thought. The result was a story 'welche auf wunderliche, ironische und fast parodistische Weise den alten deutschen Wilhelm-Meisterlichen Bildungsroman, dieses Produkt unserer großen bürgerlichen Epoche zu erneuern unternimmt'.[6] In the archetype of the German *Bildungsroman*, Goethe's *Wilhelm Meister*, the central action takes the form of a journey, a literal journey that very soon takes on a symbolic character as the young hero travels through life, generally via a series of errors, from immaturity to maturity. This tortuous journey is punctuated by a series of landmarks or stages in the development of the hero's understanding of his place in the world. In this process his personality is 'formed' ('gebildet') in the sense of gradually assuming its pre-destined form. As Goethe saw it, the development of the individual personality ('Dämon') was, or ought to be, dictated by innate, organic laws: 'Und keine Zeit und keine Macht zerstückelt/ Geprägte Form, die lebend sich entwickelt'.[7]

In order to succeed, such a process demands self-reflection on the part of the protagonist, the hard-won ability to reflect critically on oneself, and thereby to choose which qualities should be supported and which should be curtailed, and which forms of activity offer the most productive channels for the individual's characteristic energies and talents. In this process of self-formation, the hero is often helped by the love he receives from and feels for others, and by the guiding hand, often unseen, of pedagogically inclined father-figures (including the narrator) who have an interest in seeing his talents develop productively. The stages in the formation of the protagonist derive their significance, in

---

5   *Dichter über ihre Dichtungen, Bd 14 I-III: Thomas Mann*, ed. by H. Wysling (Munich, Frankfurt a. M., 1975–81), Vol. 1, p. 465.

6   'Lübeck als geistige Lebensform'. *Über mich selbst. Gesammelte Werke in Einzelbänden*, ed. by P. de Mendelssohn (Frankfurt a.M., 1983), p. 46.

7   'Urworte. Orphisch. Dämon.' All references to Goethe are from *Goethes Werke. Hamburger Ausgabe in 14 Bänden*, ed. by E. Trunz (Hamburg, 1956). Here to Vol. 1, p. 359; subsequent references to this edition take the form *GW*, etc.

part at least, from the social development to which he will be able to contribute ever more effectively, the more fully he develops his personality. Personal progress is linked to the advance of society at large.

That *Der Zauberberg* exhibits some of the most important features of the classic *Bildungsroman* is plain enough. Hans Castorp's story, we are informed in the very first sentence, is being told to us 'nicht um seinetwillen [...] sondern um der Geschichte willen, die uns im hohen Grade erzählenswert scheint' (p. 7). In other words, we are about to read the kind of exemplary, socially significant story that is typical of the genre. The outward action, such as it is, takes the conventional form of a journey. Castorp is introduced to us traveling by train from his home in Hamburg across Germany and high up into the Swiss Alps, where he plans to spend a short holiday visiting his cousin Joachim, who is undergoing treatment for tuberculosis, before returning to resume his studies for a career in marine engineering.

From the outset, however, Castorp's journey into the mountains differs from that of Goethe's Wilhelm Meister or Keller's 'grüner Heinrich', in that he has not consciously been harbouring since childhood the kind of artistic ambitions that cause his predecessors to strike out on a non-bourgeois path at the earliest opportunity. Castorp's conformist intention, by contrast, is to return home 'ganz als derselbe [...] als der er abgefahren war' (p. 8). Despite appearances, however, there is already something of the artist lurking beneath the fashionable overcoat of this pampered son of Hamburg. While Castorp's technical drawings of ships are competent at best, his sensitive rendering of the sea beneath them reveals a painterly talent fed by something much more profound than technical proficiency.[8] This pre-disposition in Castorp to develop the non-conformity of the artist is accompanied and supported by others: a childhood attraction to a Polish schoolfriend Pribislav Hippe contains the germ of his fatal attraction to the Russian beauty, Clawdia Chauchat, while an early infection of the lung has left him with a proclivity to develop the tubercular symptoms he exhibits at the 'Berghof'. All three interwoven predispositions have as their strongest link a common attrac-

---

8   Mann, whose own art was often inspired by childhood memories of the sea, once
     observed: 'Das Meer ist keine Landschaft, es ist das Erlebnis der Ewigkeit, des
     Nichts und des Todes, ein metaphysischer Traum', 'Lübeck als geistige Lebens-
     form', loc.cit., p. 46.

tion to death, a tendency that has been reinforced in Castorp over time by a vague sense that the world around him affords no binding answers to certain troubling questions about the ultimate point of life and hence of the hard work normally required to sustain it.

Although the need for self-development has to be awakened in Castorp in the course of his journey, this initially reluctant 'Bildungsreisender' (p. 925) fairly soon finds himself straying at least as far off the path of conformity as any of his predecessors in the genre. In his case, admittedly, his adventurous travel is mainly spiritual, for, like Rip van Winkel or 'Zwerg Nase', he does not leave the 'Berghof' for seven whole years, partly on account of its, for him, easily affordable comforts (in this respect Castorp remains a self-indulgent son of the propertied bourgeoisie to the end), partly because of the absorbing 'experiments' and illusions to which he devotes himself during his stay, but principally partly because of Clawdia Chauchat. While there, he spends much of his time 'in horizontaler Lage', half-dozing on his beloved 'Liegestuhl' on the balcony outside his bedroom. During these long periods of dreamy rumination Castorp's thoughts wander off down all manner of cosmological, metaphysical, and physiological tracks, inspired on the one hand by the new knowledge he now has the leisure to acquire through reading and from the disquisitions of Settembrini (his first mentor) and Naphta (the second), and on the other by infatuated contemplation of Madame Chauchat's shadowy image, for whose gauze-covered arm Castorp developed a metonymic obsession within hours of his arrival at the 'Berghof'. As he undertakes this imaginary odyssey, Castorp less resembles Goethe's Wilhelm Meister than he does a comically reduced version of Faust who, under the magical tutelage of Mephistopheles, is transported high and low through 'die kleine, dann die große Welt' in order to satisfy his desire to understand 'was die Welt im Innersten zusammenhält' (*GW*, Vol. 3, p. 80).

As these few instances of allusions to other works, and kinds, of literature (with which the *Zauberberg* is packed to bursting point) make clear, Mann's treatment of the *Bildungsroman* tradition is playful. One of his many jokes is to pair his small-scale Faust with Settembrini as a benevolent 'Satana' (p. 81), a man whose approval of Castorp's inclination to live by the principle 'placet experiri' (p. 139) is heavily qualified by the reservations of a prudential rationalist. Nevertheless Settembrini's role as Castorp's first (and last) mentor points clearly to the novel's

genealogical descent from the classic *Bildungsroman* of the eighteenth
century. Settembrini is a man of the Enlightenment, a missionary of
'Fortschritt', intellectual and moral, political and social. One of his principal functions in the *Zauberberg* is to remind the reader constantly of
this notion of life as progress, as an upward journey via identifiable
landmarks towards a succession of goals, both for the individual and for
humanity. In practice, admittedly, Settembrini's insistence that Castorp's
journey through life ought to follow a pattern of progress largely provides a foil against which to identify and measure the idiosyncratic
patterns of movement traced by his increasingly recalcitrant tutee. On the
other hand, while Settembrini's rationalistic optimism regularly comes
off second best in his dialectical duels with the sharper-minded, radical-
reactionary Naphta, and although he is mocked as a mere 'organ-grinder'
by Castorp, the latter ultimately finds him a more sympathetic and trustworthy human being than the cleverer Jesuit (whose 'sharpness', paradoxically, points to his greater affinity to the Satanic). The narrator
signals a similar sympathy, or even identification, with Settembrini
when, at the point of his leave-taking from the 'Sorgenkind' Castorp, he
too puts a finger to his eye to wipe away a tear (p. 1006). Is, then, the
Zauberberg, for all its playfulness, ultimately less of a parody than a
renewal of the *Bildungsroman*? Is Hans Castorp's journey to be understood as a story of progress? [9] If so, of what kind, and which episodes
might qualify as 'landmarks' to mark it out as such?

One such episode occurs at a relatively early point in Castorp's
stay, namely the period during which he takes on the role of the Good
Samaritan towards some of the most gravely ill patients in the sanatorium. Another, even stronger candidate for 'landmark' status is the
episode described in the chapter entitled 'Schnee' about two-thirds of
the way through the novel. Each of these is worth considering in turn.

9   This question has divided commentators more than any other. Hans Wysling, for
     example, is one of the doubters: 'Die drei Gedankenexperimente [...] vermögen
     Castorps Leben keine neue Richtung zu geben. Der *Zauberberg* bleibt ein
     décadence-Roman – mit Gegenimpulsen'. 'Probleme der *Zauberberg*-Interpre-
     tation', *Thomas Mann Jahrbuch*, 1 (1988), 25. T. J. Reed, by contrast, sees the
     complicated, contradictory genesis of the work as resulting in an 'echten und ernst-
     haften Exemplar einer Gattung, zu der greifen mag, wer an sich selbst, an seiner
     Umgebung oder seiner Zeit irre geworden ist', *Thomas-Mann-Handbuch*, ed. by
     Helmut Koopmann (Stuttgart, 1991), p. 117.

Castorp's works of charity are undertaken as an act of protest against what he regards as the uncaring attitude towards the emotional needs of the dying at the 'Berghof'. But do they mark a development towards independent judgement – the capacity for 'Urteil' and 'ribellione' Settembrini keeps demanding – either of his own behaviour or of the values and organisation of 'Berghof' society? Certainly, Castorp's shocked reaction to the callous hypocrisy he perceives in the practice of removing the dead at night from the sanatorium and generally passing over their removal in a conspiracy of silence, is one of many signs of his inability or refusal to conform to the accepted norms of life at the sanatorium, symptoms of his 'Gewöhnung daran, daß er sich nicht gewöhnte' (p. 662). Nevertheless, his actions can equally well be seen as an extension of the reverential attitude to death he brought with him into the mountains, having acquired it at an early age when the deaths of his parents and grandfather followed one another in quick succession. In his attempt *not* to conform to the unfamiliar norms of life at the 'Berghof', Castorp may simply be relapsing into conformity to the values and forms of behaviour inculcated in him in the social sphere in which he was raised. If so, it bears witness not to freedom but to conditioning.

Just as importantly, Castorp's campaign of good works does not do justice to the conflicting feelings he has had about death since childhood, a conflict that has been revived by his stay on the mountain. Profoundly impressed as he was by the 'true' image his grandfather had supposedly assumed in death once he had been laid out in state with his head supported by the starched ruff of his high ancestral office, the young Hans was also alert to other, quite different and anything but dignified aspects of the inert figure, above all its waxy corporeality and the distinct odour of decomposition that the heavily scented flowers in the room could not quite mask. This conflict in Castorp's perceptions and feelings is raised to a new pitch of intensity ('Steigerung') in the heady, oxygen-deprived atmosphere of the Magic Mountain. When he first hears of the nightly transport of the cadavers by bobsleigh to their place of disposal, for example, Castorp is seized by an uncontrollable fit of laughter:

> Und plötzlich geriet er ins Lachen, in ein heftiges, unbezwingliches Lachen, das seine Brust erschütterte und sein vom kühlen Wind etwas steifes Gesicht zu einer leise schmerzenden Grimasse verzog. (p. 17)

As a respectable son of the Hamburg-protestant bourgeoisie, Castorp is shocked by his own involuntary reaction, but the same pattern keeps repeating itself as he encounters one grotesquely ambivalent feature of 'Berghof' life (and death) after another. Castorp's motives for showing kindness to the sick and dying doubtless include an element of altruism, but his conscious intentions can no more hide the presence of other, unadmitted and perhaps inaccessible motives than the flowers surrounding his grandfather's bier can banish the smell of decay.

As much as he is concerned to succour the dying, Castorp is evidently bent on dealing with the disquietingly 'inappropriate' feelings aroused in him by numerous features of disease and death 'up here' in the mountains, where the human body and its disposal are the focus of a profitable industry and where conditions are not conducive to the pious reserve expected of a decent young gentleman in the 'Flachland'. Because his charitable acts are an attempt to master contradictory experiences by simplistic means, they hardly qualify as steps on a path of progress towards a more mature, morally complex response to the world. Rather the episode is one of many that cast doubt on his later claim to be 'Herr der Gegensätze'. It is Settembrini, of all people, who is given the task of questioning Castorp's conduct during this episode. He asks sarcastically whether Castorp is looking for 'Rechtfertigung durch gute Werke' (p. 433). Justification for what? For his fascination with the details of death? Perhaps for the fact that the role of the Good Samaritan gives him an excuse to remain here – and thus stay close to Clawdia Chauchat? Is his pity for the suffering an outlet for self-pity in his role as unrequited lover? At all events, the transience of Castorp's charitable work suggests that Settembrini is right to suspect that it does not have an entirely altruistic source – or, at the very least, if it *is* morally motivated behaviour, that it does not indicate a major landmark in the shaping of his personality.

What then of the later chapter entitled 'Schnee', at the end of which Castorp declares: 'damit hab' ich zu Ende geträumt und recht zum Ziele' (p. 695)? Does his belief that he now has reached his 'goal' mark the culmination of Castorp's 'Bildungsweg'? The events of this chapter can certainly be read as a triumph over decadence, in that Castorp has deliberately brought himself into closer contact with death by skiing far off-piste so that he has to battle for physical survival when a sudden snowstorm takes him by surprise. As he takes shelter from the blizzard behind an isolated herdsman's hut, the combination of exhaustion, cold and his own foolish decision to warm himself with a drink of port threaten to pull him down into a sleep that could so easily prove to be the twin brother of death. What that unwise or more probably disingenuous drink of port suggests, however, is that Castorp has embarked on this foolhardy adventure not simply to face death as an external enemy but in order to expose himself more fully than ever before to the internal threat presented by his own decadent fascination with and indeed attraction to death, a threat that has been intensified at the 'Berghof' by his failure to secure the love of Clawdia Chauchat. In as much as Castorp is finally able to wrench himself out of his slumber, stand up again on his skis, and make his way back to the sanatorium, he passes his self-imposed test by choosing life over the seduction of death. By so doing he appears to confirm Settembrini's verdict that the decision to go off skiing on his own is a sign of inward health and strength: 'Zwei Jahre hier und noch dieses Einfalls fähig, – ah, nein. Ihr Kern ist gut, man hat keinen Grund, an Ihnen zu verzweifeln. Bravo, bravo!' (p. 663).

Settembrini's endorsement may echo the eighteenth-century optimism of the 'Prolog im Himmel' from *Faust* ('Ein guter Mensch in seinem dunklen Drange/ Ist sich des rechten Weges wohl bewußt') (*GW*, Vol. 3, p. 18), but the novel as a whole does not lend the same degree of authority to his judgement. There is irony, for example, in the fact that Settembrini identifies himself with 'Mercurio' (p. 663) at precisely this moment. Mercury, after all, is the Roman name given to the Greeks' tricky messenger god Hermes, one of whose principal functions is to convey the souls of human beings to the realm of death. Not that there is any deliberate malevolence in Settembrini's encouragement to Castorp to go out skiing in defiance of sanatorium rules, but the effect of the Hermes allusion (one of hundreds in the novel) is to suggest (contrary to Settembrini's optimistic rationalism) that no simple distinction is possible between health and sickness, strength and decadence, an action undertaken in the name of life and one directed at death, since the one can so easily masquerade as or transform itself into the other in this world of ambiguous, ambivalent and 'vexatorisch' phenomena. Castorp's decision to go out to confront death may indeed be a sign of his robust 'Kern', but he may equally well have persuaded himself that his adventure has a healthy motive in order – subconsciously – to yield to the temptation of death. As the novel establishes Castorp's own sly gift for self-deception and self-justification from the very beginning of his stay on the mountain, there is every reason to view his words and conduct in 'Schnee' just as sceptically as in the preceding and following chapters.

The 'goal' supposedly reached by Castorp at the end of his adventure in the snow is a self-given commandment, '*Der Mensch soll um der Güte und Liebe willen dem Tode keine Herrschaft einräumen über seine Gedanken*' (pp. 694–95), of which Thomas Mann said that he intended this to be the message of the novel.[10] Some such spiritual goal or landmark had indeed to be aimed for if the novel was to be a renewal of the *Bildungsroman*, and a path of progress imagined that would somehow lead across or through the abyss opened up by the First World War. Yet while Mann doubtless wanted to deliver such a message of hope in the post-war years, what one might call his conscience as a writer ensured that this message was refracted in such a multi-faceted prism of irony that, at most, it offers belief to those who already have faith and doubt to those who are sceptical.

The most obvious objection to the notion that Castorp's adventures in the snow mark a decisive stage in his personal formation is the fact that he begins within hours to forget his experiences and fail to understand his own conclusions. Once back in the 'hochzivilisierte Atmosphäre des "Berghofs"', his enormous appetite displaces his recent preoccupation with grand moral questions: 'Was er geträumt, war im Verbleichen begriffen. Was er gedacht, verstand er schon diesen Abend nicht mehr so recht' (p. 697). In itself the objection need not be decisive, as the effects of the experience could lie at a deeper level of the psyche and prove to have longer-term formative effects. In a sense this is true, but not in a sense that is compatible with the classic Enlightenment notion of moral 'Bildung'.

The reference to the 'hochzivilisierte Atmosphäre' of the sanatorium has quite specific implications in the discursive world within which Mann's thought had evolved during the years of the novel's genesis. In his essays in defence of the national cause during the war Mann had repeatedly elevated the values of spiritually profound 'Kultur' above those of materialistic, comfort-loving 'Zivilisation', claiming that Germany was a land of tragic 'Kultur', whereas the nations of the western Entente

10   *Thomas Mann–Robert Faesi Briefwechsel* (Zürich, 1962), p.16.

were capable only of the shallow optimism of 'Zivilisation'.[11] Seen in this context, Castorp's re-absorption into the 'zivilisiert' atmosphere of the 'Berghof' may not simply signify his return to the banal, and perhaps common-sense normality of the dinner-table after his exalted dreams and rhetoric in the snow, but rather mark his seduction away from the insights into the true nature of 'Kultur' he acquired during the blizzard and back into the inauthentic life of the international bourgeoisie.

The larger, as yet hidden implications of Castorp's development only emerge in the final chapter of the novel, when he is shown staggering across a battlefield, singing snatches of a Schubert setting of a song by Wilhelm Müller ('Der Lindenbaum'), a veritable embodiment of patriotic German 'Kultur' fighting to defend its spiritual birthright against a hostile world. Although this final scene is extremely brief, its interpretative importance can hardly be overstated, since it casts a long shadow back through the entire novel. Once Mann had decided that the novel would end with Castorp's entry into the war, he retouched certain details from the beginning of the story to point forward to this conclusion. In order to make the end of Castorp's seven-year stay at the 'Berghof' coincide with the outbreak of the war, for example, the start of his visit to Joachim was moved from May to August.[12]

Read in the light of the war-chapter, the 'Schneekapitel' can be seen to contribute to a form of 'Bildung' quite at odds with the enlightened conception of moral progress advocated by Settembrini, namely a late *Romantic* one. Castorp's conclusion in the midst of the blizzard, after all, is that the 'Sonnenleute' by the sea are 'höflich und reizend zueinander [...] im stillen Hinblick auf eben dies Gräßliche' (p. 693), 'dies Gräßliche' being the tearing apart of an infant no distance from the gentle scenes of sociability by the shore. At the heart of the culture imagined by Castorp is not simply a general awareness of death and suffering in the world but, crucially, their incorporation into sacrificial ritual: the child's dismemberment (echoing the fate of Dionysos zagreus) takes place in a temple where this community of 'Sonnenleute' has its abominable cult.

---

11 'Die deutsche Seele ist zu tief, als daß Zivilisation ihr ein Hochbegriff, oder etwa die höchste gar sein könnte', 'Gedanken im Kriege'. *Von deutscher Republik.* Thomas Mann, *Gesammelte Werke in Einzelbänden*, ed. by P. de Mendelssohn (Frankfurt a. M., 1984), p. 17.

12 For details of this and other changes, see James F. White, *The Yale 'Zauberberg'-Manuscript, Thomas-Mann-Studien*, Vol. 4 (Berne and Munich, 1980).

The affinity with Nietzsche's conception of the Dionysiac foundations of all true culture is unmistakable, as is, consequently, the problematic character of Castorp's three-part dream. According to Nietzsche, the ancient Greeks were prompted to create Apolline images of heroic, beautiful or godly life on Olympus as a means of coping with their unusual sensitivity to suffering.[13] At a deeper level, he argued, these Apolline images were actually illusions serving a dark, Dionysiac Will that pulsed within the Greeks, inducing them to carry on living heroically and positively until the time had come for Fate to destroy them much as the child is consumed by the hags.[14] What Castorp learns during the blizzard, then, is not simply that he must venerate life, but also that violent death, no matter how horrific, must be accepted as the necessary, sacrificial basis of any truly cultured and 'fromm' conduct of life.

Thomas Mann cast his own defence of Germany's 'cultured' war aims from 1914 onwards in precisely these terms. Understood as part of a Romantic rather than an enlightened 'Bildungsweg', the 'Schneekapitel' becomes a profoundly disturbing landmark on Hans Castorp's journey. Contrary to what he resolves in the third, abstract part of his dream – 'Ich will dem Tode keine Herrschaft einräumen über meine Gedanken' (p. 694) – obsession with death continues to lie at the heart of Castorp's attitude and conduct for the remainder of the novel, whether in his fascination with Mynheer Peeperkorn's attention-seeking pursuit of pleasure to the point of self-destruction (or sacrifice, as Peeperkorn prefers to think of it), in his growing passion for music, or finally in the exalted manner in which he welcomes the outbreak of war as an opportunity to redeem his life in an act of sacrifice:

Er sah sich entzaubert, erlöst, befreit, – nicht aus eigener Kraft, wie er sich mit Beschämung gestehen mußte, sondern an die Luft gesetzt von elementaren Außenmächten, denen seine Befreiung sehr nebensächlich mit unterlief. Aber wenn auch sein kleines Schicksal vor dem allgemeinen verschwand, – drückte nicht dennoch etwas von persönlich gemeinter und also von göttlicher Güte und Gerechtigkeit sich darin aus? Nahm das Leben sein sündiges Sorgenkind noch einmal an, – und

13   The title of Mann's novel may even have been suggested to him by a key passage of *Die Geburt der Tragödie*: 'Jetzt öffnet sich uns gleichsam der olympische Zauberberg und zeigt uns seine Wurzeln'. *Die Geburt der Tragödie*, §3. (Nietzsche, *Werke*, ed. by G. Colli and M. Montinari (Berlin, 1972), p. 31).

14   See *Die Geburt der Tragödie*, § 21.

nicht auf wohlfeile Art, sondern eben nur so, auf diese ernste und strenge Art, im
Sinn einer Heimsuchung, die vielleicht nicht Leben, aber gerade in diesem Falle
drei Ehrensalven für ihn, den Sünder bedeutete, konnte es geschehen. Und so
sank er denn auf seine Knie hin, Gesicht und Hände zu einem Himmel erhoben,
der schweflig dunkel, aber nicht länger die Grottendecke des Sündenberges war.
(p. 1000)

If one of the chief effects of Castorp's experiences in the snow is to
make him accept the necessity of death as sacrifice, however gruesome,
even as he asserts the values of form, dignity and friendliness, the result
of his 'Bildung' is to leave him – in his emotional orientation – not very
far from where he began when he set off to visit Joachim at the outset,
which is to say still profoundly in awe of death, despite its repulsive
features. While listening to the Schubert song late at night at the 'Berghof', so the narrator assures us, Castorp had come to recognise the need
to transcend the love of death that lurked in the depths of this innocent-
seeming 'Volkslied' (pp. 690–91). Yet when he actually goes to war
with this song on his lips, it is utterly unclear that or how Castorp's
actions represent the kind of 'Selbstüberwindung' through which some
new form of love, uncontaminated by the seductions of death and darkness, might emerge from the 'Weltfest des Todes' on the battlefields of
Europe. Castorp, we are told, sings phrases from the song 'bewußtlos',
'in stierer, gedankenloser Erregung' (p. 756), demonstrating not a trace
of the complex, critical understanding of the song's profound implication
in the ambitions of imperial Germany that Thomas Mann, from a post-
war point of view, felt compelled to project back into the mind of the
pre-war generation. Early in his stay at the 'Berghof', Castorp had
observed from his balcony a woman adjusting her steps unconsciously to
the rhythm of some trivial music played by the 'Kurkapelle'. When
the orchestra of war finally strikes up the dance of death down on the
'Flachland', the melody Castorp hears speaks to him of a yearning for
rest in death that lies deeper than the critical voice of reason, and he too
moves, just as unconsciously, to its rhythm.

As he leaves Castorp stumbling amidst the shellfire, the narrator
asks a question that puts not just the Romantic and the Enlightenment
conceptions of 'Bildung', but also his own rather forced attempts to put a
positive gloss on Castorp's development, into doubt: 'Wird auch aus
diesem Weltfest des Todes, auch aus der schlimmen Fieberbrunst, die
rings den regnerischen Abendhimmel entzündet, einmal die Liebe stei-

gen?' (p. 1006). This question, formulated in the very last sentence of the novel, could conceivably have an open ring to it, were it not for the preceding paragraphs. One of them describes the detonation of a shell:

> Das Produkt einer verwilderten Wissenschaft, geladen mit dem schlimmsten, fährt dreißig Schritte schräg vor ihm wie der Teufel selbst tief in den Grund, zerplatzt dort unten mit gräßlicher Übergewalt und reißt einen haushohen Springbrunnen von Erdreich, Feuer, Eisen, Blei und zerstückeltem Menschentum in die Lüfte empor. Denn dort lagen zwei, – es waren Freunde, sie hatten sich zusammengelegt in der Not: nun sind sie vermengt und verschwunden. (p. 1003)

Did Mann perhaps have Goethe's faith in the indestructibility of the personality (as suggested above in the quotation from 'Urworte. Orphisch') in mind when he wrote this description of 'zerstückeltem Menschentum'? At all events, Settembrini's enlightened faith in science as a means to human progress is challenged by the exploding shell, 'das Produkt einer verwilderten Wissenschaft', that rips apart human beings in mechanical imitation of the hags dismembering the child in the temple. Yet Castorp's Apolline-Dionysiac apotheosis of culture is called into question no less clearly on the very same page:

> Das junge Blut, mit seinen Ranzen und Spießgewehren, seinen verschmutzten Mänteln und Stiefeln, man könnte sich humanistisch-schönseliger Weise auch andere Bilder erträumen in seiner Betrachtung. Man könnte es sich denken! Rosse regend und schwemmend in einer Meeresbucht, mit der Geliebten am Strande wandelnd, die Lippen am Ohr der weichen Braut, auch wie es glücklich freundschaftlich einander im Bogenschuß unterweist. Statt dessen liegt es, die Nase im Feuerdreck. Daß es das freudig tut, wenn auch in grenzenlosen Ängsten und unaussprechlichem Mutterheimweh, ist eine erhabene und beschämende Sache für sich, sollte jedoch kein Grund sein, es in die Lage zu bringen. (p. 1004)

Far from dignifying or justifying violence (as Mann's 'Gedanken im Kriege' had done in 1914), the fact that it is possible in imagination to convert the reality of warfare into some tragic-mythical vision of life's beauty heightened by the presence of death is now seen to provide no justification for waging or engaging in war as an occasion for sacrifice. The 'junges Blut' that is destroyed, by cold calculation, in the war, would have been equally beautiful and worthy of veneration, had it been permitted to live rather than be torn to fragments by high explosives.

While the echoes of the 'Schneekapitel' in the closing scene of the novel are perhaps the most powerful device used by Mann to cast a critical light on the results of Castorp's 'Bildungsweg', they are supported by many other features of the narration. In the 'Schneekapitel' itself, for example, the circularity of Castorp's imagined 'Fortkommen' in the blizzard is just one irony amongst many which suggest that his spiritual and intellectual progress may be equally illusory. Thus, while Castorp is making his way towards the high-sounding conclusions of his three-fold dream, the narrator repeatedly describes his mental processes as 'unklar', 'verworren', 'gewagt und kraus', as 'faseln', or as embodying things that he had 'sich vorgefabelt'. Whereas Castorp claims ultimately to be 'Herr der Gegensätze' that present themselves to his mind, he is described throughout this episode as being at the mercy of conflicting physical, emotional and intellectual impulses, just as he had been from the moment he first left the train in Davos:

> So wirkten die zweideutigen Ausfälle, die er nur matt bekämpfte. Jene Mischung aus Müdigkeit und Aufregung, die den vertrauten Dauerzustand eines Gastes bildete, dessen Akklimatisation in der Gewöhnung darin bestand, daß er sich nicht gewöhnte, hatte sich in ihren Bestandteilen so weit verstärkt, daß von einem besonnenen Verhalten gegen die Ausfälle nicht mehr die Rede sein konnte. (pp. 678–79)

Ultimately, it is true, Castorp's survival instinct proves stronger than the deadly pull of drowsiness, and it is helped to this victory by his capacity for critical reason, 'gewissermaßen einer fremden, unbeteiligten, wenn auch besorgten Person' (p. 677), but it is not Settembrini's 'ragione' alone that gets Castorp out of difficulties. Rather it is the fact that Castorp is who he is: a young man in good health (despite the 'feuchte Stelle' that has given him the excuse he needed to dally at the sanatorium), one who has been shaped by multifarious influences throughout his life, and one whose love for Clawdia Chauchat, however unsuccessful so far, gives him a reason for wanting to survive the snowstorm (just as the disappointment of his love will give him reason to sacrifice his life in war, still sporting the beard he acquired at the 'schlechten Russentisch'). Change any one of these factors and the outcome of his struggle in the snow could have been very different.

This point, trivial enough in itself, is important as far as the Enlightenment project of 'Bildung' is concerned. In that scheme of things, the individual was conceived as an exemplar of mankind, a particular instance of a universal human capacity for development, at the core of which lay a common set of attributes and values: reason, sensibility, morality. The post-war, pro-republican Thomas Mann wanted to believe in the general human potential for progress just as strongly as his creature Settembrini. But the Thomas Mann who completed the novel in 1924 had not – could not – shed entirely the general way of looking at life he had acquired long before, even if he did now want to evaluate things differently. As someone whose own intellectual formation took place during the last quarter of the nineteenth century, Mann had learned at an early stage to appreciate the combined effects of heredity and circumstance on the shaping of views and values. He had also learned from Nietzsche and Schopenhauer to understand the workings of subconscious impulse, both negative and affirmative, to be keenly aware of the human need for and susceptibility to illusions of various kinds, and to appreciate the changing perspectives in which life can be seen, depending on hope or despair, health or decadence, or the countless other factors that distinguish one human being from another or even determine different stages in the evolution of a single life.

The *Magic Mountain* is pervaded by precisely this awareness of the particularity of each human life, and of the shaping influence of factors that, at best, are only partly under the control of the individual, however devoted to self-formation and self-overcoming. It is not possible to conceive of a single way of looking at things or a universal set of values to which the wide range of oddly assorted beings (from Frau Stöhr to Naphta, from Peeperkorn to Settembrini, from Clawdia Chauchat to Adriatica von Mylendonk) who populate the pages of the novel might subscribe, or by which their lives might be encompassed. One of Mann's favourite literary quotations was Hamlet's comment to his father's ghost: 'Thou com'st in such a questionable shape'. For Mann these words summed up the singular, perhaps ultimately incomprehensible given-ness of the human personality, an awareness that made him deeply sceptical about the long-term efficacy of all resolutions to lead life differently and better. Tonio Kröger's promise to Lisaweta ('Ich werde Besseres machen')[15] was succeeded in a few years by the collapse of Gustav von Aschenbach's attempt to base his life and art on a self-given moral imperative. Equally, Castorp's vow in the snow ('Ich will

15   'Tonio Kröger'. *Frühe Erzählungen. Gesammelte Werke in Einzelbänden*, ed. by
       P. de Mendelssohn (Frankfurt a. M., 1981), p. 341.

gut sein') was followed just six years later by the failure of the mature and critical narrator of 'Mario und der Zauberer' to remove his children from the scene of Cipolla's hypnotic, Dionysiac manipulations of the audience's subconscious impulses.

'Du mußt dein Leben ändern' is how Rilke summed up the effect that genuine 'Bildung' ought to have on the individual.[16] Nietzsche, Thomas Mann's chief intellectual mentor, had preached the same doctrine: unless the process of self-formation altered a person's approach to life in a fundamental way, the result would be to produce a 'Bildungs-philister' rather than a truly cultivated personality.[17] In *Der Zauberberg* Castorp is afforded every opportunity to pursue the goal of 'Bildung', and his experiences at the 'Berghof' undoubtedly affect him powerfully, giving him a much more sophisticated understanding of life than he had on his arrival. But the outcome of the process is not, as Thomas Mann would have wished it to be, a landmark in the moral formation of an entire generation, except in the sense that it presented an exemplary case from which warning lessons might be learned. The 'Bildung' achieved by Hans Castorp on the Magic Mountain, one that prepared him to accept the necessity of sacrificing life in the name of an idealised vision of culture, was more likely to lead into the abyss of the First World War than to lead his generation out of that abyss and towards different ways of living and feeling. That is not to say, however, that *Der Zauberberg* is not a landmark in the history of the German novel. It is indeed such a landmark, precisely because it makes clear why the *Bildungsroman*, a genre developed at the end of the eighteenth century, could not provide an exemplary model of conduct after the profound intellectual and social changes that had taken place in the nineteenth and early twentieth centuries. By transforming the *Bildungsroman* into a *Zeitroman*, by diagnosing what had become of the idea and project of 'Bildung' under a new set of intellectual, social and historical circum-stances, *Der Zauberberg* took the intellectual novel in Germany a decisive step forward.

---

16   'Archaischer Torso Apollos'. *Gedichte 1895 bis 1910.* R. M. Rilke, *Werke,* Vol. 1,
      ed. by M. Engel and U. Fülleborn (Frankfurt a. M., 1996), p. 513.
17   See Section 2 of the first of Nietzsche's *Unzeitgemäße Betrachtungen*, 'David
      Strauss. Der Bekenner und Schriftsteller', op. cit., pp. 160–69.

CAROLIN DUTTLINGER

Kafka, *Der Proceß*

Der Proceß, written in 1914–15, is one of the most famous German-language novels of all time, an undisputed landmark not simply in German, but also in world literature. That said, the term 'landmark' has a rather grand ring to it, suggesting a carefully crafted, self-contained masterpiece. In fact, however, *Der Proceß* has always fascinated readers precisely because it resists such categories. Not only is it an unfinished work that was never published during the author's lifetime, but many editions later its manuscript continues to pose numerous unresolved challenges. The boundaries of Kafka's text are far from clear, and since its publication in 1925 its reception has been intertwined with heated debates about what does and does not constitute the corpus of the novel. *Der Proceß* is thus a landmark of German literature despite – or indeed because of – its lack of completion: its inherent openness has kept editors, readers and critics puzzled about the text, its shape and structure, quite apart from its meaning and interpretation.

In this essay I will explore such issues by focusing on those parts which are commonly relegated to the margins – of both the published text and our understanding. For this purpose, I will focus primarily on the so-called 'fragments', that is, on those parts of the text which, in Malcolm Pasley's critical edition of 1990, appear separately, at the end of the volume. While this position suggests that they are somehow accidental to the text and its meaning, a closer look reveals that these chapters – some more fragmentary than others – open up new and different perspectives on Kafka's novel. To read *Der Proceß* in this way raises challenging questions about the text, its shape and conception, and uncovers a precarious dynamic between part and whole, margins and centre, fragmentation and closure. Furthermore, such issues are thematised within the text, in a manner which brings out their ambiguity; while the narrative is underpinned both structurally and thematically by a desire for unity and coherence, it also displays a marked suspicion of such ideas and their effect on the creative process.

Kafka's desire for closure and unity is embedded in his writing strategy. The manuscript indicates that he wrote the opening and final chapters first (he might have even written them in parallel),[1] thereby giving his text a fixed narrative frame and, most importantly, a conclusion. As if to underline this achievement, the chapter describing Josef K.'s execution is simply called 'Ende' – something which Kafka failed to achieve in his first novel, *Der Verschollene* (1912–14). The bulk of this text, written in 1912, unfolded as one continuous narrative which eventually breaks off and is left unfinished – a fate which also awaited Kafka's final novel, *Das Schloß*.

When writing *Der Proceß*, Kafka attempts to fend off the spectre of another unfinished novel. Even if the order in which he wrote the chapters cannot be definitively reconstructed, the chapters 'Verhaftung' and 'Ende' are closely linked in thematic terms, thereby providing a tightly structured narrative frame for the rest of the novel. The concluding chapter is set exactly one year after K.'s arrest; what is more, it is informed by a pervading, uncanny sense of repetition which lends the action a sense of defeatism and inevitability. As at the beginning, Josef K. is visited at home by two court officials, although the two shambolic guards from the opening chapter are now replaced by two robot-like 'Herren' who are unresponsive to any pleading or questions. Once again, there is an emphasis on clothing, yet while K. was arrested in his nightshirt, a year later he awaits his executioners in a sombre black suit and

1   Observing an overall increase of the words-per-page ratio in other texts written over the months during which Kafka worked on *Der Proceß*, Malcolm Pasley argues that this pattern can be reapplied to the novel manuscript, offering an indication of the order in which different parts were written. According to this approach, the chapters known as 'Verhaftung' and 'Ende' were the first to be written. (See Pasley, 'Entstehung', in Franz Kafka, *Der Proceß: Apparatband*, ed. by Malcolm Pasley (Frankfurt a. M., 1990), pp. 71–129 (pp. 78–9; 111).) The validity of this approach has been challenged by Roland Reuß, one of the editors of the *Historisch-Kritische Ausgabe* of Kafka's works, who argues that the writing process depends on too many factors to be analysable through statistical analysis. That said, Reuss likewise assumes that the first and last chapters were written early on, even if he challenges Pasley's assumption that 'Verhaftung' was written before 'Ende', arguing that they might well have been written in parallel. (See Roland Reuß, 'Zur kritischen Edition von "Der Process" im Rahmen der Historisch-Kritischen Franz Kafka-Ausgabe', in *Franz Kafka-Hefte* 1 (Frankfurt a. M., Basel, 1995), pp. 3–25 (pp. 3; 6–8; 10).)

new gloves. This time K. is dressed for the occasion, and as the novel draws to a close, Kafka's protagonist no longer struggles against the predetermined course of the trial and its narrative.[2]

Even though the novel's narrative frame of arrest and execution thus lends it an inner coherence, within the text itself such notions of framing and unity are invested with a sense of claustrophobia. Once the trio has left the house, K.'s executioners hook their arms into his:

> Gleich aber vor dem Tor hängten sie sich in ihn in einer Weise ein, wie K. noch niemals mit einem Menschen gegangen war. Sie hielten die Schultern eng hinter den seinen, knickten die Arme nicht ein, sondern benützten sie, um K.'s Arme in ihrer ganzen Länge zu umschlingen, unten erfaßten sie K.'s Hände mit einem schulmäßigen, eingeübten, unwiderstehlichen Griff. K. gieng straff gestreckt zwischen ihnen, sie bildeten eine solche Einheit, daß wenn man einen von ihnen zerschlagen hätte, alle zerschlagen gewesen wären. Es war eine Einheit, wie sie fast nur Lebloses bilden kann. (p. 306)[3]

The structural concept of *Einheit*, of (narrative) closure and coherence, is here transplanted into the action. K.'s body is forced into a strangely rigid position by his executioners, and this unity of bodies takes on an eerily inhuman, even lethal quality. Only lifeless things, the text implies, can enter into such a complete fusion, and this sense of objectification is underlined by the verb *zerschlagen*, which is more applicable to objects

2   Another recurrent motif is that of windows; in the opening chapter, K. feels exposed to the gaze of the old woman, who watches his arrest from the house opposite, where she is later joined by an old and a younger man. In the final chapter, in contrast, most of the windows opposite are dark, and the one lit window does not frame any watchful – and potentially compassionate – observers but two toddlers whose position ('hinter einem Gitter [...], noch unfähig, sich von ihren Plätzen fortzubewegen') mirrors K.'s own entrapment. (Franz Kafka, *Der Proceß*, ed. by Malcolm Pasley (Frankfurt a. M., 1990), p. 305–6. References henceforth to this edition. Prior to K.'s execution, finally, a window recurs as a symbol of (futile) hope (p. 312).

3   In a letter to his future fiancée Felice Bauer of 11/12 February 1913, Kafka describes and even draws a very similar grip with which he holds Felice in a dream underpinned by a 'Mischung von Trauer und Glück'. (Franz Kafka, *Briefe and Felice und andere Korrespondenz aus der Verlobungszeit*, ed. by Erich Heller and Jürgen Born (Frankfurt a. M., 1976), p. 294.) In *Der Proceß*, written in the months after the break-up of their engagement, this grasp recurs as a clear sign of entrapment.

than to living bodies. At this poignant moment in the narrative, the notion of *Einheit* thus triggers thoughts of fragmentation as a violent, and similarly destructive, reaction against this deadly union.

It is no coincidence that this passage occurs in a chapter which embodies Kafka's rigorous striving for narrative closure. In fact, on more than one level, this episode anticipates the ending of the novel. Having been physically and mentally absorbed by his trial, Josef K. submits himself freely to his own elimination within, and through, the narrative. The text's conclusion, its 'Ende', coincides with the gruesome termination of human life, the ultimate seal of narrative closure.[4]

In *Der Proceß*, unity and coherence are thus not straightforwardly positive concepts but are associated with the restrictive nature of court and trial.[5] A similar tension between unity and fragmentation underpins the novel's narrative structure. Although Kafka attempted to give his novel a fixed frame, this does not ensure its coherence. The action linking arrest and execution does not reveal a clear sense of progression or teleology; rather, the overall atmosphere is one of stagnation, futility and repetition, an effect reflected in the continuing debates about the 'correct' order of these middle chapters. While such uncertainties affect what is commonly regarded as the novel proper, they play an even greater role in relation to the so-called fragments – those parts of the novel which most stubbornly resist integration into a narrative whole.

---

4   This congruence between the end of the text and that of the protagonist ties in with the novel's narrative perspective. A third-person narrative, the text is mostly narrated through K.'s eyes, and hence the death of the protagonist logically spells the conclusion of the story. That said, in other texts, such as 'Ein Hungerkünstler' (1922) and in particular *Die Verwandlung* (1912), whose narrative perspective is similar to that of *Der Proceß*, the death of the protagonist does not immediately bring about narrative closure but is followed by a brief epilogue. Kafka did, however, reject the ending of *Die Verwandlung* as 'unlesbar' and 'unvollkommen fast bis in den Grund' (Franz Kafka, *Tagebücher*, ed. by Hans-Gerd Koch, Michael Müller and Malcolm Pasley (Frankfurt a. M., 1990), p. 624).)

5   Throughout the novel, K.'s trial leads him into enclosed, claustrophobic spaces, such as the law offices, Titorelli's studio or the lumber room in 'Der Prügler'. The bad air which often fills such places lends this sense of entrapment a physical immediacy.

It is difficult, if not impossible, to draw a clear distinction between complete and incomplete chapters.[6] By focusing on these so-called fragments, I do not therefore want to suggest that a categorical distinction between main part and fragments is possible or even desirable. Rather, my approach attempts to redress the imbalance in reception between the novel's 'centre' and its margins created by existing editions. A renewed focus on these marginalised texts might offer less canonical routes of interpretation, providing a different perspective on Kafka's writing process and the conceptualisation of his novel.

For this purpose, I will focus on three of the six texts which in Pasley's critical edition are included in the appendix. In different ways and for different reasons, these pieces chapter the unity of Kafka's novel – its neat progression from arrest to execution – by expanding the boundaries of the text in temporal, spatial and psychological directions. While these pieces thus challenge established distinctions between the margins of the text and its core or centre, they also resist interpretative certainty: the insights they offer remain tantalisingly ambiguous, hinged between utopia and dystopia, desire and domination, wish-fulfilment and disaster.

The episode entitled 'Staatsanwalt' is noteworthy for two reasons. Not only is it the only chapter which is set before the start of Josef K.'s trial, but it also reverses the power dynamics which underpin interpersonal relations in the rest of the novel. Chronologically speaking, this chapter is set just prior to K.'s arrest; in fact, were it not for this episode, the novel's timeframe would be identical to its title. If the 'Staatsanwalt'

6   In this respect I disagree with Max Brod and Malcolm Pasley, who both distinguish between 'complete' and 'incomplete' chapters. In their respective editions, they exclude the so-called 'fragments' from the main text and reprint them in a separate section at the end – a distinction which is rejected as arbitrary and misleading by the editors of the *Historisch-Kritische Ausgabe* (see Reuss, 'Zur kritischen Edition', pp. 10–5). Indeed, some of the chapters which are commonly included in the main body of the novel, such as 'Kaufmann Block / Kündigung des Advokaten' and 'Im Dom', end very abruptly and might well be unfinished, whereas some 'fragments' are rather long and self-contained. The piece 'B.'s Freundin', for instance, which is included in the main text by Brod but not by Pasley, is longer than both 'Der Prügler' and 'Ende'; indeed, the latter, which in Pasley's edition only amounts to seven printed pages, is shorter than, or of equal length to, three of the six 'fragments'. The fact that Kafka was fond of very short prose narratives, which he published alongside longer stories, makes a distinction on the grounds of length particularly problematic.

chapter thus expands the temporal framework of the novel, it also marks an exception from the pervading atmosphere of rivalry and aggression. Yet while the chapter offers us a glimpse of K.'s life before his arrest which in many ways is very different from his experiences during the trial, the chapter also illustrates that K.'s dealings with the court do not start with his arrest. Even before his trial, K. maintains close links with court representatives, and in particular with Hasterer, a senior figure within this institution.

The court representatives featured in this chapter are not the remote and inaccessible figures we find elsewhere in the novel. K. gets to know them in the relaxed, informal context of their *Stammtisch*, and although he is an outsider to this group, he is by no means ignorant of its inner hierarchies: K. 'war überhaupt [...] allen gegenüber sehr höflich und bescheiden und er verstand es, was noch wichtiger als Höflichkeit und Bescheidenheit war, zwischen den Rangabstufungen der Herren richtig zu unterscheiden und jeden seinem Range gemäß zu behandeln' (p. 331). Although K. is not a member of the legal profession, moreover, he is not treated as an ignorant outsider; quite to the contrary, his external view is highly valued:

> Als geschäftlicher Fachmann war er bald anerkannt und seine Meinung in solchen Dingen galt – wenn es auch dabei nicht ganz ohne Ironie abgieng – als etwas Unumstößliches. Es geschah nicht selten, daß zwei, die eine Rechtsfrage verschieden beurteilten, K. seine Ansicht über den Tatbestand abverlangten und daß dann K.'s Name in allen Reden und Gegenreden wiederkehrte. (pp. 328–9)

Thus K., who during his trial will be constantly puzzled by the workings of the court, and whose attempts to confront this institution fail on every level, is here elevated to the level of an external advisor. What is more, this chapter breaks down the division between bank and court which K. is later so anxious to maintain; he even hopes that this connection 'auch in der Bank Vorteil bringen konnte und außerdem konnte er zum Gericht persönliche Beziehungen anknüpfen, die immer nützlich waren' p. 328).

On the whole, then, K.'s engagement with the court in the 'Staatsanwalt' chapter reverses his experiences during the trial, where we find him confused, excluded and mistaken, in turns boastful and intimidated, but never at eye-level with the court. Another, even more significant deviation from this norm, however, becomes apparent in K.'s friendship with the attorney Hasterer. Throughout the novel, K.'s dealings with both men and women are never based on friendship or affection, but are invariably governed by some underlying aim or purpose. Women are regarded as sex objects and possible allies in the struggle against the court; sexuality in turn serves as the battleground on which K. tries to defeat his male opponents. This pattern is reversed in the 'Staatsanwalt' chapter, where male solidarity offers an antidote against the divisive power of women.[7]

After their *Stammtisch* evenings, Hasterer and K. often go back to the attorney's flat: 'Diese Abende waren Hasterer so lieb, daß er nicht einmal auf sie verzichten wollte, als er während einiger Wochen ein Frauenzimmer namens Helene bei sich wohnen hatte' (p. 332). Indeed, Helene senses the competition from K. and tries to interrupt the men's conversation by attempting to seduce first Hasterer and later K. Unlike later in the novel, however, K. is steadfast in his solidarity:

[Helene] erreichte damit nur, daß K. sich nächstens weigerte zu Hasterer zu gehn, und als er nach einiger Zeit doch wieder hinkam, war Helene endgiltig fort-geschickt; K. nahm das als selbstverständlich hin. Sie blieben an diesem Abend besonders lange beisammen, feierten auf Hasterers Anregung Bruderschaft und K. war auf dem Nachhauseweg vom Rauchen und Trinken fast ein wenig betäubt. (p. 333)

The inebriating pleasures of homosociality take over from the thrills of heterosexual seduction, a reversal aided by the fact that Helene is not the most attractive of women. She is described as 'eine dicke ältliche Frau mit gelblicher Haut und schwarzen Locken, die sich um ihre Stirn ringelten' (p. 332), and both her body shape and her sexually forthright manner are reminiscent of Brunelda in *Der Verschollene*. Both women are depicted as monstrous and repulsive, and as such they pose no apparent threat to the virtue of Kafka's bachelor protagonists. Yet while Helene's age, physical appearance and old-fashioned clothes make her

---

7   Hasterer's seniority does not impact on his friendship with K.; on the contrary, 'wenn in ihrem Verhältnis äußerlich manchmal einer überlegen schien, so war es nicht Hasterer, sondern K., denn seine praktischen Erfahrungen behielten meistens Recht, da sie so unmittelbar gewonnen waren, wie es vom Gerichtstisch niemals geschehen konnte' (p. 329).

an unlikely object of desire, these attributes point into a rather different direction. Helene comes across as a rather maternal figure, and this, together with Hasterer's obvious seniority, lends this triangle an Oedipal character. All of this makes it all the more remarkable that the 'Staats-anwalt' chapter does not result in the kind of male rivalry so prominent throughout the novel. Indeed, this episode sheds a different light on K.'s personality and his stance towards male authority figures, revealing a deeply rooted desire for solidarity, friendship and paternal acceptance which, with the onset of the trial, gives way to aggression and sexual competition.

The chapter thus lies at margins of *Der Proceß* both chrono-logically and in terms of its overall atmosphere, yet despite these differ-ences it also displays one crucial continuity: even before his arrest, K.'s life is intertwined with the court and its representatives. Put differently, there is no state 'before the law' in Kafka's novel; even though K. remains an outsider to the law, his life prior to his trial is characterised by an even more intimate association with the court than after his arrest, when K. tries everything in his power to escape the grasp of this institution and forms no lasting bonds with any of the people, male or female, whom he encounters.[8]

Compared to the rest of the novel, then, this chapter appears almost like a wish-fulfilment. It resembles some happy dream of friendship and respect which is then crushed by brutal reality.[9] As it turns out, K.'s friendship with Hasterer is of no use in his trial. The 'Staatsanwalt' is only briefly mentioned in 'Verhaftung', and despite their apparent close-

---

8   This paradoxical state of being both intimately linked to the law and yet excluded from it is mirrored in the priest's parable about the man from the country. As Jacques Derrida remarks, 'Before the law, the man is a subject of the law in appearing before it. This is obvious, but since he is *before* it because he cannot enter it, he is also *outside the law* (an outlaw)'. (Jacques Derrida, 'Before the Law', in *Acts of Literature*, ed. by Derek Attridge (New York, London, 1992), pp. 181–220 (p. 204).)

9   In other words, it is the *function* of the court, rather than its impact on K.'s life, which changes with the onset of the trial. The *Stammtisch* and the friendship with Hasterer offer a respite from the dog-eat-dog mentality of K.'s work at the bank; his trial, in contrast, condenses all the negative aspects of K.'s daily existence: the sense of hierarchy and competition at work and his instrumentalising attitude towards women.

ness K. never turns to him for support or advice.[10] All of this should lead us to reconsider the status of this chapter as fragmentary; perhaps the reason why this episode was not developed any further was precisely its positive, almost utopian quality, which jarred with the rest the novel. That said, although this chapter seems at odds with the work as a whole, the sudden shift from happiness to disaster, from solidarity to isolation, is not entirely unheard of in Kafka's writings. *Der Verschollene* is characterised by a similar alternation between utopia and dystopia, as scenes of oppression, rejection and punishment are interspersed with fairytale-like moments of rescue and acceptance.[11] It would appear that Kafka gestured towards something similar in *Der Proceß* but then departed from this model in favour of a more unified and coherent, but also bleaker and more unrelenting, narrative framework.

Where the 'Staatsanwalt' chapter expands the scope of the novel in temporal terms, the piece 'Fahrt zur Mutter' gestures towards a spatial expansion, although this is never actually realised within the text. Its curtailed events take place towards the end of the narrative and would have probably been inserted in between the chapters 'Im Dom' and 'Ende'. The episode is set two weeks prior to K.'s thirty-first birthday (p. 351), on the eve of which he will be executed; in fact, it is informed by an atmosphere of impending doom and a sense that things are drawing to a close. Like the 'Staatsanwalt' chapter, it depicts the protagonist in an unfamiliar light: K. appears emotional and even sentimental, quite in contrast to his otherwise detached and pragmatic attitude.

Revealingly, none of the protagonists in Kafka's novels has any active family ties. Karl Roßmann is cast out by his parents, and although K. in *Das Schloß* claims to have a family, this claim is never verified. Josef K. is the only protagonist in the novels who makes an active attempt to see his mother (he is also in contact with his uncle and cousin). As it turns out, however, this plan is less a symbol of close family links than an attempt to resurrect a neglected relationship. At the beginning of the chapter, K. suddenly realises that he has not seen his

---

10 When K. threatens to call Hasterer in his dealings with the inspector, the latter stresses the pointlessness of such an undertaking, 'es müßte denn sein, daß Sie irgendeine private Angelegenheit mit ihm zu besprechen haben' (p. 23).

11 The tone of the 'Oklahoma' chapter, which was written in parallel to *Der Proceß*, is by comparison more ambivalent, thus illustrating the change in Kafka's overall approach.

mother for almost three years, even though he had promised to visit her once a year on his birthday. This piece of information is highly revealing. K.'s thirtieth and thirty-first birthdays act as important temporal markers within the novel, coinciding with his arrest and execution. In K.'s life, then, the trial takes the place of family ties which might otherwise structure – or restrict – his existence.

The date of the birthday ties together the apparently remote fields of trial and family, suggesting a contrasting, or indeed complementary, relationship between the two. This association between family and trial is not, of course, entirely unheard of in Kafka's writings. In several texts preceding *Der Proceß*, it is the family, rather than an official law court, which acts as the site of accusation, condemnation and punishment.[12] In *Der Proceß*, by contrast, except for the time marker of K.'s birthday, there seems to be no apparent link between his mother and his trial.[13] Indeed, for K. a visit to the mother promises a break from his case, as well as from the competitive climate at the bank. His mother is convinced that K. is in fact the bank director (p. 355), a belief well suited to prop up his fragile ego. What makes the mother so attractive is precisely her lack of understanding of her son's day-to-day life. Not only does she live away from the city in what is described as an 'unveränderliche[s] Städtchen' (p. 335), but she is almost blind and would therefore be unable to scrutinise and judge K. in the way that he is constantly scrutinised and judged by others.

Yet this is not the whole story, and in other respects K. feels quite alienated from his mother. In recent years she has become 'unmäßig fromm' (p. 352), and her association with the church serves as an unpleasant reminder of K.'s recent unsettling encounter with the priest in the cathedral. In the chapter 'Im Dom', religion is portrayed as a sphere to which K. has no access and which resists his rational, instrumentalising approach; the mother's association with this context removes her from her son's grasp and understanding.

12   Examples include Georg Bendemann in 'Das Urteil', who is sentenced to death by his own father, Gregor Samsa in *Die Verwandlung*, who encounters a very similar fate, and Karl Roßmann in *Der Verschollene*, whose parents condemn him to a life of exile.
13   Unsettlingly, the uncle seems closely informed about K.'s trial and even gets actively involved by recommending his case to his friend, the lawyer Huld; K. is not the only one in his family to maintain personal ties to the court.

On one level, then, the visit to his mother can – like the Hasterer episode – be read as a case of wish-fulfilment; once again, the narrative gestures towards emotional closeness, in this case not that of a father–son relationship but of the even more intimate bond between mother and child. Within the narrative, however, this prospect is undercut by various obstacles both within the plot and beyond. K. himself is mistrustful of his own intentions, regarding his desire to see his mother as a symptom of his weakening self-control: 'er hatte neuerdings unter anderem Unerfreulichem eine gewisse Wehleidigkeit an sich festgestellt, ein fast haltloses Bestreben allen seinen Wünschen nachzugeben – nun, in diesem Fall diente diese Untugend wenigstens einem guten Zweck' (p. 352).

However, it is the text itself which provides the ultimate obstacle to this plan. The chapter ends with K. getting into a taxi which is supposed to take him to his mother, but here the narrative breaks off; Kafka's protagonist will leave the city only for his execution. Just as K.'s friendship with Hasterer does not outlast a single chapter, his desire to escape from his trial into the bosom of the family is equally curtailed. Indeed, in this case, the potentially positive turn of events is not actually narrated but merely alluded to, and Kafka's narrative strategy of self-censorship is paralleled by the protagonist, who mobilises his psychological defences against unwanted emotions. As it turns out, this armour of willpower and self-control is broken down in another curtailed episode which offers the most overt, but also most surreal, example of wish-fulfilment in Kafka's novel.

The chapter 'Das Haus' is one of the strangest parts of *Der Proceß*, comparable only to 'Der Prügler' in its dream-like character, but also its voyeuristic, homoerotic undertones. Yet while the scenes of violence and humiliation in 'Der Prügler' have a distinctly nightmarish character, events in 'Das Haus' appear to take a more positive turn towards the end.

K. is so worn out by his trial that he often stays behind after work, recovering on the sofa in his office. Falling into a semi-sleep, he allows himself to indulge in daydreams about his trial. In these dreams, K. wanders through the corridors of a law court, where he first of all encounters Fräulein Bürstner surrounded by other tenants from his boarding house. Disengaging himself from this silent group, he is confronted with a sight both alluring and unsettling. In the antechamber to a court room, he observes a mysterious stranger, who is dressed like a bullfighter and whose appearance greatly fascinates K.:

> Gebückt umschlich ihn K. und staunte ihn mit angestrengt aufgerissenen Augen
> an. Er kannte alle Zeichnungen der Spitze, alle fehlerhaften Fransen, alle
> Schwingungen des Röckchens und hatte sich doch nicht sattgesehn. Oder vielmehr
> er hatte sich schon längst sattgesehn oder noch richtiger er hatte es niemals
> ansehen wollen aber es ließ ihn nicht. 'Was für Maskeraden bietet das Ausland!'
> dachte er und riß die Augen noch stärker auf. (p. 350)

K.'s scrutiny of this stranger takes on a compulsive, voyeuristic dimension; in particular, he becomes obsessed with the matador's 'kurzes [...]
Röckchen' which lends the man's appearance a camp, effeminate character.[14]

K.'s voyeuristic infatuation leads over into another scene which
continues the theme of eroticised submission. From the matador, K.'s
thoughts switch to the painter Titorelli, and he pictures himself kneeling
in front of the painter. In this pose, K. pleads to Titorelli, and while it
does not become clear what he is pleading for, K. makes every effort to
persuade the painter through verbal as well as physical means; stroking
Titorelli's cheeks, K. 'bemühte sich nicht allzusehr, er war fast lässig, er
zog die Sache aus Genusssucht in die Länge, er war des Erfolges sicher.
Wie einfach war die Überlistung des Gerichtes!'.[15] Here K. transfers his
technique of seduction from women to men, and more specifically to a
court representative. Indeed, he seems fairly confident of his persuasive
powers; although he is physically subservient to Titorelli, K. feels in
control of the situation and even seems to take pleasure in his own
subjugation.

It is at this point that the tone of the chapter changes. K. has apparently succeeded with his pleading, for Titorelli takes him by the hand
and hurries with him through the corridors of the law court. As K. soon
realises, this walk involves a very different form of movement: rather
than walking, he seems to glide 'auf und ab [die Treppen] ohne jeden
Aufwand von Mühe leicht wie ein leichtes Boot im Wasser', and he
comes to the conclusion 'dass diese schöne Art der Bewegung seinem

---

14   This fusion of exoticism and homoeroticism is familiar from the 'Prügler' episode,
     where the two naked guards are whipped by a leather-clad man who is 'braun
     gebrannt wie ein Matrose und hatte ein wildes frisches Gesicht' (p. 111).
15   Franz Kafka, *Der Proceß: Apparatband*, ed. by Malcolm Pasley (Frankfurt a. M.,
     1990), p. 346. References to this edition are henceforth abbreviated to '*PA*'.

bisherigen niedrigen Leben nicht mehr angehören könne' (*PA*, p. 346). At this point, another change occurs:

> Das Licht, das bisher von rückwärts eingefallen war, wechselte und strömte plötzlich blendend von vorn. [...] Wieder war K. auf dem Korridor des Gerichtsgebäudes, aber alles war ruhiger und einfacher, es gab keine auffallende Einzelheiten, K. umfaßte alles mit einem Blick, machte sich von T[itorelli] los und gieng seines Weges. (*PA*, pp. 346–47)

The suddenly brighter light is reminiscent of the priest's parable about the man from the country, in which a 'Glanz' seems to emanate from the law in the moments before the man's death (p. 294). In this story, the light marks the end of the man's life and hopes; in K.'s daydream, in contrast, it has a rejuvenating, empowering effect, enabling K. to see more clearly, to gain a (perceptual) sense of control over his surroundings. He disengages himself from Titorelli, freeing himself from his guidance and authority, and as if to underline this sense of a new beginning, he finds himself dressed in

> ein neues langes dunkles Kleid [...], es war wohltuend warm und schwer. [...] In dem Winkel eines Korridors, an dessen einer Wande [sic] grosse Fenster geöffnet waren, fand er auf einem Haufen seine frühern Kleider, das schwarze Jakett, die scharf gestreiften Hosen und darüber das Hemd mit zittrigen Ärmeln ausgestreckt. (*PA*, p. 347)

In the text, these events are described as a 'Verwandlung' (*PA*, p. 346); K.'s new clothes, as well as his new way of walking and seeing, suggest that he has left behind his old existence. Yet although this is all very evocative, no clear explanation is provided as to what is actually happening; as the text mysteriously states, K. 'wusste, was mit ihm geschehen war, aber er war so glücklich darüber, dass er es sich noch nicht eingestehen wollte' (*PA*, p. 347). The adversative 'aber' creates a tension between K.'s happiness and the cause of his transformation. The bright light streaming towards K. lends the scene a metaphysical dimension, as does the shedding of his old clothes, that is, of his old self. The same is implied by K.'s new floating movement which distances him from his previous 'niedriges Leben' (*PA*, p. 346). While K.'s elated response reveals this dream to be a wish-fulfilment, his unwillingness to confront the underlying cause of this physical and spiritual renewal points in the direction of a death wish. Exhausted by the strains of bank and court, K. craves a release from his trials and tribulations – a release only possible by means of a complete transcendental escape. The fact, however, that this part of the dream continues to be set in the law courts suggests that even this renewal does not in fact transcend the trial but is rooted within its laws and confines.[16]

The chapter 'Das Haus' is situated even further at the margins of *Der Proceß* than other 'fragmentary' episodes. Starting with the scene between K. and Titorelli, Kafka actually deleted this entire section from the manuscript – a decision which perhaps reflects the sexually charged nature of this episode. The real transgression, however, takes place not in this homoerotic encounter but in the subsequent transformation; the chapter's erotic transgressions are symptomatic of a more general break-down of K.'s psychological defences, as his daydream offers a glimpse into his hopes and fears. Indeed, it is this alternative ending dreamed up by its protagonist which disrupts the novel's most rigid barrier: the narrative frame of arrest and execution which entraps reader and pro-tagonist through its predetermined lethal conclusion. By deleting the last part of this chapter, Kafka removes the prospect of an alternative con-clusion, however imaginary. That said, the deleted ending resurfaces in Kafka's writings a few years later. Various parts of this episode recur in a story which was published three years later and which bears a curi-ous, both close and remote, relationship to *Der Proceß*.

The short story 'Ein Traum' was never part of the novel manuscript and is never mentioned by Kafka in this context. It does not feature in any of the lists of literary projects which Kafka drew up prior to 1916, and it is only published, together with other stories, in the *Landarzt* col-lection of 1917. Yet although there is no explicit, external link between *Der Proceß* and 'Ein Traum', the short story is linked to the novel, and in particular 'Das Haus' through various intertextual connections, which far extend beyond the name shared by both protagonists.[17]

---

16   When K. eventually meets his death, of course, this scene triggers no sense of
      release or redemption but merely a sense of shame, the one thing said to outlive the
      protagonist.
17   Malcolm Pasley argues that 'Ein Traum' could not possibly have been associated
      with *Der Proceß* because of differences in narrative perspective. He claims that the
      short story is narrated 'aus der Perspektive eines Erzählers […], der den Inhalt des
      Traumes kennt und gleichzeitig die Außensicht hat' (Franz Kafka, *Drucke zu*

Framed by the opening sentence, 'Josef K. träumte' (*D*, p. 295), the story describes a dream which is set not in a law court but in a cemetery. One aspect, however, which immediately connects this dream and the one in 'Das Haus' is the protagonist's mode of movement. The cemetery has running across it 'sehr künstliche, unpraktisch gewundene Wege, aber er [K.] glitt über einen solchen Weg wie auf einem reißenden Wasser in unerschütterlich schwebender Haltung' (*D*, p. 295). In 'Das Haus', by comparison, Josef K. glides up and down the stairs of the law court 'wie ein leichtes Boot im Wasser' (*PA*, p. 346).

In 'Ein Traum', the protagonist is then suddenly attracted by one particular tomb which 'übte fast eine Verlockung auf ihn aus und er glaubte, gar nicht schnell genug hinkommen zu können' (*D*, p. 296). Here the next parallel occurs; when he gets to the tomb, Josef K. encounters an artist who is 'nur mit Hosen und einem schlecht zuge-knöpften Hemd bekleidet; auf dem Kopf hatte er eine Samtkappe; in der Hand hielt er einen gewöhnlichen Bleistift, mit dem er schon beim Näherkommen Figuren in die Luft schrieb' (*D*, p. 296). This artist resembles Titorelli, K.'s guide in 'Das Haus', who in the novel is described as wearing only trousers and an unbuttoned night shirt (p. 192). The artist in the short story seems to be a cross between a painter and a writer; with his 'gewöhnlichen Bleistift' he writes golden letters onto the tombstone of this freshly dug grave. This is not an easy task; after a long struggle, the artist finally writes the first letter, 'J', of the name of the person to be buried. Only when Josef K. starts to dig into the loose soil, uncovering a dug-out grave, and lets himself fall into it, does his full name appears on the tombstone; as the story concludes, 'Entzückt von diesem Anblick wachte er auf' (*D*, p. 298).

Lebzeiten: Apparatband, ed. by Wolf Kittler, Hans-Gerd Koch and Gerhard Neumann (Frankfurt a. M., 1994), pp. 357–8. References to this edition are henceforth abbreviated as '*D*'.) However, not only is the predominantly personal perspective of *Der Proceß* interspersed with moments of more detached narration, but the narrative of Kafka's short story is far more subjective than Pasley claims. K.'s impression, for instance, that the tomb he is walking towards 'wurde ihm verdeckt durch Fahnen, deren Tücher sich wanden und mit großer Kraft aneinanderschlugen; man sah die Fahnenträger nicht, aber er war, als herrsche dort viel Jubel' (*D*, p. 296) lend the text a hallucinatory quality which is diametrically opposed to the conventions of objective narration.

Thus Kafka's story makes explicit what is only alluded to in the chapter 'Das Haus': the attraction of death as a wish-fulfilment. Here, the open windows which K. comes across at the end of 'Das Haus' have metamorphosed into an open grave, both offering an escape from the entrapments of human life. At the same time, the idea of death as liberation is even further displaced when it (re)appears in Kafka's story; not only has the daydream become an actual dream, thus further removing it from reality, but the entire set-up is deleted from the novel and transplanted into a separate text. Yet the link with the novel remains, not least through the name of the protagonist, and so we can read 'Ein Traum' as a kind of supplement, as a text situated at the furthest margins of Kafka's novel, where it acts as a repository for ideas which were expelled from the narrative of *Der Proceß*.

On the whole, then, Kafka's novel is grounded in tensions between openness and closure, unity and fragmentation. Those chapters which have been marginalised as fragments open up new narrative and critical perspectives which point beyond the novel's tightly structured framework of arrest and execution. That said, the scope for expansion inherent in these episodes remains limited within and by the narrative, curtailed perhaps by a mechanism of self-censorship in which certain divergent plot-lines are not fully integrated and developed. Ultimately, of course, it is fruitless to speculate whether Kafka would have extended these chapters and whether he would have included them into a published version. Their exclusion from the main body of the novel in editions past and present, however, is a contestable move based on a restrictive and perhaps outdated notion of the self-contained work – and hence of an ideal of unity whose downsides are highlighted within the narrative. To read Kafka's *Proceß* from its supposed margins, in contrast, enables a fuller appreciation of this text with all its divergent strands and inner tensions, and prevents this landmark from becoming a dusty, faded monument.

PETER HUTCHINSON

Hesse, *Der Steppenwolf*

Hesse's breakthrough as a Modernist writer came as a result of two life- transforming events towards the end of the First World War. The author's first novels had relied almost completely on the nineteenth-century tradition – a third-person narrator, authorial omniscience, and a coherent plot – but mental crisis, psychoanalysis, and intensive engagement with the works of Freud and Jung led to a new approach to writing, to the attempt to recreate in art some of the experiences and insights of analysis. Thus, on the very first page of *Demian* (1919) Hesse rejected the notion of the authoritative, omniscient author and urged a search for inner knowledge. *Siddhartha* (1922) likewise took its readers on a spiritual journey, exploring ways to fulfilment through breaking away from one's origins and repeatedly changing the search for one's goals. This quest for the essence of life, as well as the need to be different, unorthodox, at times shocking, was taken over into *Der Steppenwolf* (1927), which provokes its readers in a number of ways, and not solely thematic. This novel too was born of personal and mental crisis,[1] and like those mentioned above, owes much to an interest in psychology. Thomas Mann may treat Freud light-heartedly, indeed, irreverently, in *Der Zauberberg*, gently mocking some of his ideas on sexuality. Hesse, however, takes the findings and theories of both Freud and Jung utterly seriously, seeing them not only as a means to understand, but also as cure and as

---

1   Details of Hesse's condition in the mid-twenties are provided in the standard general surveys by, for example, Mark Boulby, *Hermann Hesse: His Mind and Art* (Ithaca, N.Y., 1967) and Joseph Mileck, *Hermann Hesse: Life and Art* (Berkeley, Los Angeles, London, 1978). This particular crisis is also reflected in a collection of poems which actually contains the concept in its title, *Krisis: Ein Stück Tagebuch*, in *Sämtliche Werke*, Vol. 4, ed. by Volker Michels (Frankfurt a. M., 2001), pp. 211–46. (All further quotation from this edition.) These poems, and other relevant material, are also available in the helpful collection *Materialien zu Hermann Hesses 'Der Steppenwolf'*, ed. by Volker Michels (Frankfurt a. M., 1972).

inspiration. His post-war work represents the first major attempt to explore in literature the value of psychoanalysis – and especially Jung's 'analytical psychology' – for the understanding of individuals, human relationships, archetypes, and the unconscious. And *Der Steppenwolf* is the best example.[2] The groundbreaking status of the novel is further enhanced through the means by which the author chooses to convey his message: ideas of the sort contained here do not lend themselves to the traditional mode of writing a novel – their nebulousness needs to be expressed in a way which reflects a sense of striving, uncertainty, hope, and *partial* breakthrough.

The simple plot is narrated from several points of view, but the image of the protagonist which emerges is consistent. Harry Haller, a rootless and depressive intellectual aged forty-eight, determined to commit suicide on his fiftieth birthday, visits an unnamed town which has similarities with Basle. He lodges in bourgeois surroundings, despite his ambivalence to this setting, and occasionally converses with the nephew of his landlady. He leads an unstructured existence in which he regularly turns to alcohol, and on one of his evenings out he is handed a strange 'tract' which turns out to be an uncannily accurate analysis of his 'wolf of the steppes' mentality. On another, clearly inebriated occasion, his life is suddenly transformed through an encounter with a call-girl, Hermine, and her circle, especially another prostitute named Maria and a jazz saxophonist, Pablo. Recognising the need to overcome his inhibitions and to accept that the division of his personality is far more complex than that into two simple parts of 'man' and 'wolf', he learns to dance, accept modern music, and also his own sexuality. The culmina-

---

2   There are, of course, earlier works that acknowledged the insights of the new discipline, but they are usually modest in their aims. Thomas Mann, for example, partially explores Freud's theories, especially those of *Totem und Tabu*, in *Der Tod in Venedig* (1912), but the text exploits a wide range of sources, and the psychoanalytical element is far from striking. Mann was later to exploits Jungian ideas, although in a restrained manner, in his *Joseph* tetralogy. For details of this, and of the general relationship between Mann and Jung, see Paul Bishop, 'Thomas Mann and C. G. Jung', in *Jung in Contexts*, ed. by Paul Bishop (London, 1999), pp. 154–89. For a recent general volume on Hesse, with an up-to-date bibliography on *Der Steppenwolf*, see Sikander Singh, *Hermann Hesse* (Stuttgart, 2006). The most exhaustive study of the novel is that by David G. Richards, *Exploring the Divided Self: Hermann Hesse's 'Der Steppenwolf' and its Critics* (Columbia, 1996).

tion of his experiences is a drug-induced exploration of various sides of his personality and his past. The novel concludes with his disappearance into a new existence, leaving behind him a pile of 'notes' – the work with which the reader is now presented.

The reception of *Der Steppenwolf* was mixed, often hostile, and much of its seemingly escapist message was not welcome to many Germans of the late nineteen-twenties, especially the middle-aged, who felt lost under the breakdown of old values in a new and uneasy 'democracy', the recent experience of hyperinflation, lack of political stability, a mixture of insecurity, hope, and cynicism. The escapist features of the novel were, however, bound to be appealing to some, even though they were seen as shocking by others: most obviously, perhaps, the flight to a different world, one in which economic and political problems are rarely seen,[3] one of sexuality and drugs. Here we find an exploration of 'love' in a broad sense, unorthodox means of fulfilment, alternatives to the traditional view of happiness, satisfaction, and society's norms. There is tolerance of alternative life styles and the advocacy of an existence, in some ways irresponsible, never explored since the Romantics, over a century before. Here is a central character who openly admits he uses wine and opium to relieve his misery, and who has turned his back on a world in which he feels an 'outsider' (to quote the term actually used in the novel). For its age this was a deliberately scandalising work with its views on free love and sexual relations across generations. It was also something of an elitist novel, one which encouraged intellectuals above all to come to recognise their unconscious and to explore, analyse, and become stronger through an understanding of the dark side of their psyche. It was also a highly personal novel in which the author was working out aspects of his own life and complexes. As he put it in a letter to his friend Carl Seelig, '[ich] muß nun in mir selbst aufräumen und muß vor allem das alles, was ich früher weggelogen oder doch

---

3   For an alternative view, i.e. that the political and social dimension is significant, see, for example, Paul Bishop, 'Hermann Hesse and the Weimar Republic', in *German Novels of the Weimar Republic: Intersections of Literature and Politics,* ed. by Karl Leydecker (Rochester, N.Y., 2006), pp. 45–60. Bishop produces a careful and very useful list of elements which may be regarded as part of a general social critique (pp. 51–56), but these are presented through the eyes of two figures whose judgment is questionable: Harry Haller and his landlady's nephew.

verschwiegen hatte, anschauen und anerkennen, alles Chaotische, Wilde, Triebhafte, "Böse" in mir'.[4]

The novel marked a turning point in German literature in other respects. Partly in its attitude to the reader, who is left uncertain as to the nature of what is being described – there is deliberate obfuscation of reality and fiction, in addition to clear fantasy and drug-induced hallucination. The interplay of these was too much for those readers who were still bound to the nineteenth-century norm, who had not yet arrived in a Freudian, Jungian environment, and who found the concepts of projection, complexes, or subject-matter like schizophrenia, or madness, too bewildering, or distasteful. Like *Der Proceß* and *Der Zauberberg*, this novel is sometimes surrealistic, it is a reaction against Naturalism and Realism, and above all against the rational. Its closest description may be as a form of neo-Romanticism, a search for the essence of life, and for the individual, in the irrational, the unconscious, and the world of dreams. As such it can offer no clear conclusions, and the 'open' ending reflects the way in which only partial fulfilment has been achieved: the protagonist has more, and painful, stages to go through before he can truly find himself, and this is the resolve of the final page: 'ich [...] war gewillt [...] die Hölle meines Innern nochmals und noch oft zu durchwandern' (p. 203) As it was for the Romantics, life must be a perpetual striving.

The novel is striking too in its mixture of styles, registers and even genres (report, memoir, autobiography, verse, tract), its range of narrators, its repeated emphasis on analysis, argument, and discussion rather than action, and its inclusion of sections which obviously comment on other sections, such as a 'Tractat', which suddenly appears and which provides an alternative image of the central figure. As such the work is clearly Modernist in that it is concerned with self-referentiality, producing art which is about producing art, while at the same time it leans towards the disjointed, even the disintegrating (in its handling of drug-induced experiences). This complexity, although common in postmodernist fiction, clearly gave many of the author's contemporaries the impression the aim was to bewilder rather than to entertain or enlighten.

---

4   *Gesammelte Briefe*, ed. by Ursula and Volker Michels, 4 vols (Frankfurt a. M., 1973–86), Vol. 1, pp. 423–24.

Der Steppenwolf was, then, a complex novel by contemporary standards, giving the reader not a simple narrative but a series of different perspectives on its hero. Patrick O'Neill has suggested that the novel 'as a literary text is centrally about the way in which these several presentations of [Haller's] situation intersect and mutually reflect one another'.[5] This view is only possible, however, on an ideal second reading. A standard first reading would rather suggest that the novel reveals the possibilities of using several narrators, all of whom are in some ways unreliable. The first is, ironically, closest to the traditionally 'reliable' guide in that he represents a social class for which precision, pedantry, openness, etc. is crucial. He is the nephew of the landlady who accepts as a lodger the self-styled 'wolf of the steppes', and he recalls his memories of this figure with a mixture of emotions. Harry is described by this narrator in considerable detail, and in retrospect this outline might be seen as a parody of traditional methods of characterisation. Once more, but again only in retrospect, we see the *partiality* of this narrator's perspective: his biased status as a bourgeois, his obsession with detail, his concern for the superficial, his fussiness, all reflected in the long and heavy sentences in which he records his memory of Harry Haller. Harry represents almost the opposite of what the nephew stands for, and yet the latter displays open sympathy and frequent admiration for this person quite outside the scope of his normal life. (This is the sort of person who should learn something from the adventures of the protagonist, but, rooted as he is in his bourgeois existence, it is clear he has not been able to do so.)

This 'Vorwort des Herausgebers', less than a tenth of the novel, prepares the reader for the next stage, the view from the 'wolf of the steppes' himself, 'Harry Hallers Aufzeichnungen'. It begins in a seemingly ordered world in which an ageing, purposeless intellectual reflects on his situation, but it carries a portentous sub-heading which is quite new for German literature: 'Nur für Verrückte' (p. 27). The style of the opening sentence is the complete opposite of that of the editor's 'foreword'. Whereas the latter had opened with a flat, informative sentence of some twenty-two words, Haller's opening comprises one hundred and ten, a leisurely, flowing sequence which is above all suggestive of an

5   *Acts of Narrative: Textual Strategies in Modern German Fiction* (Toronto, Buffalo, London, 1996), p. 58

unhurried, self-indulgent, purposeless life-style. The writing continues in a reflective and gently descriptive way, there is little narrative drive, until the reader is again disturbed by an unexpected and worrying warning. Haller deciphers a flickering sign, which suddenly appears above a door he has never previously noticed in an ancient wall, as an invitation and a threat: the enticing 'Magisches Theater / Eintritt nicht für jedermann / – nicht für jedermann' is followed by letters he slowly makes out on the wet pavement: 'Nur – – für – – Ver – – rückte!'

The reader is presented with a puzzle: does this sign, and do the letters reflected on the pavement, really exist? Are they a figment of Haller's imagination? Is this the beginning of the possibly fantastic dimension the 'editor' has cautioned us about ('einerlei, wie viel oder wenig realen Lebens ihnen [Hallers 'Aufzeichnungen'] zugrunde liegen mag' (p. 27))? Haller has not been drinking at this stage, although he certainly has been by the time he encounters a comparable sign, a street-seller with a placard carrying the words 'Anarchistische Abendunterhaltung! / Magisches Theater! / Eintritt nicht für jed... (p. 40). The man gives Haller a booklet, does not want payment, and quickly disappears. The booklet carries the title 'Tractat vom Steppenwolf', and it carries a significant sub-title 'Nur für Verrückte'. Its subject is, of course, none other than Harry Haller himself, and his dilemma of being caught between man and wolf.

By this point the reader's uncertainty over Haller's view of the world has reached a peak. 'Madness' has become a motif, but has the world gone mad, or has Haller? A single surprising episode would not disturb us unduly, but the accumulation of such bizarre events is unsettling. What exacerbates our difficulty is that the impossible is put forward in the language of the everyday, and with the incredulity of a rational participant, thus tempting us into belief. The problem is that we can certainly trust various elements of what we read, for they confirm events which have been recorded by a conventionally reliable narrator, the landlady's nephew. But other events leave us uncertain. To the twenty-first century reader such a situation is common. The 'view from the madhouse' is well established. For the nineteen-twenties, however, this approach had few precedents, although an obvious one is Kafka. The Romantics had often set their stories in clearly fantastic worlds, but there was usually little doubt about what was real and where imagination took over; for much of Hesse's text hallucination is mingled unconcernedly with the real. This is the beginning of the attempt to disorient the reader, and, as Haller's adventures develop, to scandalise the bourgeois. Throughout the text Hesse is playing with the reactions of conservative, tradition-bound readers by setting bizarre, improbable events against a traditional background of sharply observed reality and clear delineation of character.

In early editions of the novel, the slim volume which Harry is handed, the 'Tractat vom Steppenwolf', is given a separate, coloured, cover, it is printed on different, cheaper paper, and it is in a different font; this device was actually opposed by the publisher, but Hesse insisted on it, providing the first instance of such a technique in German literature. The intention is to give the impression Haller really was handed this by a third party, just as, say, Goethe gave early readers of *Werther* the illusion of reality by providing a footnote suggesting he had changed certain names (for reasons, it is implied, of decorum). That tract's title is significant. Changing the German 'Traktat' to the more Latin-sounding 'Tractat' gives the impression of dignity, and the concept is in fact better translated as 'tract' rather than 'treatise', even though its author may finally refer to it as a 'Studie'.[6] Like the standard religious or philosophical tract, this one is 'preaching', it is advocating new forms of lifestyle, new ways in which many others, not simply the hero, can achieve knowledge and self-understanding. The rest of the novel goes on to show some of these ways, culminating in their dramatic presentation in a 'Magic Theatre'.[7]

6   Parick O'Neill draws attention to the fact that Haller refers in his 'Auf-zeichnungen' to a 'Traktat', but the piece itself actually bears the title 'Tractat' [standard German spelling would demand a 'k']. Further, Haller seems to make a threefold 'mistake'. He refers to the title as 'Traktat vom Steppenwolf. Nicht für jedermann', but this is not what features on the 'tract' itself, which bears the simple 'Tractat vom Steppenwolf' and has as an *epigraph* 'Nur für Verrückte' (p. 60). O'Neill does not follow up these careful observations. Is Hesse simply being careless, or is he signalling some form of game? Is this, perhaps, an indication of Haller's clear inability to act as a reliable narrator, or is there, in the shift from 'k' to 'c', playful mockery of Wittgenstein's *Tractatus logico-philsophicus* (1922), which was first published as *Logisch-philosphisches Traktat* (1921), and of which the most famous line is the final one, 'wovon man nicht sprechen kann, darüber muß man schweigen'?

7   Helga Esselborn-Krumbiegel sees the relationship between Tract and Magic Theatre more precisely, noting 'im Magischen Theater herrscht die Tendenz vor,

The language of the 'tract' is again different from anything that has preceded. It begins with the formulaic introduction to the fairy tale ('Es war einmal...') and for a few sentences retains a simplistic, light-hearted, ironic tone which suggests its study of the Steppenwolf will be rudimentary. But it develops into a more serious discussion, trying to diagnose Haller's problems and arguing that he is not divided into the discrete elements of wolf and bourgeois, but, like all individuals, he embodies a wide range of possibilities within his breast. The language is plain and forthright, the mood is detached and totally different to what has preceded, and the statements are authoritative, sometimes being made in the 'ich' form, at other times in the 'wir' – at times, however, there is a sense of flippancy, if not facetiousness, as we sense the author laughing at Haller, a point which will become more important later. Many of the points made here link with what has preceded or will follow, and there are four of particular importance. They are part of the admonitory tone of this novel, which seeks to change viewpoints, par-ticularly with regard to conventional thinking on society. Above all, they have relevance to the position of the artist and the modern reader.

The first of these is that the bourgeois obsession with protecting himself is self-defeating; a lifestyle of moderation, balance, and adher-ence to the norm will preclude intensity of experience in either direction, both joy and sorrow (pp. 54–55). Second, developing the ability to laugh is the best way to transcend one's situation (pp. 57–58). Third, suggesting the 'Steppenwolf' consists of two distinct sides is a gross oversimplification since, like all individuals, he consists of hundreds, indeed, thousands (pp. 60, 62). And finally, in order to gain immortality one must constantly be prepared to sacrifice oneself by stripping off layers of one's personality ('Hüllenabstreifen', p. 64). Although these ideas are related in the first instance to Haller, they clearly hold rele-vance for others. In fact, the tract contains a large number of ideas which bear relevance to the life of any intellectual, a point underlined by the generalising tendency and repeated use of the word 'Seele'. This 'study'

---

die Seelenvielfalt Harry Hallers im angeschauten Bild erfahrbar zu machen, im 'Traktat' dominiert dagegen die abstrahierende Theorie' (*Hermann Hesse: Der Steppenwolf* (2nd revised ed., Oldenbourg, 1988), p. 88). I would suggest that everything following the encounter with Hermine is to be seen under the shadow of the 'Tractat', however.

of Haller's intellect is in fact almost a launching pad for a series of generalisations about life, about the intellect, psychology, and philosophy. It also contains hints about how these ideas are to be understood, and in this respect features at a higher level of the so-called technique of 'mise-en-abîme'. At its simplest, this is merely a 'story within the story', but at a more demanding level it represents a complex duplication, an insertion which reflects – or distorts – thematic aspects of the main work. Thus in André Gide's *Les Faux-Monnayeurs*, for example (a novel which appeared in 1926 and which Thomas Mann praised alongside *Der Steppenwolf* and Joyce's *Ulysses* for their experimental boldness), a character is writing a novel entitled *Les Faux-Monnayeurs*. The 'Tractat vom Steppenwolf' is more complex than this, for Hesse's insertion not only draws attention to aspects of his hero's condition, but also to ways of understanding the role of this insertion and interpreting the novel as a whole.

The clearest suggestion here comes after the discussion of the multiple aspect to the personality of the 'Steppenwolf' and of the difficulties which face the writer in trying to capture the essence of the individual. Although it might seem that certain forms of writing produce successfully unified figures – and here Hesse is clearly rejecting Naturalism and Realism – it is only a naively aesthetic stance which could see these as anything other than superficial – 'eine billige Oberflächenästhetik' (p. 62). By contrast, Indian literature has always revealed the complexity of the individual, and this achievement can be seen in some modern (western) writing. Any writer who wants to achieve this, however, 'muß sich entschließen, einmal die Figuren einer solchen Dichtung nicht als Einzelwesen anzusehen, sondern als Teile, als Seiten, als verschiedene Aspekte einer höhern Einheit (meinetwegen der Dichterseele)' (p 62). The idea of multiple aspects to personality has already been raised, but the most striking words here are those which have been enclosed within brackets, ostensibly to suggest their relative unimportance. In fact these three words are central to an understanding of the 'tract' and the novel as a whole: the apparently dismissive reaction ('meinetwegen') is rather a provocation in view of the highly charged concept which follows. The author is explicitly opening the novel to biographical, Jungian interpretation. This work *is* about the 'Dichterseele', and specifically about that of someone whose initials are 'HH'. The parallels between the lives of Haller and Hesse have often been noted.[8]

The tract takes up around the same space as the foreword, and it is followed by a poem which Haller recalls writing and of which he has been reminded by the tract. This too can be seen as a sort of mirror of the central figure, but in a totally different light and spirit. The poem is facile in conception and content, presenting a pathetic, sentimental self-image, while the weak versification characterises the author as a failed poet. It also shows the need for change: this self-pitying figure desperately needs the advice of the 'Tractat'. But the following section of the 'Aufzeichnungen' shows the problems of putting it into practice.

Thus far there has been little action. As in many of his mature works, Hesse here prefers reflection and, of course, 'character'. As Mileck puts it, 'Hesse the storyteller played second fiddle to Hesse the portraitist, and as usual, the portraitist preferred inner to outer depictions; the cultural to the physical world, the psyche to the body' (p. 194). Nevertheless, the story does now gather some impetus, for soon afterwards Haller thinks he recognises the man who has given him the tract and who recommends to him, if he has 'Bedürfnisse' (the sexual dimension is plain), a visit to the 'schwarze Adler'. Haller then bumps into a former acquaintance, a university professor, who invites him for dinner. That occasion proves a disaster: the professor denounces a 'Harry Haller' who has questioned German war guilt, not realising the very man is sitting before him, while Haller himself cannot resist condemning an idealised portrait of Goethe which is treasured by the professor's wife. Depressed by the evening, Haller leaves, drifts from pub to pub and eventually ends up, apparently by chance, at the pub 'Zum schwarzen Adler'.

The reader may have been disoriented by the earlier section with the references to 'only for the mad', but the evening with the professor, very much in the line of traditional narrative, has restored the illusion of realism. The novel now swings back to the realm of fantasy – although only gradually – as Haller experiences in this lively pub an encounter with an attractive young woman, Hermine, who has an uncanny insight into his mind and who diagnoses Haller's problems quite

8   See, for example, the commentary by Joseph Mileck, op. cit., in particular pp. 174–81.

simply. He needs her, she suggests, 'um tanzen zu lernen, lachen zu lernen, leben zu lernen' (p. 108). The combination of activities is significant. Under her guidance and inspiration, he changes his whole attitude to life, moderating his indignation at seemingly vulgar aspects of modern living, learning to dance, to appreciate the gramophone, and to enjoy sexual adventure with Hermine's beautiful and sensual friend Maria. Both she and Hermine are part-time prostitutes, and in depicting the life of 'happy prostitutes' Hesse breaks boundaries and scandalises. Haller's experiences reach a climax after a masked ball to which he has been invited, after which he is encouraged by Hermine's friend, the relaxed and carefree saxophonist Pablo, to experiment with a drug-inspired entry into a 'magic theatre', another place which is 'nur für Verrückte'; here Harry re-lives earlier experiences from a different perspective, entering a series of different doors onto events and memories which reveal repressed aspects of his psyche, betray the aggressive side of his personality, etc. On entering the final door of the theatre, he sees Hermine and Pablo lying together after having made love, and, unable to tolerate seeing Pablo with his ideal, he stabs her. For this 'confusion' of real and imaginary, he is condemned to eternal life and told he must learn how to laugh. The novel concludes with Haller recognising his future path, his need to strive for the attitude towards life held by those who have become 'immortal' – notably figures like Mozart and Goethe; he sees the fulfilling existence which awaits him, signalled in the simple 'Pablo wartete auf mich. Mozart wartete auf mich.' Such an indeterminate conclusion was bound to disappoint tradition-bound readers, but its implications seem obvious: Haller has indeed moved on in his search, leaving this manuscript behind him. The past these 'Aufzeichnungen' describe is one of those layers, 'Hüllen', he has managed to peel off in his search for individuation.

The impact of Jung on Hesse's work is evident in *Demian*, his first novel to break through into a new mode of writing, one of quest, searching for the self by exploring, in obviously symbolic manner, the depths of the unconscious. Prior to this Hesse had undergone extensive psychoanalysis by a disciple of Jung in 1916–17[9] (seventy-two sessions,

---

9   For further details, see David Richards, *The Hero's Quest for the Self: An Archetypal Approach to Hesse's Demian and other Novels* (Lanham, London, New York, 1987), p. 1.

for up to three hours each), he had read widely in Jungian and Freudian theory, and he had actually written an essay on writing and psycho-analysis. In this essay, 'Künstler und Psychoanalyse' (1918), he had made four major points.[10] First, that in Freud and Jung he had found a confirmation of his observations and intuitions; second, that psycho-analysis confirms the value of his belief in the imagination and in litera-ture; third, that psychoanalysis allows a more intense relationship with one's own unconscious; and finally, that analysis demands self-honesty, and recognition of what has been repressed. The final section quotes extensively from a letter by Schiller to Körner, which advocates not interfering with the process of literary creation. The implications for Hesse's own writing are clear: the repressed should be allowed to emerge unchecked before shaping into literary form should take place. The most forceful endorsement of psychoanalysis comes, however, in a diary entry some three years later: 'Mir wurde zum Weg der Heilung und Entwicklung nächst den asiatischen Lehren (Buddha, Vedanta und Lao-Tse) die Psychoanalyse, welche wir nicht als eine Heilmethode ansehen, sondern als wesentliches Element der "neuen Lehre", der Entwicklung eines neuen Stadiums der Menschheit, in der wir stehen.'[11]

In *Demian* the influence of Jung manifests itself prominently in dreams and symbols. In *Der Steppenwolf* the traces are more subtle and

10   *Werke*, Vol. 14, pp. 351–56. Hesse claimed greater influence from Freud than Jung, but this is not to my mind evident in the novels. As David Richards suggests, 'it is not uncommon for artists to attempt to hide their sources and minimize the importance of influences in order to increase the impression of their own origin-ality' (op. cit., p. 7). Edward Timms, in a sharp analysis of Hesse and psycho-analysis, has argued that while *Demian* can be seen as a 'Jungian' novel, *Der Steppenwolf* is 'Freudian'. Although Timms' analysis is remarkably sensitive and soundly based, on this point I feel he fails to clinch his argument. None of the distinctly Freudian theories of sexuality (in particular, the Oedipus complex and early sexual experience as the source of all neuroses) are emphasised in the novel. (See 'Hesse's Therapeutic Fiction', *Modernism and the European Unconscious*, ed. by Peter Collier and Judy Davies (Cambridge, 1990), pp. 165–81.) By the time of writing *Der Steppenwolf*, Hesse may have been embarrassed by what he had confided to Drs Lang and Jung; he is in fact quite savage towards the former in his scurrilous poem 'Abend mit Dr Ling', written in the winter of 1925–26 (*Werke*, Vol. 4, pp. 231–32).

11   Diary entry for ca. May/June 1921, reprinted in *Materialien zu Hermann Hesses 'Siddhartha'*, ed. by Volker Michels (Frankfurt a. M., 1975), p. 29.

more varied. By this point Hesse had undergone analysis by Jung himself (1921), and he had praised the latter's *Psychologische Typen* as one of the most important works he had read in recent times (also in 1921).[12] He had in addition accepted Jung's progression beyond Freud, who saw only a 'personal' unconscious of forgotten experiences and events we wish to repress; Jung, however, had developed the idea of a secondary unconscious, one which was common to individuals over the ages and over diverse cultures, a 'collective' unconscious in which major 'archetypes' (inherited modes of psychic functioning, patterns of behaviour and understanding), could be identified. The most important of these were the animus/anima, that is, the masculine side to the female personality/the female to the male; the 'shadow', that is, the 'dark' side of the individual personality, those immoral, unpleasant, unwelcome aspects which we are reluctant to admit; the 'persona' or mask which is adopted in society, possibly in order to survive, but which can easily overwhelm the individual and become a form of prison; the Wise Old Man, who possesses a certain magic-like power and the capacity to lead or guide through particular struggles; or, of course, more obviously archetypical figures as 'the Mother' or 'the Hero'.

Whether or not Hesse had acknowledged a debt to Jung, the Jungians would have identified the psychological system of their master in *Der Steppenwolf* – just as they do in all literature. But rigorous application of Jungian categories is here inappropriate, for like all reflective writers, Hesse's independence from his source of inspiration produces a mixture of Jungian thinking and an interpretation of that thinking. His reading in addition to Jung was, after all, vast and intensive, covering literature, thought, history and art.[13] So although we may, for example, find a distinct 'shadow' in Harry's projection of the darker side of his personality into a 'wolf' – that denied, repressed side mentioned by Hesse in his letter to Carl Seelig quoted above – this binary self-division, as Harry later realises, is a false one. Likewise, the presentation of Hermine as Harry's 'anima' is far from straightforward. Although Hermine

---

12   *Sämtliche Werke*, Vol. 18, pp. 256–7.
13   No fewer than five volumes of the *Sämtliche Werke* are devoted to his essays and reviews, ranging over poetry, drama and prose, thought, art and history, classical and modern, German and foreign, western and oriental. Hesse was also very active as an editor. For material specifically related to *Der Steppenwolf*, see the *Materialien zu Hermann Hesses 'Der Steppenwolf'*.

appears to him principally in sexual form, an Oedipal element is hinted at in the two references to her *maternal* qualities. At the masked ball, she dresses as a man, and as Harry searches for her here, he suddenly thinks he recognises a friend from his youth, Hermann. The description is significant: '*Er* lächelte. "Harry? Hast du mich gefunden?" Es war Hermine…' [my italics] p. 157. Hesse seems to be playing with the idea, already in Freud, that gender is not to be seen as a binary male/female, but as a spectrum. Towards the end of the masked ball, however, Hermine's role as anima emerges in almost mystical form, as she becomes part of Harry: 'Vor ihrem Blick, aus dem meine eigene Seele mich anzuschauen schien, sank alle Wirklichkeit zusammen, auch die Wirklichkeit meines sinnlichen Verlangens nach ihr. Verzaubert blickten wir einander an, blickte meine arme kleine Seele mich an' (p. 163). Further examples of an extension of Jungian thought are clear in the Magic Theatre, which is presented to the reader as a descent into the psyche. Pablo, perhaps the Jungian archetype of the Wise Old Man (or 'Magician') emphasises, repeatedly, that in his 'Magic' Theatre Harry will find nothing but himself:

> Sie wissen ja, wo diese andre Welt verborgen liegt, daß es die Welt Ihrer eigenen Seele ist, die Sie suchen. Nur in Ihrem eigenen Innern lebt jene andre Wirklichkeit, nach der Sie sich sehnen. Ich kann Ihnen nichts geben, was nicht in Ihnen selbst schon existiert, ich kann Ihnen keinen anderen Bildersaal öffnen als den Ihrer Seele. Ich kann Ihnen nichts geben, nur die Gelegenheit, den Anstoß, den Schlüssel. Ich helfen, Ihnen Ihre eigene Welt sichtbar machen, das ist alles. (p. 165)

The language, over-emphasis on the 'soul', and the approach are clearly that of the analyst. But art is never simply psychoanalysis – or analytical psychology. Indeed, as already suggested, like many intellectuals who are drawn to Jung, Hesse takes what suits his purposes. And as he had argued in his 1918 essay on literature and psychoanalysis, art allows *creative* solutions to the problems produced by the repressed psyche.

Another dimension in which *Der Steppenwolf* may be seen to be a landmark lies in its attitude towards the reader. For despite the serious subject-matter, this novel adopts a playful attitude; it reflects a Modernist approach to the handling of form, and indeed, as Patrick O'Neill puts it, 'there are very few narratives, German or otherwise, in which narrative discourse itself is so flamboyantly – and so playfully – foregrounded'.[14] The notion of 'play' is in fact hinted at through the regular use of the concept 'Spiel' in the course of the novel, and at the masked ball which prepares Haller for the Magic Theatre, the hero at one point comes to a sudden insight:

> Und doch war alles nur Maskenspiel, war nur ein Spiel zwischen uns beiden, flocht uns beide enger zusammen, entzündete uns beide füreinander. Alles war Märchen, alles war um eine Dimension reicher, um eine Bedeutung tiefer, war Spiel und Symbol. (p. 183)

This seems overwritten, forcing a deeper interpretation than the superficial. It is surely not simply the literal situation which is being described here, an event in which the face – and thus the individual – is covered by a mask and thus loses identity. The wider significance is clinched by the unexpected, and in some respects rather puzzling final word. There has been threefold reference to 'Spiel', but the sentence is extended to include 'und Symbol'. Is this a hint by the author, a gentle reference to the central plank of Jungian ideas, maybe to Jung's first major work on dreams and symbols, *Wandlungen der Symbole*? The characters are themselves symbols, the use of masks may remind us of the original meaning of 'persona'. The reference to the 'Märchen' takes us back to the Romantics.

In both its message and its form, *Der Steppenwolf* was breaking boundaries. Yet despite its successful play with language, perspective, and ideas, as well as its desire to shock contemporaries into a new way of viewing the mind, the novel does have weaknesses. It is essentially a 'male' novel, for example; it fails to consider the female psyche. The analysis contained in the 'Tract' is unnecessarily long, and parts of the 'Magic Theatre' may become tedious – Hesse seems content to pursue his experiments for too long at a time. The novel has also not stood the test of time as well as other near contemporary works like *Der Zauberberg* or *Döblin Alexanderplatz*, and Hesse's popularity has regularly been sociologically rather than artistically driven. For modern readers in particular, this novel may seem *insufficiently* experimental, too half-hearted in its exploration of the psyche, lacking true boldness in its conception and structure, only taking us to the brink of approaching the

---

14   *Acts of Narrative*, p. 57.

world anew. And in its content too, we may feel slightly cheated. As Martin Swales has pointed out, the novel's 'answer to modern disarray is troublingly dependent on traditional high bourgeois culture (Goethe, Mozart)'.[15] Perhaps Hesse is too anxious to reveal aspects of the psyche in a comparatively rational manner – and also too good at pastiche – to feel justified in wholehearted experiment. Indeed, Mary Stewart has suggested that the novel is less radical than it seems, and that it is possible to argue that 'the reader is not taxed enough, if the goal of unsettling our thinking to the point where we abandon traditional categories, and even thought itself, is serious.'[16] She argues that although individual sections may in themselves be experimental, it is easy for us to slip into an 'omniscient' mode, almost becoming an 'integration point' for the novel as a whole. For the modern reader, accustomed to more radical and consistent play with tradition, this is certainly the case; but we must recall that for Hesse's German contemporaries it was far less so. For them, as for particular, highly responsive, generations in such dissimilar societies as the USA and Japan, Hesse's strength lay in his ability to change views of life by urging us to see not the goal, nor the achievement, but the path. That path is unclear, bordered as it is by symbols and motifs which are ambiguous, which serve to reflect others and which thus complicate as much as clarify. In emphasising the problems of searching, Hesse is showing there is no common, model, or ideal way. In the process of inner exploration individuals must find their own road, not that of others. Only by this means will individuality be possible. With this message, couched in commensurate form, *Der Steppenwolf* must be recognised as an important milestone in the education of the reader into different ways of reading, and, of course in the German journey to Postmodernism.

15   'New Media, Virtual Reality, Flawed Utopia? Reflections on Thomas Mann's *Der Zauberberg* and Hermann Hesse's *Der Steppenwolf*, in *Hermann Hesse Today*, ed. by Ingo Cornils and Osman Durrani (Amsterdam, New York, 2005), pp. 33–39 (p. 37).

16   'The Refracted Self: Hermann Hesse, *Der Steppenwolf*', in *The German Novel in the Twentieth Century*, ed. by David Midgley (Edinburgh, 1993), pp. 80–94 (p. 92).

ANDREW WEBBER

Döblin, *Berlin Alexanderplatz*

First published in newspaper serial and then in book form in 1929, *Berlin Alexanderplatz* tells the story of Franz Biberkopf – 'meines kleinen Menschen in Berlin' (p. 192),[1] as the narrator calls him. At the start of the novel, he is released from prison after serving a sentence for the killing of his girlfriend. Returning to the city, he resolves to become 'anständig' and tries various kinds of street vending before sliding back into crime. His partner in crime and in relationships with women, the ambiguous Reinhold, pushes him out of a getaway car, and he loses an arm. He seems to settle down to a new life with the prostitute Mieze, but Reinhold seduces and kills her, apparently as further punishment for Biberkopf. Our hero, or anti-hero, is admitted to an asylum, comes close to death, and is reborn at the end of the novel.

What is so extraordinary about the text is its dynamic representation of Berlin in its Weimar heyday and of the inner life and outer dealings of its protagonist. It is at once deeply engaged with both place and person, and holds these at a certain distance, not least through the aesthetic method of montage. In his discussion of the novel, Walter Benjamin recognises montage as the distinguishing feature, the 'Stilprinzip' that organises Döblin's radical transformation of the novel genre into a new form of epic narration.[2] Benjamin sees Döblin as turning the modern novel out of the constraining, private regime of the book into the epic mode of public speech. This new epic narrative takes the form of montage in order to give voice to the multiplicity and contradictions of the modern condition at large. Montage always works through breaks in continuity, but, as Benjamin insists, Döblin's montage is never wilful.

1   All references are to Alfred Döblin, *Berlin Alexanderplatz: Die Geschichte vom Franz Biberkopf*, ed. by Werner Stauffacher (Zürich and Düsseldorf, 1996).
2   'KRISIS DES ROMANS: Zu Döblins *Berlin Alexanderplatz*', in *Gesammelte Schriften*, ed. by Rolf Tiedemann and Hermann Schweppenhäuser (Frankfurt a. M., 1991), Vol. 3 (ed. by Hella Tiedemann-Bartels), pp. 230–36 (p. 232).

It is sociological document and aesthetic form, its many parts organised around recurrent motifs, both documentary and formal.

Following Brecht's description of Döblin's radicalisation of writing practices, *Berlin Alexanderplatz* is a decentred work, influencing the structural logic of his own works of epic theatre, where part and whole are dialectically related, at once reciprocal and separate: 'sodass ein Ganzes in rapider Entwicklung entsteht, das aus sehr selbstständigen Einheiten geformt ist'.[3] This applies, in particular, to the internal and external perspectives of the text, the exploration of psychology through environment, 'die Vertiefung der introspektiven Methode durch Ausbau einer extraspektiven' (ibid). My discussion of *Berlin Alexanderplatz* will focus in particular on this methodological interaction between introspective and extraspective dimensions: the construction of character in and through the mediation of environment, a new version of one of the determining characteristics of the novel genre.

A key feature of any landmark text, signposting it on the literary-historical map, is its title. Even the most conventional titles can point up less obvious aspects. The titles of novels may typically adopt the names of their protagonists, as in eponymous texts that feature in this volume like *Effi Briest*, *Buddenbrooks*, or *Der grüne Heinrich*; or the names of places, as in *Der Zauberberg*; or an event or a theme, as in *Der Proceß*. But each of these names of works also carries extra implications. *Effi Briest* is also the inscription on the tombstone at the end of the novel, setting her story under the sign of death as a maiden; *Buddenbrooks* at once names a particular family and the dynastic family as theme – it carries the name in the corporate style of the family firm; *Der grüne Heinrich* adds to the name proper the allegorical greenness that – as Martin Swales argues in his essay – carries ambiguous symbolic value for the novel; and *Der Zauberberg* is not just an invented name for a place, but also a theme, a trial, or a process for its protagonist, just as *Der Proceß* is both a theme, a trial or a process, and a place or procession of juridical places for its protagonist. These landmark titles, then, all name their texts in multiple ways, point in more than one direction. A key aspect of each is that they incorporate both introspective and extraspective dimensions: private lives and their social implantation.

3   'Über Alfred Döblin', in *Werke: Große Berliner und Frankfurter Ausgabe*, ed. by Werner Hecht et al., 30 vols (Frankfurt a. M., 1988–2000), Vol. 23, p. 23.

The title *Berlin Alexanderplatz* appears ready to be taken as read, a simple pointer. Like *Der Zauberberg*, this is a novel named after a place-name, suggesting from the start a concern with toponymy. And, indeed, *Berlin Alexanderplatz* is preoccupied with place-names as it charts the peregrinations of its protagonist on the streets of Berlin, reads addresses from a telephone book (pp. 52–53), or lists the stops of a bus-route or a tramline that it encounters. While the place-name in Döblin's title seems more actual than that of Mann's novel, it too is mythological in its reach: the Alexanderplatz is a key *topos* – or figurative site – in what has been called the 'Mythos Berlin'.[4] As much as any other great city, indeed more than most, Berlin is a mythological as well as an actual place, and the exuberant but also deeply fraught city-life of the Weimar years is a key element in that mythology. If mass modernity came relatively late to the German-speaking countries, in the Weimar period the metropolis as prime site of that modernity becomes the privileged place of narrative of all scales, and not least the novel. While 'Fontanopolis', the Berlin of Fontane in the last decades of the nineteenth century, was still in transition towards the status of modern metropolis, the Berlin of the 1920s fully embraced that status, as 'Weltstadt'. And *Berlin Alexanderplatz*, named after one of the landmark squares of the twentieth-century city, is a landmark of German novel writing, not least in those terms. If the nineteenth-century German novel tradition was more or less lacking in the metropolitan scale of Dickens or Balzac, here is a novel that redeems that lack after the fact, puts epic city-writing on the German map and German city-writing on the international map.

At the same time, this is a landmark novel in its relationship to other media. It is not of course the first novel to be serialised in a newspaper. However, this novel also thematises newspapers as medium, shows their economy of circulation, their ideological power, their penetration of mass consciousness, at a time when the news media are more prolific and potent than ever before. And *Berlin Alexanderplatz* also has a fundamental relationship to the new technological media of urban modernity, responding to the challenge they pose for the time-honoured art of literature. Soon after its publication, the novel was both recast in 'Hörspiel' form and made into a film, and the new media of radio and

4   See *Mythos Berlin: Zur Wahrnehmungsgeschichte einer industriellen Metropole* (Berlin, 1987).

cinema are presupposed in the form of the narrative, its broadcasting of the polyphonic voices and sounds of the city (its 'Geräuschwellen' (p. 87)), and its adoption of a highly visualised montage technique in the narrative perspective. The novel cultivates a form of what Döblin as early as 1913 in his 'Berliner Programm' called 'Kinostil',[5] the sort of intensive sequencing of image that is demanded by the accelerated and complex *mise-en-scène* of modernity. By the late 1920s, the speed and convolution of urban experience was all the more intense, and film technique massively advanced. The development of sound film enabled a coordination of sight and sound in the representation of the spectacle of modernity. Early reviews described the novel as a 'geschriebener Film',[6] suggesting that it pre-empted the sound-film version through the narrative technique of a 'tonfilmischer Aufnahmeapparat'.[7] The novel is seen and heard as a city symphony, a sound-cinema counterpart to Walther Ruttmann's 1927 film *Berlin: Die Sinfonie der Grosstadt*, and as such a landmark of the new media age.

The novel focuses its mapping of the metropolis and its media networks on one of its ordinary residents. The subtitle of the novel is 'Die Geschichte vom Franz Biberkopf', thus aligning it with the eponymous works mentioned before – or perhaps more especially with a pseudonymous title like Hesse's *Der Steppenwolf*. It is indeed like *Der Steppenwolf* in its application of a mythical man-animal name to its protagonist, representing the modern human condition in allegorical form as that of a beast that has wandered into and is astray in the city. As Hesse's novel is the literary case history of a kind of Wolf-man, so Döblin's is that of a man – Biber-kopf – with animality hybridised into his psyche. As much as the works of Hesse, Kafka, Mann, or Musil, Döblin's novel is informed by an, albeit ambivalent, attachment to psychoanalytic thinking and method, and the symbolic fact of becoming animal in the head embodies that attachment. There will be more to say about the name Biberkopf in this respect in due course.

5   'An Romanautoren und ihre Kritiker: Berliner Programm', in *Schriften zu Ästhetik, Poetik und Literatur*, ed. by Erich Kleinschmidt (Olten and Freiburg im Breisgau, 1989), pp. 119–23 (p. 121).

6   Herbert Ihering, in his review of Jutzi's film, *Berliner Börsen-Courier*, 9 October 1931, taking up his earlier review of the novel as 'Wortfilm', *Berliner Börsen-Courier*, 19 December 1929.

7   Kurt Pinthus, in his review of Jutzi's film, *8 Uhr-Abendblatt*, 9 October 1931.

Franz Biberkopf is a proletarian figure, and his story thereby breaks with the bourgeois privilege of the novel tradition, especially in its *Bildungsroman* form. In this class political sense, too, this is a landmark work. As Benjamin suggests, the milieu of 'Ganoventum' into which Biberkopf moves is a parallel social order to the petit bourgeoisie. Biberkopf's rise and fall in that alternative order can be said to parody the conventions of the *Bildungsroman*. When Benjamin calls it 'Die äußerste, schwindelnde, letzte, vorgeschobenste Stufe des alten burgerlichen Bildungsromans',[8] the term 'schwindelnd' is nicely readable as both dizzying and swindling, suggesting that Döblin's version of the genre is in itself a swindle, double-dealing in its contract with the reader, in keeping with the professional standards of the criminal parody of bourgeois culture.

While *Berlin Alexanderplatz* puts its protagonist through a certain form of sentimental education after the *Bildungsroman* model, the type and degree of personal formation that it achieves goes against the tenets of that tradition. It is as much a novel in the picaresque tradition, a *Schelmenroman*, as it is a *Bildungsroman*, describing the adventures and misadventures of an itinerant rogue seeking rehabilitation but always a prey to recidivism. And the ostensibly educated or reformed version of the ex-rogue Biberkopf that emerges at the end of the novel is a neutralised and estranged automaton, a man of the masses. While the institutions and discourses of medicine and the law make their judgements upon him, their diagnostic and corrective measures remain external to his case. At the end, we, in turn, get barely a glimpse into the social and ethical knowledge, the 'Bildung' that the protagonist might have acquired, as the 'Geschichte vom Franz Biberkopf' runs out. The novel acts to question the knowability of people and things, adopting a mobile and deeply ambiguous view of the human condition and of the modern world that humanity has created for itself.

I said that *Berlin Alexanderplatz* has a place-name for its title, but before we go further, it would be as well to reconsider that claim. Berlin Alexanderplatz is the name less of the square as such than of its position in the transport system. It is above all a place of transit – of destination, departure, or transfer – the name of the place as seen or heard by the traveller reaching it from elsewhere or en route to elsewhere. The title

8   Benjamin, 'KRISIS DES ROMANS', p. 236.

puts this focal square of the city, known not least for its railway station, under the sign of transition. The protagonist of the novel is a one-time 'Transportarbeiter', and the novel itself is a work of transport, with repeated recourse to forms of transportation, both public and private. Individual and mass movement is a key feature of the Alexanderplatz. It is not by chance that Biberkopf has to travel to this, his proper location, at the start of the novel. Under the railway, underground, or tramway sign, 'Berlin Alexanderplatz', marking the landmark square as mobile, the place in question is transformed into what the urban theorist Marc Augé in his discussion of the supermodern city has called a 'non-place': a site of flow, intersection, and exchange rather than of stable topographical identity.[9] So, if this novel is a landmark of the arrival of German culture in metropolitan modernity, it also marks that arrival as subject to mobility, to transition and displacement – the fundamental conditions of modern city life in both positive and negative terms. The stimulation and the alienation, vitality and morbidity, inherent in those conditions are the prime concern of *Berlin Alexanderplatz*.

Döblin's novel is a key document of what can be called Berlin's imaginary, establishing the Alexanderplatz and the territory around it as a constitutive site of the city. As any visitor to Berlin will know, words from the novel are displayed on the unprepossessing *Plattenbau*, the 'Haus der Elektroindustrie', on one side of the square, encouraging the contemporary city-dweller or visitor to see a correlation between the place and the book of the place. Thinking back to Benjamin's reading, this gesture nicely represents the conversion of the book into epic, public form. Indeed, *Berlin Alexanderplatz* emerges out of a Weimar culture that is instrumental in establishing a connection between urban environment and text. Thus the work of such as Benjamin and Franz Hessel establishes the city as a complex and shifting sign system, a montage of text and image, requiring constant critical acts of reading.

This is the logic that informs the only actual intermedial montage of the text, the famous point at which Biberkopf's entry into the city is represented by a sequence of iconic institutional images (pp. 49–50). The sequence is introduced by the emblematic figure of the Berlin bear, representing the city and – as popular etymology would have it at least –

9   *Non-Places: Introduction to an Anthropology of Supermodernity* (New York and
     London, 1995).

constructed into its name, much as the beaver is into Biberkopf. The bear certainly seems an appropriate stand-in for this bearish Berliner, seeming to represent both the city and Biberkopf's act of entry into it. The sequence is followed first by a town planning document, concerned – suitably enough – with the attachment of a sign to a street-wall and then by a complex account of one of the key sites of the novel, under the title 'Der Rosenthaler Platz unterhält sich'. It is a bewildering montage of that square's activities, and the fluctuating networks of meteorological, technological, and human traffic in which it stands, its complexity in ironic counterpoint to the code of icons and the planning document. The icons work in the manner of a primer, a basic set of words and images to guide the city-reader in his negotiation of the urban image-text. To enter the city is to enter the variations of this pictographic text. We can only speculate, with critic Alexander Honold, on whether it is part of the text's play with established models of novel-writing that this book about Berlin culminates in the asylum at Berlin-Buch.[10] There is always potential for the book of the great city to go mad with the kind of information overload that features when the Rosenthaler Platz 'unterhält sich', entertains or converses with itself, and enters into the dynamic and crossed networks of urban intercourse.

The city had never been more publicly imaged and textualised than in this period, and the illuminated commercial signs of what became known in the Weimar period as the 'Stadt des Lichts' and the 'Litfaß-säule', often itself illuminated, are key features of this metropolitan word-image text. In the investigation of the case of Mieze's murder, both the police and Biberkopf resort to the 'Litfaßsäule' to see and read what is happening. When the detectives cannot track down Reinhold, we read 'Und wenn sich etwas ereignen sollte, dann wird mans schon sehn, dann wirds an der Litfaßsäule stehn.' (p. 345). The rhyming of 'sehn' and 'stehn' here, a common feature of this novel full of jingles of one kind or another, not least rhyming couplets in the 'Moritat' style. It establishes the advertising column, indeed advertises it, as a place for standing and seeing, a medial equivalent of the 'Moritat', the ballad of dark deeds

---

10 Honold notes how the novel's mutilation motif is reprised 'in einer Anstalt mit dem sprechenden Ortsnamen "Berlin-Buch"' ('Der Krieg und die Großstadt: *Berlin Alexanderplatz* und ein Trauma der Moderne', in *Internationales Alfred-Döblin-Kolloquium Berlin 2001*, ed. by Hartmut Egge and Gabriele Prauß (Berne, 2003), pp. 191–211 (p. 208)). Early in his career, Döblin worked at Buch asylum.

performed on the street. Biberkopf too needs to stand and see and read: 'Ich muß runter, an die Litfaßsäule. Ich muß det sehen. Ich muß det lesen' (p. 384). Rather than simply recording urban events, the text-image column comes to take on the character of one in itself: 'Er begafft die Litfaßsäulen, als wären die ein Ereignis' (p. 237). It is the same metonymic logic as operates when the protagonist registers 'Schilder, die Kinos waren' (p. 31); in the medial networks of the city, the medium or the sign takes the place of what it represents. The cover designed by Georg Salter for the first edition of *Berlin Alexanderplatz*, itself of course an advertising image, represents the conjunction of space, text, and figure that is at work in the novel. Typography and topography, or topology, are merged here to contextualise the stations of Biberkopf's story, as if in a stylised map of the text.

The mobile Alexanderplatz into which Biberkopf is inscribed is characterised as another place, or place of the other. While close to the official centre of the city, the Alexanderplatz is also off-centre. Carrying the name of the Russian Tsar Alexander I, it seems disposed to look to the East, and so represents what is other to the comfortable bourgeois enclaves of the City-West. The novel makes an ideological shift to the territory and concerns of proletariat and petit bourgeoisie and the mobile territory between the two. Biberkopf's sales patter is programmatic here: 'Warum aber im Westen der feine Mann Schleifen trägt und der Prolet trägt keine?' (p. 68). At the same time, his focal space of the workers' and petit-bourgeois districts of Berlin Ost is surrounded by migrant and underworld sub-cultures. It is the site of the police headquarters, but also of criminal activities. The Alex – as the square was and remains popularly known – was also, by a logic of metonymy or spatial associ-ation, the familiar name for the *Polizeipräsidium* that stood there. Alex is, as it were, both the Berlin criminal and the Berlin policeman.

The shortened, familiar form of 'Alex' might also lead us to look at the other components of the place-name: '-anderplatz' as 'other-place'. It is worth noting that Döblin recurrently associates the place and what occurs on and around it with 'andere', 'ändern' and their cognates. It would appear to be the representative place for encounters with otherness in Berlin. This involves both the migrant and the criminal as urban other, the underworld or otherworld figures that populate Döblin's novel, and also the principle of change for which the Alexanderplatz stands. The Alexanderplatz is one of the historic marketplaces of the city and so marked out as a place of exchange, of traffic of all kinds. It is in its character as a place of exchange that Ernst Bloch in a feuilleton piece on Berlin sees the exemplary function of the Alexanderplatz in Döblin's novel. The place of exchange demands mediation in a literary form that is mobile and various, that of montage: 'hier hat die Montage des Döblinschen "Alexanderplatz" ihren eigenen Platz [...] in fast boden-loser Vertauschbarkeit'.[11] This mode of representation that works through exchange marks the 'Platz' out as indeed an '-anderplatz', a place of transformation that allegorically names its function.

A collaborative work of 1928 by the leading Weimar photographers Sasha Stone and Otto Umbehr, also known as Umbo, has the title *Der Alexanderplatz im Umbau*, and this is indeed something of a collocation: reconstruction and the Alex belong together. The work suitably casts the environmental montage in the form of photomontage, shifting normal planes and perspectives into new relationships, in a technique akin to Döblin's textual montage. Throughout its twentieth-century history and until the present day, the Alexanderplatz is a paradigmatic place of reconstruction and resurfacing in a city that has been subject to constant 'Umbau'. A series of photographs from Döblin's own album feature variations on the same scene of excavation, a signature feature of the novel. This digging-work constantly opens up perspectives on what is conventionally concealed, on subliminal material and structures, indi-cating that the novel is strategically aimed at exposing such insights. This is what we saw Brecht call the exploration of introspective dimen-sions via the extraspective. It represents Döblin's attachment to the archeological method of psychoanalysis, on both collective and individ-ual levels, and opened up in particular in the interaction between interior monologue and the external sights and voices of the city. In each case, the work of excavation has constructive intentions, but it also reveals uncertainties and dangers.

While 1920s Berlin is conventionally associated with the glamorous sheen of what Janet Ward has called 'Weimar Surfaces',[12] the 'Hundert blanke Scheiben' (p. 16) that Biberkopf encounters on his re-entry to the city, here we see those surfaces opened up for inspection and always ready to undermine the sleek glamour of appearance. This breaking up of

11 'Berlin aus der Landschaft gesehen', *Frankfurter Zeitung*, 7 July 1932.
12 *Weimar Surfaces: Urban Visual Culture in 1920s Germany* (Berkeley, 2001).

surface and volatile collapsing of layers applies at once to the city and its people, with the two regularly cross-referenced. It is in the subversive nature of the substratum to be projected above ground, so that Biberkopf is haunted by the possibility of the roofs of houses falling down on him like a hat from a head or like the proverbially unsettled sand upon which Berlin is built, 'wie Sand schräg herunter' (p. 131), as the urban environment is turned on its head. The threat is that the protagonist might be hit on the head – 'kriegt er eins aufs Hauptgebäude' (p. 314) – much like the buildings under demolition. The threat of the hammer that hangs over Biberkopf follows this logic of his construction, or destruction, into the fabric of the city. The warning 'Achtung Baustelle' (p. 132) thus seems to apply to all levels of the urban environment and the place of the city-dweller within it, who is always subject to pressures of bursting and collapse from that environment.

Franz Biberkopf once worked in cement as well as in transportation, and he is thus doubly built into this construction site. A comparison might be made here with another novelistic world altogether, that of Goethe's *Die Wahlverwandtschaften*, as discussed in Nicholas Boyle's essay. Biberkopf is linked with the industrial material and traffic of the urban environment in a system of elective relationships between the human and non-human elements of the modern metropolis. Where Goethe's pre-industrial, feudal, landscape novel puts the emphasis on elementary affinity, however, albeit in crossed forms, Döblin's industrial novel of mass metropolitan modernity puts it upon volatility and alterity. Under the pressure of what comes to bear upon him, we read how Biberkopf bends 'und zuletzt wie ein Element, das von gewissen Strahlen getroffen wird, in ein anderes Element übergeht' (p. 414).

Like *Die Wahlverwandtschaften*, and indeed many another novel, the structure of *Berlin Alexanderplatz* is determined by the relationship between place and personal narrative – 'Die Geschichte vom Franz Biberkopf'. If the Alexanderplatz, also known as Alex, is a familiarised, popular place, the colloquial 'vom' here indicates that Biberkopf is or will also become a familiar, popular figure – 'der Franz Biberkopf'. Yet in both cases, that familiarity is subject to estrangement through change. The paradox of the place is also that of the person. Biberkopf himself is the object of 'Umbau', of decimation and reconstruction, in the course of his story. After his ostensible street accident, we read: 'Franz ist steinern' (p. 223) and 'Franz liegt eisern still.' (p. 224). The man of the city has been constructed into the urban materials of stone and iron. When his fate is programmatically set out in the prologue to the novel, it is accordingly in the language of urban reconstruction. Biberkopf will by the end of the novel stand once more upon the Alexanderplatz: '*sehr verändert, ramponiert, aber doch zurechtgebogen.*' (p. 11). Like the place on which he stands, its buildings and street furniture, the resilient Berliner will have been beaten and bent into a new shape. The story of Biberkopf is cast between this sort of urban materialism and the sort of creaturely life that is implied in his name, through the beaver as emblematic builder-animal. But the novel's appeal to the creaturely is not simply constructive. The corollary of the hammer that falls on streets or buildings or Biberkopf is the slaughterhouse knife, as we shall see.

Let us look at the first few pages of the novel to see how the relationship between person and place is established under the sign of otherness and transition. The opening pages of novels of course often serve to establish place, persons, and their relationship. Here that establishment is in transition. Biberkopf, who has been serving time outside the city limits in Tegel jail, re-enters the city and rejoins his home territory as a migrant figure, still psychologically attached to the walls of the prison. Biberkopf's encounters with the 'Ostjuden', early twentieth-century Berlin's principal immigrant community, at the start of the novel are telling here. His behaviour mimics that of itinerant Jews: 'Er ist von Haus zu Haus geloffen. Auf einen Hof hat er sich gestellt und hat gesungen.' (p. 20). It is as though he is performing a version of the travelling Yiddish theatre-shows that were staged in the 'Hinterhöfe' of this area. Nachum accepts Biberkopf back into Berlin in a fashion that imitates the historical entry of Jews into the city. As Jewish visitors and migrants to Berlin had had to enter the city through the Rosenthaler Tor, not far from the Alexanderplatz, a gated entrance that came to be administered by the resident Jewish community, so Biberkopf who has been performing in a 'Hof' in the Sophienstraße, just off the Rosenthaler Straße, is received at its gate by Nachum, who recognises him as a 'Zugereister' (p. 21): 'Der Jude nahm ihn am Tor in Empfang' (p. 18). Biberkopf is an archetypal, indigenous Berliner who no longer belongs to his city. He is in the position of the other, the other guest adopted by an itinerant host: 'ein Gast bringt den andern' (p. 19).

This opening excursion has a programmatic character. *Berlin Alexanderplatz* joins other great Modernist novels in this series – notably *Der*

Zauberberg and *Der Proceß* – as allegories of travel, transposing that time-honoured form for the exploration of identity to the dense, multi-cultural geography of the great city of modernity. And by its attachment to the category of the other, the scene establishes alterity as the native terrain of the novel. Biberkopf is aligned with the immigrant Jews as expatriated 'Bewohner Babylons' (p. 21), introducing the leitmotif of Berlin as latter-day Babylon, a great city under the sign of ruin and expulsion. Like Kafka's Josef K., who is put under arrest by a man in travel clothes, Biberkopf is always an exile in his hometown. He will in fact have to re-enter the city repeatedly in order to be in it again.

His relationship to the city is also represented in his relationships to its cultural diversity. Not only does he consort with the Jews of the *Scheunenviertel*, but he is also both drawn to and repelled by both homo-sexual and criminal subcultures. On the one hand, Biberkopf is drawn to the plight of homosexuals under the strictures of paragraph 175, to the extent that his lover, Lina, comes to doubt his sexuality. In keeping with the kind of linguistic confusion that is associated with Babylon, Biber-kopf's resistance to a homosexual identification is nicely expressed in Yiddish, as his panicked reaction to this taboo territory is mimicked by the narrator: 'Er zog in einem großen Schlamassel ab, die Sache kam ihm so wenig koscher vor, daß er Lina kein Wort sagte und sie abends versetzte.' (p. 74). Biberkopf's ambivalent relations with the minority cultures of Berlin-Babylon are expressed in a confusion of tongues.

A key element of the novel's representation of modern urban life is in the form of linguistic exchange of this kind. It is seen and heard both in the idiom of Franz Biberkopf and the colloquium of other voices, both diegetic and extradiegetic, that run through the novel. Döblin's narrator speaks as a ventriloquist of such other voices and their non-standard lexicons and grammars. The Berlin dialect that characterises the novel is the language of the marketplace as the place of popular politics, of public speaking in its different forms, as opposed to the 'Quatsch-bude' of the Reichstag (p. 266). Biberkopf may profess to be no 'Volksredner' (p. 70), but when he sells his wares he also speaks a ver-sion of the language of the demagogue with his appeal to proletarian politics. And he is a 'Volksredner' in another sense: he speaks for the people through what Benjamin suggests is the megaphone of Berlin,[13]

---

13   'KRISIS DES ROMANS', p. 233.

the public colloquium of its popular voices. As the representative common man and *vox populi* in this public arena, subject of and to the economics and politics of a city in foment, Biberkopf is a sort of Berlin allegory, the city's everyman. His function is both to be the novel's primary speaker and the common ear for the many voices of the city.

In the modulation of focalising and vocalising roles, moving between foreground and background and negotiating with others and with his environment, Biberkopf is a figure of exchange. He trades in material commodities and in ideological positions, adopting and promoting one after the other in an exchangeable system. Commerce is the driving force of the city, especially on and around the great market-place that is the Alexanderplatz, and not least in the speech that is transacted there. Such transactions of speech on and around the Alexanderplatz provide many of the set-piece scenes of the novel, and they are mobilised by the traffic that is another feature of the place. Passengers become pedestrians and then passengers again in other forms of transport, and as they pass from one side to the other, the same people are converted from one form of mock-epic exodus into another: 'Das Gesicht der Ostwanderer ist in nichts unterschieden von dem der West-, Süd- und Nordwanderer, sie vertauschen auch ihre Rollen [...] Sie sind so gleichmäßig wie die, die im Autobus, in den Elektrischen sitzen.' (p. 168). As a marketeer on and of that place, Biberkopf is caught up in all sorts of commercial transactions: doing commerce with the stuff of life ('Obsthandel'), with information ('Zeitungshandel'), and with the body ('Mädchenhandel'). He himself embodies the principle of exchange, as he exchanges one kind of goods for another. He operates both in the official economy and the unofficial, where 'Obsthandel' is a cover for the parallel black-market of crime.

A key complex in the urban marketplace is the 'Viehhof' and 'Schlachthof', which represents the consumer system of the city as turning on a ritual of violence. The 'Viehhof', with its 'Viehstraßen' (p. 140) acts as a kind of *mise-en-abyme* for the city, a representative site that reflects in its spaces of 'Hof', 'Markt', and 'Straße' what goes on in the city at large. The slaughterhouse is understandable as a heterotopia in the sense developed by Michel Foucault.[14] Foucault's heterotopia or other spaces are those institutional sites which at once represent the

14   'Of Other Spaces', *Diacritics* 16 (Spring 1986), 22–27.

prevailing order and invert or carnivalise it. They expose the contradictions that haunt the fantasy of social control and surveillance that Foucault famously exemplified through the architecture and rhetoric of the panopticon (represented in the novel by the 'panoptischer Bau' of the Polizeipräsidium). His examples for heterotopia include such sites of confinement as the prison and the asylum, and in *Berlin Alexanderplatz* those other places of the social order are indeed networked with the slaughterhouse. As a heterotopical system, they serve as extensions of the allegorical function of the Alexanderplatz as other place. Alongside the construction of human life in the city into its technology and architecture is its becoming animal and the reduction of life to the bare life of the organism. The struggle between crime and the law in the novel is represented as a kind of animal farm, where the 'Bullen' are up against underworld figures repeatedly described as 'Ochsen' (e.g. p. 148). In a process of reciprocal montage, references to criminology are constructed into the account of the 'Schlachthof', while the world of urban crime is cast as animal market and slaughterhouse.

As already suggested, it is arguably no coincidence that 'Biberkopf' is named after an animal, or an animal part. Just as his arm is forfeited in a traffic accident and exchanged for a prosthesis, so the head highlighted by his name is subject to a system of exchange. The montage of the novel's form correlates not only with the construction and mapping of the city but also with a montage of the body, which correlates in turn with the ideological reconstruction of the human subject. As one of the chapter headings has it – *Ein anderer Mensch kriegt auch einen anderen Kopf* (p. 246). One form that this exchange takes is the disparaging of figures in the novel as animal-heads, as when newspaper vendors as innocents in the trading system of the city are cast as 'Kalbsköppe' (p. 253). Other transformations are also brought into play, as Biberkopf becomes 'Ziberkopf, Niberkopf, Wiedekopf' (p. 335) and then, in the asylum, is transacted into 'Wiedehopf' and 'Gliedertropf' (p. 423). The exchanging of the protagonist's emblematic identity culminates in the sort of madness that replaces the head-name at will for the nonsense of 'Gliedertropf' – translatable as limbsfool, a foolish form of 'Gliedermann' or puppet, with detachable arm and head.

When Reinhold sacrifices Biberkopf, it is in the style of the animal market allegory. His iron hand deals an 'eiserner Schlag' to the arm of Biberkopf, whom he calls a 'Rindsvieh' (p. 211). Biberkopf is the sacrificial animal of the market-city, and also both perpetrator and victim of a form of hyperbolic, but inwardly panicked masculinity. It is a version of the crisis of traditional masculine identity in the wake of the First World War (Biberkopf's amputation can be understood as an after-effect, and indeed comes to be performed as, the damage to male bodies done there) and in a time of mass unemployment. Men like the members of the 'Pumskolonne' find alternative work, but the bonds in this type of 'Männerbund' are fraught with insecurity and resentment. When Reinhold takes Franz's arm from him, it is treated as a symbolic castration (making him an 'Eunuch' (p. 242)). The love between the two men is a threat to the homosocial order of the criminal subculture. When it ceases to be displaced into the exchange of women, through their 'Mädchenhandel', it comes to a crisis and the sacrificial slaughter first of the phallic arm and then of the woman that Biberkopf still enjoys, Mieze. The sexual order of the text is fundamentally destabilised by the 'other' that is desire between men. For Biberkopf, Reinhold is that other: 'während er mit Eva tanzt, liebt er zwei: die eine ist seine Mieze, die er gern da hätte, der andere ist – Reinhold.' (p. 299). This othering is what can only ultimately be contained, it seems, by the violence of the slaughterhouse, the exchanging of the human values of care for the other that run through the text with the bare life violence that also racks it.

The end of the novel is rife with the language of othering, preparing for the programmatic return of the other Franz Biberkopf – 'sehr verändert' – to the Alexanderplatz. Biberkopf undergoes a change into another condition that is a brutal, psychopathological counterpart to the mystical transition into the 'anderen Zustand' of Musil's *Mann ohne Eigenschaften*. The identification with animals that has run through the novel as the measure of the brute otherness in human nature is now made fully explicit in Biberkopf's deathbed illumination: 'ich bin kein Mensch, ich bin ein Vieh', and redoubled, as even the animal identification has to be negated: 'Ein Untier' (p. 442). At the end of his story, Biberkopf thus attributes himself to the same non- or unspecies as Gregor Samsa in Kafka's classic Modernist tale of personal alteration, *Die Verwandlung*.[15] The other that he becomes at this point is of course

15   For discussion of this categorisation under the sign of 'un', see Andrew Webber, 'Kafka, *Die Verwandlung*', in *Landmarks in German Short Prose*, ed. by Peter Hutchinson (Berne, 2003), pp. 175–90 (p. 180).

both same and different, like the constantly other Alexanderplatz. When he returns to stand once more on that place, and the narrator records the encounter in 'erlebte Rede', it seems that the changed place and the changed man are one, converged in the 'er ist da': 'Und auch sonst ist viel los am Alex, aber Hauptsache: er ist da.' (p. 449).

At the close of the text the market-place has been exchanged for another place, a military parade-ground or battle-field: '*Und Schritt gefaßt und rechts und links und rechts und links, marschieren, marschieren, wir ziehen in den Krieg, es ziehen mit uns hundert Spielleute mit, sie trommeln und pfeifen, widebum, widebum, dem einen gehts grade, dem andern gehts krumm, der eine bleibt stehen, der andere fällt um, der eine rennt weiter, der andere liegt stumm, widebum, widebum.*' (p. 455). Whether the de-individualised Biberkopf, shoulder to shoulder in a mass march to war at the close of the text, will go left or right, will stand or fall, be the one or the other – 'der eine' or 'der andere' – remains as open as the fate of Hans Castorp in *Der Zauberberg*, going to war to different music. The phonetic effects of Biberkopf's marching tune – its '*widebum, widebum*' – complete the soundscape of the city novel. They chime both with the 'Rumm rumm' that was the rhythm of the steam ram on the Alexanderplatz (p. 165) and with the 'Wumm-wumm' of the fateful storm in the woods, its chaotically destructive march echoing with the impact of 'Flieger-bomben' (p. 354). The final march accommodates both the drive of the city and the drive of nature, each of them always echoing the compulsive rhythms of the death drive, battering human life from 'rumm' to '*krumm*'. The 'wide-' of '*widebum*' in the march seems to echo at once with 'wieder', marking the impact again and again in a repetition compulsion, and with the 'Wiede' that was substituted into the exchange system of Biberkopf's name. And the '-bum' also chimes with '*stumm*', with the mutism of the dead as ultimate other ('*der andere liegt stumm*'), and so with the deathly silence into which the repetitions and variations of the polyphonic text are about to fall. In this, too, its recording of the mortal march of history, its allegorical vision of bare life driving on in the face of death, this is indeed a landmark novel of its time and place, but also one with a more universal reach.

DAVID MIDGLEY

Musil, *Der Mann ohne Eigenschaften*

Der Mann ohne Eigenschaften, the first volume of which appeared in 1930, has come to be recognised as one of the most significant contributions to the development of the European novel in the twentieth century. The waves of intense scholarly interest that it has attracted over the last fifty years – which have variously focused on its critique of the intellectual culture of its time and its exploration of existential issues, as well as the qualities of its writing and its distinctive approach to the business of narration[1] – are testimony to the rich texture of the work. In a essay such as this I shall not attempt to reflect all the dimensions of this critical interest, nor to add a further dimension of my own. Rather, I shall concentrate on those aspects of the text that make it such a distinctive and innovative contribution to the novel.

In his recent book on the broad heritage of European fiction, *The Curtain*, the Czech novelist Milan Kundera speaks of *Der Mann ohne Eigenschaften* as an existential encyclopaedia of its time, in which each chapter is a discovery, and in which the intellectual content, far from detracting from the character of the work as a novel, brings about an enrichment of the possibilities of 'what only the novel can do'.[2] It is very much in that spirit that I want to discuss the work here, but in order to understand what Kundera's claim really signifies we need to recognise the peculiar – and complex – ideational tensions at work within Musil's

---

1   For recent surveys of the secondary literature, see Christian Rogowski, *Distinguished Outsider: Robert Musil and his Critics* (Rochester, NY, 1994); Tim Mehigan, *The Critical Responses to Robert Musil's 'The Man without Qualities'* (Rochester, NY, 2003).

2   '*L'Homme sans qualités* est une incomparable encyclopédie existentielle de tout son siècle. [...] c'est chaque chapitre en lui-même qui est une surprise, qui est une découverte. L'omniprésence de la pensée n'a nullement enlevé au roman son caractère de roman; elle a enrichi sa forme et immensément élargi le domaine de ce que *seul le roman* peut découvrir et dire.' Milan Kundera, *Le Rideau* (Paris 2005), p. 89; available in English as *The Curtain*, transl. by Linda Asher (London, 2007).

text. We need to grasp the relationship between the cultivated detachment of the protagonist, Ulrich, which is announced in the work's title, and the critical depiction of late Habsburg Austria which is also a salient feature of the text. We also need to understand the relation between the powerful evocation of a historical world in Volume I and the introspective, abstract, and ultimately inconclusive investigations that came to dominate Musil's work on subsequent volumes, leaving *Der Mann ohne Eigenschaften* an unfinished fragment of some 1600 pages at the time of the author's death in 1942. But above all we need to recognise the relation between the general preponderance of intellectual analysis within the text and the distinctive approach to narration that Musil adopted.

Notoriously, the opening paragraph of the work evokes the technical terminology of weather-forecasting and climate description, only to conclude by saying that the situation could just as well be described with the words, 'Es war ein schöner Augusttag des Jahres 1913' (p. 9).[3] The second paragraph evokes the specific sounds and smells that make the 'Reichshaupt- und Residenzstadt' Vienna instantly recognisable to anyone who knows it, only to brush this information aside in its turn with the comment that the precise location is not important and that this city is constituted out of the same ingredients as any other large city: 'Wie alle großen Städte bestand sie aus Unregelmäßigkeit, Wechsel, Vorgleiten, Nichtschritthalten, Zusammenstößen von Dingen und Angelegenheiten' (p. 10). In a similar vein, we are introduced to a pair of characters on the street, only to be told that they are not in fact the persons named, and that even if they were, we would still be left with the puzzle of who they really are: 'Angenommen, sie würden Arnheim und Ermelinda Tuzzi heißen, was aber nicht stimmt [...], so steht man vor dem Rätsel, wer sie seien' (p. 10). All this is happening in a chapter which is pointedly presented as one that does not lead anywhere – 'Woraus bemerkenswerter Weise nichts hervorgeht' – and which introduces a section of the text (the first nineteen chapters) that is disdainfully entitled 'Eine Art Einleitung', while the larger second part (consisting of one hundred and four chapters) evokes a world in which

---

3   Page numbers incorporated in the text refer to Robert Musil, *Gesammelte Werke* (Reinbek bei Hamburg, 1978), Vol. 1.

no particular event seems to emerge as especially significant from the general buzz of activity in which 'Seinesgleichen geschieht'.

Clearly, then, this is a text which pointedly flouts the conventions of precise setting, of defined personalities, and of action, but which in doing so nevertheless introduces us to the specific time and place, and the upper-class social ambience, of late Habsburg Vienna. For all the playfulness with which it deploys narrative conventions, the text does evoke a fictional world – that world of 'Seinesgleichen geschieht' – which approximates to what might well have been being done and said in the salons of Vienna on the eve of the First World War; and it is precisely that evocation of what might have been happening, along with the intimations of what is going to happen historically, come what may, that keeps Musil's text in touch with the familiar conventions of the novel, even as it challenges them. Moreover, the irony of hindsight is intermittently permitted to show through in the form of allusions to the conflict in the Balkans which is not yet formally recognised as war (p. 359), to the fact that plans of battle are going to become a common feature of everyday conversation within a year (p. 374), to the practice of field punishments that would also soon become familiar (p. 517) – or in the confident assertion by a senior Austrian bureaucrat that it would take a 'Weltuntergang' to promote the political career of a visiting Prussian industrialist (p. 96).[4] It is above all these reminders of the specific historical timeframe of the narrative that should make us wary of assimilating *Der Mann ohne Eigenschaften* to the 'postmodern' conceptions of fiction that became prevalent in the 1980s and 1990s.[5]

---

4   The industrialist in question is modelled on the historical figure of Walter Rathenau, the Jewish heir to the AEG concern, who became Germany's foreign minister for a period after the First World War, and was assassinated by fanatical Geman nationalists in 1922.

5   See especially the discussion of *Der Mann ohne Eigenschaften* in Rolf Günter Renner, *Die postmoderne Konstellation: Theorie, Text und Kunst im Ausgang der Moderne* (Freiburg im Br. 1988), pp. 124–42. For a critique of recent trends in Musil reception, see David Midgley, 'Zur Vereinnahmung Robert Musils für das postmoderne Denken' [forthcoming: IVG, Paris 2005]; also 'Zu den wiederkehrenden Aktualitäten von *Der Mann ohne Eigenschaften*', in Pierre Béhar and Marie-Louise Roth (eds), *Musil an der Schwelle zum 21. Jahrhundert. Internationales Kolloquiuim – Saarbrücken 2001* (Musiliana 10) (Berne, 2005), pp. 287–300.

We should be similarly wary of the mystique that is sometimes attached to the fact that Musil's text was never completed. It is true that many chapters of *Der Mann ohne Eigenschaften* display some kind of in-built resistance towards moving the plot forward – either because a particular moment in the relationship between characters is being used as a pretext for reflective disquisition, or because of Ulrich's reluctance to become involved in public events – and that Musil was highly conscious of the senses in which his novel was one in which the story that was meant to be told never got told.[6] It is also true that the progress of the work was seriously hampered after 1932 by the combination of external historical circumstances and the self-absorption that overcame Musil's work on the continuation of the text. But it does not automatically follow from this that our understanding of the intrinsic qualities of Musil's text is greatly helped by resorting to Maurice Blanchot's conception of literary writing as necessarily entailing the impossibility of completion.[7] Parts I and II of *Der Mann ohne Eigenschaften* were published in 1930; and in 1932, under pressure from his publisher, Rowohlt, Musil published the first thirty-eight chapters of Part III, in which the actions of Ulrich and his sister Agathe following the death of their father are recounted with a greater sense of narrative flow than had previously characterised the text. The record of his subsequent work shows that in the period 1933–1934 Musil made attempts to continue the story-line in ways that linked events of 1914 thematically to the rise of National Socialism in the early 1930s (e.g. pp. 1436–53), but that from 1935

6   See the draft foreword in Musil, *Gesammelte Werke*, Vol. 1, p. 1937: 'Die Geschichte dieses Romans kommt darauf hinaus, daß die Geschichte, die in ihm erzählt werden sollte, nicht erzählt wird.' On the same page he states, 'Man darf die Unfertigkeit einer Sache aber nicht mit der Skepsis des Autors verwechseln.'

7   Blanchot's essay on Musil, in *Le Livre à venir* (Paris, 1959), focuses on the 'impersonality' of Musil's narrative style, both in a 'classic' sense and with regard to the possibility that Musil contemplated around 1920 of a depersonalised discourse in which writing in the first person would imply neither the perspective of the fictional character, nor that of the author, but would reflect the relationship between the two. It is Blanchot's general proposition that the very possibility of literature is predicated upon the impossibility of completing the work that has led to attempts to apply his thinking to *Der Mann ohne Eigenschaften*: see especially Anne Longuet Marx, *Proust, Musil: partage d'écritures* (Paris, 1986), pp. 164–66; on Blanchot's thinking, cf. also Simon Critchley, *Very Little… Almost Nothing. Death, Philosophy, Literature* (London, 1997), pp. 33–41.

onwards he apparently resigned himself to the fact that any effort he might make to incorporate overt allusions to contemporary politics into his fiction was bound to remain ineffectual, and focused his efforts instead on the introspective psychological investigations we find developed in the posthumous draft chapters. When he died in April 1942 he was still at work on a group of chapters which explore the fine structure of emotional connections based on Ulrich's intimate relationship with his sister (pp. 1204–39). It might be said that, as Hitler's 'tausendjähriges Reich' took over in the external world, Musil had turned to the quasi-mystical 'tausendjähriges Reich' within, which had already furnished him with his title for Part III in 1932. At the same time, the outbreak of the First World War never ceased to provide the teleological goal for the overall development of his narrative.[8]

Just as the conventional expectations of a novel provide the reference points for Musil's narrative (even if specific moments in his text refuse to gratify those expectations), so too does the normative expectation of a completed work remain a palpable reference point for the protracted and repeatedly deferred elaboration of the narrative threads that link the personal story of Ulrich to the historical society of which he is a part (albeit a relatively detached part). Moreover it is through this deferral of action and the equivocal treatment of narrative conventions that Musil creates the fictional space in which it was possible to nurture those qualities that Kundera recognises in the text: its encyclopaedic character, the accommodation of extensive reflection, and the development of each chapter into an opportunity for discovery. It is within that space that Musil can hold his various themes in tension with each other and explore the connections between them.

What, then, are the uses that Musil makes of the textual space he created in this way? One such use is a sustained critique of prevailing assumptions in pre-war Austria, to which Musil gives the unflattering name Kakanien, derived from the fact that some of its institutions were designated 'kaiserlich-königlich', suggesting the unity of authority in the Emperor, while others were called 'kaiserlich und königlich', suggesting

---

8   See Walter Fanta, *Die Entstehungsgeschichte des 'Mann ohne Eigenschaften' von Robert Musil* (Vienna, Cologne and Weimar 2000), pp. 391–532; Walter Fanta, 'Schreibexerzitien eines *Ingenieur-Dichters*', *Musil-Forum*, 28 (2003/2004), pp. 26–56: pp. 37–44.

a discrete separation of lines of authority between the Austrian Empire and the Kingdom of Hungary. Kakanien is a land of delicate balances and precarious political compromises; it lacks ambition by comparison with other European powers of the day; its internal politics are a muddle of liberalism, clericalism and Enlightenment values; and its ubiquitous bureaucracy is devoted to preserving ancient privileges and therefore wont to smother innovation (pp. 32–33). With a particular thrust against Austrian clericalism, and with a keen sense of historical irony, Musil also speaks of it as the land from which 'God withdrew his credit' (pp. 528–30). But he is no less merciless in his evocation of the political nationalism that destabilised and ultimately destroyed the Habsburg Empire, introducing a discussion of the self-conception of the ethnic groups within the Empire as 'unerlöste Nationen' with a reflection on how inappropriate such vocabulary would appear if applied to relations between individuals, continuing the exposé with the rueful thoughts of a military officer on how the lobbying of one nationalist group is impeding the modernisation of the Austrian artillery, and concluding with indications of how deeply such talk of 'Erlösung' is connected to other messianic impulses of the time (pp. 517–20).

The chief instrument by which Musil reveals the character of these messianic impulses is the brilliant comic device of a commission established to determine how best to celebrate the seventieth jubilee of Emperor Franz Joseph. Conceived in a spirit of Austro-Prussian rivalry – since the jubilee is due in 1918, the year in which Prussia will be celebrating the mere thirtieth jubilee of its Kaiser, Wilhelm II – the project is referred to throughout the text as the 'Parallelaktion'. Since Franz Joseph had in fact died in 1916, and the historical cataclysm of the First World War had ended in the demise of the monarchy in both Austria and Prussia, the irony of hindsight confers a sense of futility on the enterprise from the outset. But as a body charged with the forward planning for a major national event and concerned above all with the quest for a unifying theme for that event, the 'Parallelaktion' also provides a semi-public arena in which currents of thought that are representative of the time can be exposed to view. Its convenor is Graf Leinsdorf, a doggedly patriotic and conservative official, who has devoted his life to the neutralisation of any political force that might conceivably threaten the stability of the imperial regime, but who is now confronted with a welter of potentially destabilising proposals for a jubilee theme hatched out by organisations which relish the opportunity to 'make the world a better place' by promoting their own particular cause (pp. 138–41). He has a staunch ally in Ulrich's cousin Ermelinda Tuzzi, a *Salondame* who is generally referred to by the nickname Ulrich gives her, Diotima, which is borrowed, in a spirit of parody, from the wise woman of Plato's *Symposium*. She, we are told, promotes the view that contemporary life is overburdened with specialist knowledge and that the intellect itself is in need of redemption; and in doing so, she successfully gathers around her a range of professional experts and intellectual amateurs – politicians, bank directors, and technicians – who share that conviction (pp. 100–01). Foremost (and most welcome) among her admirers is the Prussian industrialist Arnheim, who is on the one hand presented as a figure intent on seizing his opportunities to move with the times, but who also writes books that endorse Diotima's sentiments, and who comes to see himself as taking an 'Erholungsurlaub von der Vernunft' among the riches of Viennese culture and in her company (p. 199) – although it is later rumoured that his real reason for staying in Vienna is to acquire control of the oilfields of Galicia (p. 616). They also include the Austrian general mentioned earlier, a former commanding officer of Ulrich's called Stumm von Bordwehr, who attends the meetings of the 'Parallelaktion' even though the War Ministry had not been invited to send a delegate, and who is soon putting the routines of military strategic analysis to work in the vain attempt to make an ordered assessment of the competing intellectual impulses he encounters in the civilian world of 1913 (p. 372).

The official role that Ulrich finds himself reluctantly co-opted to play, as secretary to the commission, is to manage that swarm of proposals emanating from the general public, through which the competing forces generated by economic and social modernisation are seeking a voice. Ulrich's solution itself highlights the mutually contradictory nature of these proposals: the two folders into which he organises them are labelled 'Zurück zu…' and 'Vorwärts zu…', of which the latter appears instantly repugnant to the conservative Graf Leinsdorf (pp. 233–34; cf. p. 271). Through Ulrich's network of personal acquaintances, too, the reader is made aware of some specific examples of the ideological tendencies that were making themselves felt in the pre-war world. These include a group of fervent young German nationalists whose meetings take place, ironically, in the house of a Jewish banker (p. 478; cf. 529);

their leader is the twenty-one-year-old Hans Sepp, in whom we find the militant idealism of the German youth movement combined with proclamations of an aggressive nationalist exclusivity (pp. 549–55). Late draft chapters also show Musil developing portraits of a dogmatic socialist called Schmeißer (pp. 1454–57, 1627–35) and a popular poet called Feuermaul, whose idealisation of humanity is modelled on the Expressionist poetry of Franz Werfel (pp. 1436–43). Among Ulrich's close friends we also find the passionate young Nietzschean Clarisse, who idolises a Zarathustra-like prophet figure called Meingast (modelled on the anti-rationalist intellectual Ludwig Klages), and it is Clarisse's call for an 'erlösende Tat' that prompts Ulrich to reflect on how history is not created by an 'author', nor by the sort of teleological destiny that political leaders of the time were fond of invoking, but by the combined effects of often minor and peripheral circumstances (pp. 360–61). All these cases might be said to illustrate Musil's gift for thought-provoking historical caricature, but it would be wrong to imagine that these representative figures of the time are depicted in a consistently polemical spirit, or that Ulrich, the ostensible exponent of critical reflections on many of them, is invariably presented as occupying a superior intellectual vantage point to theirs. It is rather the case that the attempts of individuals to describe contemporary experiences in the particular vocabulary that is familiar to them (the general with his strategic analysis, the *Salondame* with her comfort zones of 'soul' and 'feeling') are presented as partial attempts to grasp the nature of the world they inhabit – 'partial' both in the sense that they are necessarily limited in perspective and that they are partisan in spirit. Musil himself described the narrative style he sought to cultivate in the work as 'konstruktive Ironie', by which he meant that the evocation of one type of character or social mind-set would simultaneously reveal implications for other types in their particular social situations; and he made it clear that even the author could not be excluded from this effect.[9]

What, then, should we note about the way Ulrich himself is characterised, about the relationship in which he stands to Viennese society, and about the implications of the work's title? The notion of a 'Mann

9   'Ironie ist: einen Klerikalen so darstellen, daß neben ihm auch ein Bolschewik getroffen ist, einen Trottel so darstellen, daß der Autor plötzlich fühlt: das bin ich ja zum Teil selbst' (p. 1939).

ohne Eigenschaften' is introduced earlier in the text than any details of Ulrich's biography. It is strongly associated with the concept of 'Möglichkeitssinn', which is to say the capacity to treat the world that presents itself to us empirically as no more deserving of recognition and respect than the world as it might be (pp. 16–17). The 'Mann ohne Eigenschaften' is initially introduced to us, in fact, through the house he inhabits, which is itself indicative of the position of detachment he has adopted in relation to the social world around him: it is situated on one of the thoroughfares that connect the city centre to the suburbs and it is of elaborately mixed style, as if chosen to resist any notion of a correspondence between the character of the residence and the personality of the owner (p. 12, cf. 20). We are told on the same page that the 'Mann ohne Eigenschaften' currently 'does nothing', and among the details that we are later given of Ulrich's life, we are told that he has recently returned to Vienna at the age of 32 after an extended period of study and professional activity elsewhere, having resolved to take a year's 'Urlaub von seinem Leben' in order to decide what to do with his life (p. 47). But the circumstances in which he pursues this aim are by no means as detached from social and historical factors as this rather abstract initial description might suggest. The house in question is a small mansion ('Schlößchen') which bears clearly identifiable traces of the various architectural styles that had dominated in the seventeenth, eighteenth and nineteenth centuries respectively, whereas Ulrich has simply left it to the judgement of commercial suppliers to furnish the interior according to the conventional expectations of the day (p. 21). Moreover, the description of the house has also been used as a pretext for introducing us to Ulrich's father, whose surname is suppressed, we are told, in order to preserve him from embarrassment, and upon whose income Ulrich remains dependent. It transpires that Ulrich's desire for practical and intellectual independence is conceived in opposition to his father's firmly established position as a leading legal authority and to the sense of propriety and 'reality' with which the father is identified by virtue of that position. By the same token, the conception of Ulrich as a 'Mann ohne Eigenschaften' is defined in contradistinction to the world of citizens 'mit Eigenschaften', i.e. people with a clearly deter-mined role in the social world they inhabit (pp. 14–15). We also find his childhood friend Walter ostensibly coining the phrase 'Mann ohne Eigenschaften' as an epithet for Ulrich, precisely in order to express the peculiarly aloof relationship in which he stands to conventional perceptions of social identity (pp. 64–65); and there are even moments when the rigidly predetermined character of the social world as Ulrich experiences it is said to make him wish he were indeed a 'Mann ohne Eigenschaften' (p. 130). The sense of what it means to be a 'Mann ohne Eigenschaften', then, acquires definition only in relation to the social world from which Ulrich has set out to detach himself.

There are, however, also senses in which Ulrich's problems are presented to us as characteristic of his time and his generation. His frustration with the society he inhabits has much to do with his disappointment that all the potential for intellectual innovation and cultural renewal that had seemed to be there when he was ten years younger, i.e. around the turn of the century, now appears to have been dissipated (pp. 54–58). His friend Walter evidently shares that sense of frustration – except that Walter's conception of the problem seems to be stuck in the categories of Nietzsche's early polemics against nineteenth-century academic culture. At the precise moment when he hits on the phrase 'Mann ohne Eigenschaften' as a description of Ulrich, Walter also applies the term to a human type that he believes to be prevalent in the present age, and goes on to fulminate against the cumulative tendency towards intellectualisation and abstract calculation that he believes to be the cause of this development: in the contemporary world, he maintains, it is only Catholic priests who continue to look their part, 'Weil wir unseren Kopf noch unpersönlicher gebrauchen als unsere Hände,' and he immediately adds, 'aber Mathematik, das ist der Gipfel' (p. 64). Ulrich's own reflections on the issue bear no such animus against the depersonalising effects of economic and social modernisation, and aim rather to arrive at an adequate understanding of the developments that have brought these effects about. The relation in which Ulrich's perception of himself stands to the historical situation that both he, the protagonist, and Musil, the author, are trying to grasp, is vividly captured in the following passage from one of Ulrich's reflections:

> Hat man nicht bemerkt, daß sich die Erlebnisse vom Menschen unabhängig gemacht haben? Sie sind aufs Theater gegangen; in die Bücher, in die Berichte der Forschungsstätten und Forschungsreisen, in die Gesinnungs- und Religionsgemeinschaften, die bestimmte Arten des Erlebens auf Kosten der anderen ausbilden wie in einem sozialen Experimentalversuch [...]; wer kann da heute

noch sagen, daß sein Zorn wirklich sein Zorn ist, wo ihm so viele Leute dreinreden und es besser verstehen als er?! Es ist eine Welt von Eigenschaften ohne Mann entstanden, von Erlebnissen ohne den, der sie erlebt, und es sieht beinahe aus, als ob im Idealfall der Mensch überhaupt nichts mehr privat erleben werde und die freundliche Schwere der persönlichen Verantwortung sich in ein Formelsystem von möglichen Bedeutungen auflösen solle. Wahrscheinlich ist die Auflösung des anthropozentrischen Verhaltens, das den Menschen so lange Zeit für den Mittelpunkt des Weltalls gehalten hat, aber nun schon seit Jahrhunderten im Schwinden ist, endlich beim Ich selbst angelangt, denn der Glaube, am Erleben sei das wichtigste, daß man es erlebe, und am Tun, daß man es tue, fängt an, den meisten Menschen als Naivität zu erscheinen. (p. 150)

Ulrich's perception of the historical world he inhabits, then, is dominated by the sense that human beings now live in mass societies where the nature of their experiences and activities is more adequately represented in statistical terms than as the accomplishment of any individual will, and where the very nature of personality can be analysed in terms of a multiplicity of factors at work. The dissolution of an anthropocentric outlook, which, as Ulrich surmises, has now reached the very notion of the self, is itself the result of human intellectual activity, the outcome of a process that has taken place over centuries, and in which he himself participates as an accomplished mathematician. The consequence of this process, however, is not a descent into randomness, because it remains possible to characterise Ulrich in individual psychological terms, as Musil proceeds to do in the next chapter; and in the meantime Ulrich is shown to possess an awareness of himself as a thinking being capable of adopting an intellectual position from which he can discern (and look down on) the attitudes and assumptions of others. The quoted paragraph ends with the statement, 'mit einemmal mußte sich Ulrich angesichts dieser Bedenken lächelnd eingestehn, daß er mit alledem ja doch ein Charakter sei, auch ohne einen zu haben' (p. 150).

A further theme that the novel develops is that of the implications of this abstracted and decentred conception of human identity in the modern world for the issue of moral responsibility. The problem is touched on in a general way as early as the second chapter, where the 'Mann ohne Eigenschaften' is seen responding to the seemingly aimless bustle of the urban world with the comment that the individual is free to do as he likes because 'es kommt in diesem Gefilz von Kräften nicht im geringsten darauf an' (p. 13). In the early chapters of Part III, on the other hand, Ulrich is confronted with situations that require him to refine his thinking about specific moral issues when his sister Agathe presents him with hypothetical scenarios relating to her unhappy marriage, and more particularly when she illicitly amends their father's will in order to disadvantage her husband: in these circumstances Ulrich is compelled to reflect not only on the terms in which he would prefer to analyse human motivation (pp. 734–45), but also on how best to justify human actions retrospectively in the eyes of society (pp. 792–802).[10] Ulrich's capacity for moral engagement is also demonstrated by the fact that he uses his first visit to a high government official (a visit that will ultimately lead to his involvement in the 'Parallelaktion') to plead for clemency on behalf of a condemned man (p. 85), and the extensive treatment that the criminal case in question receives in the text is indicative of the importance Musil himself attached to the analysis of contextual evidence in the appraisal of extreme forms of human behaviour. The condemned man, Moosbrugger, has been depicted in the press as a 'Lustmörder' because it is beyond doubt that he has murdered a prostitute in a frenzied knife attack; the chapter in which Moosbrugger is introduced, however, reconstructs the story of his life as an itinerant carpenter, making it clear to what extent he has been excluded from conventional society and brutalised by the way others have treated him. It is a life in which the opposite sex has remained mysterious to him, with the result that the persistent attentions of the prostitute in question appeared aggressive to him, and that he responded to her behaviour with a mixture of desire, repulsion and panic, but also that in the course of his life he had come to identify so closely with the emotional ambivalence of his own reactions to others that his attack on her can be seen as a desperate attempt to cut himself free from a part of himself: 'er stach so lange auf sie ein, bis er sie ganz von sich losgetrennt hatte' (p. 74). What has caught Ulrich's attention is the manifest contradiction between the brutality of Moosbrugger's act and the overwhelming appearance of benevolence in his facial features when he appears in court. Whereas the press is intent on reading all manner of motivations into the smile that

10   On these aspects, see David Midgley, 'Experiments of a "free spirit". Musil's explorations of creative morality in *Der Mann ohne Eigenschaften*', in Rüdiger Görner and Duncan Large (eds), *Ecce Opus – Nietzsche Revisions in the Twentieth Century* (Göttingen, 2003), pp. 111–24.

comes over Moosbrugger's face when he knows he is being watched,[11] and the legal and medical professions can only resort to predetermined categories when assessing his fitness to plead (pp. 242–44), both Ulrich and the author are concerned to understand the process whereby the 'gärende organische Substanz' (p. 70) of Moosbrugger's existence came to be deployed in such a way as to bring his act about. As Ulrich reflects elsewhere, humanity, depending on the circumstances in which it is placed, is just as capable of cannibalism as it is of the critique of pure reason (p. 361).

As far as Ulrich's personal life is concerned, the sense of purpose he seeks might be summarised as a form of moral orientation that is consistent with the current state of knowledge provided by scientific analysis, and which does not collapse into the sort of antiquated intellectual schemes he encounters in the conventional terminology of the lawyers and psychiatrists associated with the Moosbrugger case.[12] In the course of the chapter which gives the most concentrated account of Ulrich's sense of a problem, we are told that if he were to be asked, while engaged in the pursuit of mathematical or scientific inquiry, what his goal was, his answer would be that the only question truly worth pursuing is that of how to live a good life ('die des rechten Lebens', p. 255). The same chapter also makes it clear that he is looking for ways to mediate between the language of exactitude ('Genauigkeit') as he finds it deployed in specific intellectual disciplines on the one hand, and such questions of humanity as beauty, justice, love and faith on the other, with which the exponents of those disciplines do not concern themselves (p. 250). It is also made clear here to what extent Ulrich sees himself doing battle with the woolly thinking he encounters in the world around him and which he recognises as a manifestation of reaction against the exactitude of science. The complexity of the task he has set himself and the intricacy of the emotional and psychological inquiries it involves are

11   'Es mochte ein verlegenes Lächeln sein oder ein verschlagenes, ein ironisches, heimtückisches, schmerzliches, irres, blutrünstiges, unheimliches –: sie tasteten ersichtlich nach widersprechenden Ausdrücken und schienen in diesem Lächeln verzweifelt etwas zu suchen, das sie offenbar in der ganzen redlichen Erscheinung sonst nirgends fanden' (p. 68).

12   Cf. p. 251: 'Die Moral im gewöhnlichen Sinn war für Ulrich nicht mehr als die Altersform eines Kräftesystems, das nicht ohne Verlust an ethischer Kraft mit ihr verwechselt werden darf.'

major contributory factors to the delay and uncertainty that bedevilled Musil's work on the text after 1933. As far as we can judge from the portions of the text that were completed before 1933, however, Ulrich is initially very frustrated at the lack of progress he is making with his project (pp. 256f), but he develops a new sense of resolve after the death of his father and the retreat from the social world this brings with it (p. 722).

If it is possible to discern a sense of structure in the account of how his quest proceeds, it is to be found in the models Ulrich conceives for particular kinds of approach to life, which are referred to in the text as his 'utopias'. By the time he begins his 'Urlaub von seinem Leben' he has already recognised the folly of trying to apply the scientific principle of precise experimental observation, summarised as the 'Utopie der Exaktheit' (pp. 246–47), to the sphere of the human passions and to questions of morality. Instead he has adopted a rather more literary approach, the 'Utopie des Essayismus', which entails treating any issue from a variety of angles without reducing it to a fixed concept (p. 250), but with the aim of arriving at a stable form of self-awareness. In the sense that Musil gives the term here, 'ein Essay ist nicht der vor- oder nebenläufige Ausdruck einer Überzeugung [...] sondern [...] die einmalige und unabänderliche Gestalt, die das innere Leben eines Menschen in einem entscheidenden Gedanken annimmt' (p. 253). It is unclear from Musil's posthumous notes how this ideal in its turn might ultimately have appeared in the light of Ulrich's later experiences, although there are some indications that the ending of the novel could have been planned in such a way that the 'Utopie des Essayismus' was eventually supplanted by a third model, the title of which suggests a reintegration of his approach to life with the given facts of social existence: Musil calls it the 'Utopie der induktiven Gesinnung'.[13] In any case, formulating the ideal (or 'utopia') of essayism is not the same thing as finding the 'decisive idea' around which, it is hoped, that crystallisation of one's 'inner life' into a 'Gestalt' will occur; moreover, the abundant psychological reflection that is built into the text makes it clear that any such decisive moment of self-recognition cannot be

---

13   See pp. 1877–87, where Musil also discusses further differentiations among the
      utopias Ulrich might experiment with, including those that relate more specifically
      to the life he leads in Part III, when he is reunited with his sister.

straightforwardly brought about by an act of will. In addition, Ulrich's attempts to achieve that sense of inner stability in his life are subject to intermittent distractions, not only in the form of the 'Parallelaktion' and the general vicissitudes of life, but also in the form of transient erotic encounters. Even after he has shaken off the more frivolous relationships that have initially come his way on his return to Vienna, Ulrich – young and virile as he is – continues to be made aware of his own sexual impulses, whether in his dealings with Diotima or Clarisse (who wants him to be the father of her child), or in encounters with prostitutes or other women on the streets. The intensive intimacy of Ulrich's relationship with his sister Agathe, depicted in Part III of the work, demonstrates at length that there is a continuous range of emotional experiences connecting the quasi-mystical awareness of self and world, of which the 'Utopie des Essayismus' provides at best an intellectual sketch, to the purely physical manifestation of sexuality. When the latter asserts itself in the absence of the former, the result is an emotional catastrophe: having persuaded himself that he can play the role of redeemer in the life of a significantly younger woman, the daughter of a bank director, Ulrich finds, when she visits him, that the automatic expectation of sex to which both he and she succumb prompts an uncontrollable display of revulsion on her part (pp. 562–63, 617–24). Even in the case of his relationship with his sister Agathe, an extensively drafted early scenario brings out the potential for a powerful sexual momentum to culminate in severe disappointment and disgust (pp. 1651–75).

In the text as we have it, it is the deferral of outcomes – of the search for a theme in the 'Parallelaktion', of Ulrich's search for a sense of purpose, but also of the débâcle of either quest – that creates the fictional space in which Musil can conduct the extensive investigation of his themes. It is the sense of a goal to which both the public and the private plot might ultimately move that provides the sense of overall trajectory for the narrative; and it is the manner in which Ulrich himself is shown to be feeling his way towards an articulation of insights that often provides a sense of trajectory within individual chapters. Just as the conception of the work as a whole is maintained in a relationship of tension with the idea of a novel, then, so too are the individual chapters maintained in a relationship of tension with the idea of an essay – not necessarily in the specific sense that this term acquires in the context of

Ulrich's 'Utopie des Essayismus', but in a sense that is not unrelated to it either.[14] What this involves in practice varies according to the position and function of the individual chapter within the arrangement of the whole: in Parts I and II, where the narrative evocation of the historical world of late Habsburg Austria dominates, the potential for plot development is often suppressed or deferred in favour of analytical description or reflective disquisition; in Part III, where the focus shifts to Ulrich's introspective inquiries, the reverse is often the case and the plot developments that continue to occur in the world of the 'Parallelaktion' appear as intrusions upon the efforts of the individual to arrive at a sustainable basis for giving his life a meaning.

In a late note towards an afterword for *Der Mann ohne Eigenschaften*, Musil wrote, 'ich bitte mich zweimal zu lesen, im Teil u[nd] im Ganzen' (p. 1941). The reader who engages with the text sufficiently to absorb those portions of it that were not published during Musil's lifetime is likely to find that a subsequent re-reading of individual chapters acquires an additional savour from the irony with which particular themes and motifs are treated elsewhere in the text. I hope that this brief exposition has given a clear enough sense of what the work as a whole is about for readers to discover for themselves, through their exploration of particular chapters and themes, why *Der Mann ohne Eigenschaften* enjoys the reputation it does for being an enormously stimulating – as well as a formidably ambitious – enrichment of the form of the novel in the twentieth century.

14   For a full and illuminating discussion of Musil's conception of the essay and of essayism, see Jacques Bouveresse, 'Genauigkeit und Leidenschaft: Das Problem des Essays und des Essayismus im Werk von Musil', *Musil-Forum*, 29 (2005/2006), pp. 1–56.

ROBERT VILAIN

Mann, *Doktor Faustus*

Thomas Mann's *Doktor Faustus* is modestly subtitled 'Das Leben des deutschen Tonsetzers Adrian Leverkühn erzählt von einem Freunde', but this is the only modest thing about it. It is not so much a landmark in the history of the German novel as an attempt to comprehend, describe, subsume, perhaps even redeem Germany itself. It is so German that its narrator believed it even resisted translation, claiming 'daß seine Über-setzung ins Englische sich, wenigstens in gewissen, allzu wurzelhaft deutschen Partien, als ein Ding der Unmöglichkeit erweisen würde'.[1] There is perhaps a degree of arrogance inherent in the mere attempt to write a new German Faust in the wake of Goethe's monumental creation, taking up anew what is perhaps *the* quintessentially German theme. But to undertake this using the medium that Mann repeatedly claimed was peculiarly and definitively German – music – and to set it against a historical backdrop that runs from the death of Emperor Otto III in 1002 AD, via Martin Luther and the German Reformation, to Hitler and the German catastrophe, may look little short of hubris.

The novel works on a number of levels simultaneously. One layer gives an account of the life, career and death of the composer Adrian Leverkühn, the last decade or so of which is spent in mental collapse cause by tertiary syphilis contracted, if not deliberately, then at least with full awareness of the risk, from a prostitute. Another explores a crisis of art that is not merely the individual problem of the novel's principal character but reflects Mann's views on Western European music in the first half of the twentieth century and the nature of art in general. A third layer charts Germany's decline and collapse into barbarism under the

---

1   Thomas Mann, *Doktor Faustus. Das Leben des deutschen Tonsetzers Adrian Leverkühn erzählt von einem Freunde, Gesammelte Werke in zwölf Bänden*, Vol. 6 (Frankfurt a. M., 1960), pp. 668–69. Unless otherwise stated, references are to this volume. References to other parts of the *Gesammelte* Werke are followed by the volume number and then the page.

leadership of Adolf Hitler. These layers are held together by the Faust myth and the theme of time.

The importance of the Faust figure to the first and third of those levels is manifest. In Chapter 25 Leverkühn's Faustian pact is outlined in a conversation with the Devil, whom the composer calls Sammael, the Angel of Death, but the pact merely confirms the sacrifice of health and normality that Leverkühn has already made in Chapter 19 by sleeping with the prostitute he calls Esmeralda, whose 'Zuhälter' is the Devil himself. What Leverkühn has renounced is love: 'Liebe ist dir verboten, insofern sie wärmt. Dein Leben soll kalt sein – darum darfst du keinen Menschen lieben' (p. 332). Leverkühn overtly regards himself as a Faustian figure, and his last work is a self-referential musical reconstruction of the Faust legend, *Dr. Fausti Weheklag*. Germany's Faustian pact was made in 1933 with the election of Hitler as Chancellor, but that, too, confirmed a gradual sacrifice of the nation's political and moral health made over the previous decade with the rise of National Socialism. The development and fate of Leverkühn is often linked with the history and condition of Germany.[2] After discussing the novel with Alfred Neumann, Mann notes in *Die Entstehung des Doktor Faustus*,

> Vermutlich war es die Flucht aus den Schwierigkeiten der Kulturkrise in den Teufelspakt, der Durst eines stolzen und von Sterilität bedrohten Geistes nach Enthemmung um jeden Preis und die Parallelisierung verderblicher, in den Kollaps mündender Eurphorie mit dem faschistischen Völkerrausch, was ihn am meisten beeindruckte. (*Werke*, Vol. 11, pp. 163–64)

These parallels go back nearly a thousand years to Emperor Otto III, who – in the novel only – is buried in Kaisersaschern, Leverkühn's birthplace. Otto is described by Zeitblom as 'ein Musterbeispiel deutscher Selbst-Antipathie' (p. 51), and there is some of his anti-Germanness in Leverkühn, too, who calls his compatriots 'ein konfuses Volk [...] und für die andern verwirrend': 'Die Deutschen', he says,

---

2   See for example John J. White, *Mythology in the Modern Novel: A Study in Prefigurative Techniques* (Princeton, NJ, 1971): 'Mann succeeds in insinuating that such an assignment with evil may be an inherent part of modern German's historical role: that the country was as fated to make a pact with National Socialism as Faustus or Leverkühn were to sign one with the devil.' (p. 152)

haben eine doppelgeleisige und unerlaubt kombinatorische Art des Denkens [...]. Sie sind imstande, antithetische Denk- und Daseinsprinzipien in großen Persönlichkeiten kühn herauszustellen. Aber dann vermantschen sie sie, [...] bringen alles durcheinander und meinen, sie können Freiheit und Vornehmheit, Idealismus und Naturkindlichkeit unter einen Hut bringen. Das geht aber wahrscheinlich nicht. (p. 115)

An entry in Mann's diary for May 1944 links Adrian to Otto III in respect of 'Antipathie gegen das Deutschtum',[3] and as a young man Adrian seems to have an affinity with France and England, setting their poetry to music, for example. After contracting syphilis, however, he becomes much more focused on Germany.

Some of the parallels between Leverkühn and Germany are made explicit in the novel: his artistic 'Durchbruch' and Germany's 'Durchbruch zur Weltmacht' in 1914 (p. 408), for example, his precarious health and the decline of Germany after 1918 (p. 454), the upturn of his spirits in 1919 and the establishment of the Weimar Republic and the arrival of democracy (p. 468).[4] There are contemporary cultural and political references in the proto-Nazi Kridwiss circle of intellectuals who greet the overthrow of the bourgeois humanism that Zeitblom represents with such enthusiasm (p. 485). Their embrace of the primitive, encouraged by Dr Chaim Breisacher, is echoed by the return to medieval polyphony in Leverkühn's *Apocalipsis cum figuris*: 'dieses bedrohliche Werk', says Zeitblom, aims to unveil 'das Tier im Menschen' and has

---

3   Thomas Mann, *Tagebücher 1944–46*, ed. by I. Jens (Frankfurt a. M., 1986), p. 61. Quoted by Ritchie Robertson, 'Accounting for History. Thomas Mann, *Doktor Faustus*', *The German Novel in the Twentieth Century*, ed. by David Midgley (Edinburgh, 1993), pp.128–48 (p. 142).

4   Ritchie Robertson lists a number of others, less explicit, ending with the parallel between the eleven years of Nazi rule and Leverkühn's eleven years of insanity. See Robertson, 'Accounting for History', p. 143. See also Jochen Strobel, *Entzauberung der Nation. Die Repräsentation Deutschlands im Werk Thomas Manns* (Dresden, 2000), esp. Chapter 6, 'Thomas Manns Faustroman: Eine Allegorie Deutschlands im 20. Jahrhundert', pp. 237–92 and Hans Wißkirchen, 'Verbotene Liebe. Das Deutschland-Thema im "Doktor Faustus"', in *'Und was werden die Deutschen sagen?' Thomas Manns Roman Doktor Faustus*, ed. by Hans Wysling and Thomas Sprecher (Lübeck, 1998), pp. 179–207. Osman Durrani gives a tabular summary of parallels in *Fictions of German. Images of the German Nation in the Modern Novel* (Edinburgh, 1994), pp. 109–10.

been accused both of 'blutiger Barbarismus' and 'blutlose Intellektu-
alität' (p. 496).[5]

However, more of Germany is present in this novel than contemporary or recent historical parallels. The spirit and personnel of the
Reformation feature in bold figures such as Professors Kumpf and
Schleppfuss, two of Leverkühn's teachers in Halle, the former reminiscent of aspects of Martin Luther. Nietzsche is present, too, in details
of the plot, such as a visit to a Cologne brothel and his descent into
madness – although the life of Hugo Wolf may also have contributed to
this – and in the cause of that madness, syphilis. The idea of 'creative
sterility overcome by desperate means in the absence of natural vitality
obviously draws on a facet of Nietzsche's cultural analysis'.[6] As Mann
himself points out, his Devil cites Nietzsche's *Ecce Homo*, the triangular
relationship between Leverkühn, Schwerdtfeger and Marie Godeau
echoes Nietzsche's own indirect proposals of marriage (to Lou Andreas-
Salomé and Fräulein Trampedach) via intermediaries,[7] and the final
image of Leverkühn that Zeitblom draws for us, the 'Ecce homo-
Antlitz', is famously reminiscent of Nietzsche's own physiognomy
(pp. 674–75).

Character, nation and art, specifically music, were the three aspects
of the novel that I suggested were bound together by the figure of Faust,
but the last of these is least obviously Faustian. Why should Thomas
Mann's Leverkühn be a composer rather than, say, a writer, like Gustav
von Aschenbach or so many more of the author's central fictional
creations? In a lecture entitled 'Deutschland und die Deutschen'
delivered in Washington in May 1945, Mann tells us directly:

> Die Musik ist dämonisches Gebiet [...]. Sie ist christliche Kunst mit negativem
> Vorzeichen. Sie ist berechneteste Ordnung und chaosträchtige Wider-Vernunft
> zugleich, [...] abstrakt und mystisch. Soll Faust der Representant der deutschen
> Seele sein, so müßte er musikalisch sein; denn abstrakt und mystisch, das heißt

5   The members of this circle all have real historical counterparts. See Gunilla
     Bergsten, *Thomas Manns 'Doktor Faustus'.Untersuchungen zu den Quellen und
     zur Struktur des Romans* (Tübingen, 1974), pp. 40–41.
6   Michael Beddow, *Thomas Mann:Doktor Faustus* (Cambridge, 1994), p. 10.
7   See *Die Entstehung des 'Doktor Faustus'*, *Werke*, Vol. 11, pp. 165–66. For more
     detailed assessments of the importance of Nietzsche for the novel, see Bergsten,
     Thomas Manns Doktor Faustus, or T. J. Reed, *Thomas Mann. The Uses of
     Tradition* (Oxford, 1974), pp. 367–81.

musikalisch, ist das Verhältnis des Deutschen zur Welt, – das Verhältnis eines dämonisch angehauchten Professors, ungeschickt und dabei von dem hochmütigen Bewußtsein bestimmt, der Welt an 'Tiefe' überlegen zu sein.

Worin besteht diese Tiefe? Eben in der Musikalität der deutschen Seele, dem, was man ihre Innerlichkeit nennt, das heißt: dem Auseinanderfallen des spekulativen und des gesellschaftlich-politischen Elements menschlicher Energie und der völligen Prävalenz des ersten vor dem zweiten. (*Werke*, Vol. 11, pp. 1131–32)

The association of Faust and music had already been made concretely in Oswald Spengler's *Untergang des Abendlandes* (1918–22). The section 'Apollinisch, magisch, faustisch' characterises the ancient world as Apolline (ahistorical, static), the Orient as magical (mysterious and dualistic), and the West as Faustian (historical in character, upwardly striving, dynamic).[8] In most respects Mann was profoundly hostile to the anti-cultural philosophy of Spengler, whom he once described as Nietzsche's 'kluge Affe',[9] and who is present within *Doktor Faustus* as the sinister Breisacher.[10] However, the Faustian character as described by Spengler is one that watches itself, remains constantly conscious of itself, but is one of boundless loneliness, and this is one of the first characterisations that Zeitblom gives of his friend Leverkühn: 'Ich möchte seine Einsamkeit einem Abgrund vergleichen, in welchem Gefühle, die man ihm entgegenbrachte, lautlos und spurlos untergingen' (p. 13).[11] Spengler also says that the Faustian West is characterised above all, and uniquely, by music; music, especially instrumental music, the string quartet and the violin sonata, is for him the only true articulation of Faustian dynamism. If the music he has in mind is usually heavily romantically tinged, unlike Leverkühn's twelve-tone compositions, he too dreams of an absolute form of music in geometric terms, likening the

8   See also Wolfgang Krebs, 'Kultur, Musik und der "Untergang des Abendlandes"', *Archiv für Musikwissenschaft*, 55 (1998), 311–31 (esp. pp. 318–19).

9   In a letter to Ida Boy-Ed of 5 December 1922; Thomas Mann, *Briefe 1889–1936*, ed. by Erika Mann (Frankfurt a. M., 1961), p. 202.

10   See Helmut Koopmann, 'The Decline of the West and the Ascent of the East: Thomas Mann, the Joseph Novels, and Spengler', in *Critical Essays on Thomas Mann*, ed. by Inta M. Erzageilis (Boston, MA, 1988), pp. 238–65 (esp. pp. 254–5); this essay was originally published in German in *Jahrbuch der deutschen Schillergesellschaft*, 24 (1980), 300–31.

11   See also Oswald Spengler, *Der Untergang des Abendlandes*, Vol. 1 (Munich, 1923), pp. 237–41.

ground bass to Baroque mathematics, for example. Mann's association
between the Faust legend and music is deeply rooted.

The other element that I suggested bound the novel together was the
theme of time. Mann began work on *Doktor Faustus* in 1943, exiled in
California: 'Gedanken an den alten Novellenplan "Dr. Faust". Umschau
nach Lektüre' is a diary entry for 14 March of that year; 'Faust wieder
lesen' had been entered on 4 May 1941. A plan for *Doktor Faustus*
seems to have been started on 17 March 1943, when Mann noted:
'Scham und Rührung beim Wiedersehen mit diesen Jugendschmerzen'
after noting potential parallels with 'Tonio Kröger'.[12] Interestingly
Mann was reading Stevenson's *Dr Jekyll and Mr Hyde* at the same time.
The plan can be traced back to a note on Faust from 1904 – the 'alter
Novellenplan' Mann referred to in his diary – and the theme had been a
fairly constant presence again from about 1933.[13] The novel appeared
late in 1947 in the Stockholm *Gesamtausgabe* but was not readily
available in Germany for some time after that.[14]

The novel's internal narrative operates on a number of different
temporal levels. The narrator – whose highly eloquent name is *Zeit*blom
– claims to be setting down his words during a period covering the last
two years of the second world war, 1943 to 1945, and his account of
Adrian Leverkühn's life is punctuated by military news, reflections on
the progress of the war and the imminence of Germany's defeat – he
comments on the Allied bombings, for example (p. 50), U-Boot warfare
(p. 229), and on how an American general makes the inhabitants of
Weimar walk past the Buchenwald concentration camp (p. 637). The
narrated time reaches further back, spanning the life of the composer
from 1885 to 1940, but the substance of the novel reaches even further
back than that, into Luther's Germany, into the world of the Faust chap-
books. It also reaches forward, so to speak, for it is an eschatological
novel, a work about judgement and the final destiny of the soul, not only
the death of Leverkühn but the potential for an end to music and the
possible extinction of civilisation. Finally, the nature of Leverkühn's

---

12   Diary entries quoted from Helmut Koopmann, 'Doktor Faustus', in *Thomas-Mann-
      Handbuch*, ed. by Helmut Koopmann (Stuttgart, 1990), p. 476.
13   See Hermann Kurzke, *Thomas Mann. Epoche – Werk – Wirkung* (Munich, 1985),
      p. 269.
14   Late 1948, according to a letter to Peter Suhrkamp of 2 January 1949.

musical breakthrough in the novel is that it strives for the suspension of time and the conversion of linear melodic and harmonic progress into repeated cyclical patterns.[15] The two unifying themes, Faust and time, are themselves linked, as Judith Ryan implies when writing of the presence of the Faust myth in the novel: 'what once took the guise of magic now appears as a response to a certain cultural situation, a particular juncture in the history of aesthetics and politics. Underlying these transformations, however, is the hypothesis of a perennial recurrence in which basic myths reveal themselves again in new forms'.[16]

Just such a cycle, topographical rather than temporal or mythical, emerges from the novel's earliest chapters. Adrian Leverkühn grew up on a farm not far from 'Kaisersaschern' on the Saale. Kaisersaschern has sometimes been identified as Naumburg, but it is less important to find a geographical source than to appreciate the symbolic potential of this 'mitteldeutsche Stadt' as the home of an attitude of old-German provincialism whose values are part of the Germany that Thomas Mann – and Nietzsche, whose territory this is, too – subjects to vehement critique. It is a far cry from the decadence of Munich where later parts of the novel are set. Leverkühn spends the last 18 years of his life in Pfeiffering in Bavaria, far from his family home yet in a place that is uncannily similar to it in a number of ways identified by the narrator (pp. 39–40). Serenus Zeitblom himself is the 'Z' to Adrian's 'A', a friend from the same neighbourhood, a Catholic, however (the Leverkühns are Protestant), and whilst highly educated, he is by no means as gifted as his friend and tends to blinkeredness. There is a model for this narrative relationship in E. T. A. Hofmann's parody of the *Künstlerroman*, *Lebensansichten des Katers Murr* in which a philistine cat pens his own autobiography on the back of the manuscript of a biography of his musician master.

As a boy Adrian is intellectually curious, stimulated by his father's books on flora and fauna – at least until boredom threatens to set in – and by apparent overlaps between nature and inanimate quasi-natural forms such as crystals and droplets of liquid that appear to digest other

15 See Susan von Rohr Scaff, 'Unending Apocalypse: The Crisis of Musical Narrative in *Doctor Faustus*', in *History, Myth and Music: Thomas Mann's Timely Fiction* (Columbia, SC, 1998), pp. 66–98.

16 Judith Ryan, 'The Flower of Evil. Thomas Mann's *Doctor Faustus*', in *The Uncompleted Past: Postwar German Novels and the Third Reich* (Detroit, 1983), pp. 42–55 (p. 46).

droplets. He is in some sense religious: at one point he quotes Romans 13, in some embarrassment, to the effect that 'Was von Gott ist, das ist geordnet' (p. 64), but this is in the context of a claim that 'die Ordnung ist alles' and a defence of the supreme value of 'Ordnungsbeziehungen anzuschauen', which is a preoccupation that will shape his life. Religion elsewhere in the novel is often used as an entry-point to myth.

What soon begins to consume Leverkühn is music, albeit music of a certain kind and seen in a certain way. In other words, like many of Mann's other works, *Doktor Faustus* confronts the bourgeois and the artist, the insider with the outsider, the conformist with the transgressor. This is the root of the novel, as a note from 1905 makes clear:

> Figur des syphilitischen Künstlers: als Dr. Faust und dem Teufel Verschriebener. Das Gift wirkt als Rausch, Stimulans, Inspiration; er darf in entzückter Begeisterung geniale, wunderbare Werke schaffen, der Teufel führt ihm die Hand. Schließlich aber *holt ihn der Teufel*: Paralyse.[17]

Leverkühn himself is a nimble-minded, cool-headed, ironic intellectual, prone to migraine and sudden outbursts of laughter. He is highly self-aware: 'ich bin entschieden kalt' is how he describes himself to his music teacher, Wendell Kretzschmar, 'ich bin ein schlechter Kerl, denn ich habe keine Wärme' (p. 174), prefiguring the conditions of his pact with the Devil. He is fascinated by music, not as a form of emotional self-expression but for its abstract intellectuality, the arithmetical and geometric patterns discernible in it or creatable with it. Sitting at the harmonium he plays three notes in sequence that look as if they are about to form a chord of F sharp major but thwarts that expectation by adding an E natural that brings it into the key of B major, the dominant of F sharp. 'So ein Zusammenklang', he says, 'hat an sich keine Tonart. Alles ist Beziehung, und die Beziehung bildet den Kreis' (p. 65). 'Beziehung ist alles', he says: 'Und willst du sie näher beim Namen nennen, so ist ihr Name "Zweideutigkeit"'. Music, according to Leverkühn, is 'Zweideutigkeit als System' (p. 66).

Leverkühn dislikes music that expresses fulsome feeling, rejects the conception of a work of art as '[ein] selbstgenügsam und harmonisch in sich geschlossenes Gebilde' (p. 241), and is distracted from harmony and melody by his over-sensitivity to technical devices. Adrian is not a

---

17   Quoted from Reed, *Thomas Mann*, p. 361.

practical musician, neither a performer nor a particularly keen concert-goer; first and foremost he intellectualises music. He likens it to the 'Tricks und Zwänge' of alchemy; composition resembles 'das hermetische Laboratorium, die Goldküche' (p. 177). However, music in its current state presents Leverkühn with an impasse and threatens sterility, the paralysis of his creative gifts prompted by the insight that the possibilities of traditional tonal music are exhausted. This is not a merely personal problem: 'creative sterility is no longer the psychological problem of an individual [...] it constitutes the crisis of modern art'.[18] His initial response is parody – the savage mockery of Debussy's and Ravel's musical Impressionism in his 1905 symphonic fantasy *Meerleuchten*, a work that he later disavows as a 'Demonstration koloristisch-orchestralen Könnens' (p. 202), little better than an exercise. However, its 'intellektuelle Ironisierung der Kunst überhaupt' betrays its composer's fundamental disbelief in the value of the medium and its audiences found it 'erkältend, ja zurückstoßend und empörend'. Zeitblom summarises: 'In Wahrheit war hier das Parodistische die stolze Auskunft vor der Sterilität, mit welcher Skepsis und geistige Schamhaftigkeit, der Sinn für die tödliche Ausdehnung des Bereichs des Banalen eine große Begabung bedrohten' (p. 202–03). In his letter to Kretzschmar, Leverkühn wonders 'Warum muß es mir vorkommen, als ob fast alle, nein, alle Mittel und Konvenienzen der Kunst *heute nur noch zur Parodie taugten*?' (p. 180). In the same vein, his puppet-opera *Gesta Romanorum* is effectively a parody of Wagner.[19]

Mann himself will have had some instinctive sympathy for this. Much as he admired and actively enjoyed the music of Wagner, his considered view of its implications was much more sceptical. He believed that it had potentially pernicious consequences, that its seductive emotionalism and eroticism were actually dangerous – music is 'eine nicht eben unschuldige Kunst', he wrote in *Betrachtungen eines Unpolitischen*, 'die Beschäftigung mit ihr wird beinahe zum Laster [...] zur rücksichtslos ethischen Hingabe an das Schädliche und Verzehrende'

18 Robertson, 'Accounting for History', pp. 130–1.
19 See J. M. Stein, 'Adrian Leverkühn as a Composer', *Germanic Review*, 25 (1950), 57–74 (p. 70) and Hans Rudolf Vaget, 'Amazing Grace: Thomas Mann, Adorno and the Faust Myth', in *Our Faust? Roots and Ramifications of a Modern German Myth*, ed. by Reinhold Grimm and Jost Hermand (Madison, WI, 1987), pp. 168–89 (pp. 180–1).

(*Werke*, Vol 12, pp. 74–75). Wagner's music creates weary listlessness and weakens moral fibre – a view that the National Socialists' veneration of Wagner did nothing to modify. Nevertheless, Mann also found something repellent in too much austerity and the solution to this bind that in reality presented itself, Schoenberg's dodecaphonic system, was much less palatable to him personally. There is as much Wagner in *Doktor Faustus* as there is Schoenberg.[20]

Mann came upon this solution via Theodor Adorno, whom he met in July 1943, shortly after work had begun on *Doktor Faustus*. He was lent the manuscript of Adorno's *Philosophie der neuen Musik*, which he exploited on a large scale, above all for Kretzschmar's lectures in Chapter 8, the exposition of serial music in Chapter 23 and the 'Teufelsgespräch' in Chapter 25. They met more than a dozen times and corresponded in detail and when Mann ran into trouble in December 1945 he sent Adorno the whole of his manuscript so far for comment and in tribute inscribed part of his name (Wiesengrund) into Kretzschmar's analysis of Beethoven's last piano sonata (p. 76). The features of the Devil in Chapter 25 are clearly also those of Adorno (which must have pleased Schoenberg, with whom Mann was also in contact in America and who had something of a feud running with Adorno that later also implicated Mann).

The system that Adorno opened out to Mann appeals to Leverkühn's sense of the geometrical. Dodecaphonic music is seen by Mann as 'temporally neutral', 'musically timeless', motifs 'locked into an assemblage of symmetrical correspondences which cancel the temporal relations between intervals'.[21] The twelve-tone system treats all twelve of the notes in the equal-tempered scale (an octave of black and white keys on a piano) perfectly equally. They are arranged into a particular order or 'note row', which may be used in four ways: in its original form, backwards ('retrograde'), with each successive interval inverted (a rising minor third becoming a falling minor third, for example), and as a 'retrograde inversion' (the inverted row used backwards). When Leverkühn explains it, the pattern of four possibilities is described by Zeitblom

20   He noted in his diary on 28 September 1944, whilst working on Chapter 22 of the
      novel, 'Die Dreiklang-Welt des Ringes ist im Grunde meine musikalische Heimat'
      (Mann, *Tagebücher 1944–46*, p. 106).
21   Von Rohr Scaff, 'Unending Apocalypse', p. 66.

as 'ein magisches Quadrat' (p. 257). The note-row can be started on any one of the twelve notes of the chromatic scale and each of the four ways of using it can be applied to all twelve of the rows, giving in all forty-eight permutations of the basic row: significantly there are 47 chapters and a 'Nachschrift' in *Doktor Faustus*.[22] Music constructed from these rows will use all the notes in the row in the same order (although notes may be repeated). Zeitblom sees it as a return to an older form, the variation, and Leverkühn does not disagree: 'Interessante Lebenserscheinungen', he says, however, giving another example of the cycles that characterise the whole novel, 'haben wohl immer dies Doppelgesicht von Vergangenheit und Zukunft, wohl immer sind sie progressiv und regressiv in einem' (p. 258).

The problem that had to be overcome was creative sterility; the solution proposed was, paradoxically, an unemotional, intellectual, scrupulously rational mode of composition; the means by which it is brought about, in another paradoxical twist, was sensual intoxication. This is paradoxical not least because Leverkühn has always been wary of the sensuality of music, from his first exposure to the round songs or canons sung on the farm when he was a boy by a stable-maid with flopping breasts. What transpires, again ironically, is Leverkühn's sub-mission to erotic attraction as a means of inducing a condition of creative inspiration – which ultimately provides him with the means to achieve his breakthrough from 'the chill of musical constructivism'[23] into the

22 There is much detailed work on how more intimate echoes of 12-tone musical practice have been incorporated into the narrative structure, on the arrangement of chapters within the novel and the positioning of characters, although this is probably no more than fairly simple number symbolism (see Rosemarie Pusch-mann, *Magisches Quadrat und Melancholie in Thomas Manns 'Doktor Faustus'. Von der musikalischen Struktur zum semantischen Beziehungsnetz* [Bielefeld, 1983]). Carl Dahlhaus quotes claims by Mann himself that 'Das Buch, ein Musik-Roman [...] sucht zu sein wovon er handelt', but he is adamant that 'von einer Strukturverwandschaft mit Schoenbergs Reihentechnik [...] kann nicht die Rede sein'. See Carl Dahlhaus, 'Fiktive Zwölftonmusik. Thomas Mann und Theodor W. Adorno', *Jahrbuch der Deutschen Akademie für Sprache und Dichtung*, 1 [1982], 33–49 (pp. 33–4). Mann liked to think of his works in musical terms, writing of them in *Betrachtungen eines Unpolitischen*, 'gute Partituren waren sie immer' (Vol. 12, p. 319). Ironically there is more of a Wagnerian leitmotif technique evident in the narrative texture of the novel than Schoenberg's twelve-tone rows.

23 Vaget, 'Amazing Grace', p. 181.

hellish, chaos of his oratorio *Apocalipsis cum figuris* of 1919, which Zeitblom describes as 'eine inständige Bitte um die Seele' (p. 501).

The Devil tells Leverkühn that he has engineered the meeting with Esmeralda. On a tour of the town, Adrian is hungry, but instead of being taken to a 'Gasthaus', he is led by a servant uncannily and devilishly similar to one of his theology professors in Halle to a brothel. Embarrassed by a profusion of semi-clad women, he crosses the room and strikes a few chords on the piano, and is touched briefly on the way by one particular prostitute, whom he names Esmeralda. A year later he tracks this woman down in Pressburg and insists on sleeping with her despite her admission that she is infected with syphilis, which he contracts in turn. Two doctors, eloquently named Dr Erasmi and Dr Zimbalist, die or are arrested mysteriously, so he gives up his attempt to seek treatment. It may be an exaggeration to say that he contracts syphilis deliberately, a disease that he knows will eventually destroy his mind, albeit in such a manner as to free him from intellectual inhibition, but it is nonetheless clear that some semi- or wholly unconscious psychological process is taking place, a process of which the Devil is a projection: it constitutes a decision and the formation of a pact. The link of disease and art that is so important to this novel is made well before the events in Leipzig in 1905 and in Pressburg in 1906. During their schooldays, when Zeitblom urges Adrian's music teacher Kretzschmar to restrain Adrian's intellectual ardour to spare his health, he is told, 'Ja, lieber Freund, wenn Sie für Gesundheit sind, – mit Geist und Kunst hat die denn wohl freilich nicht viel zu tun, sie steht sogar in einem gewissen Kontrast dazu, und jedenfalls hat das eine ums andere sich nie viel gekümmert' (p. 98). Mann's care in integrating each element into the Faust story is evident from the dates: Adrian sleeps with Esmeralda in 1906; he succumbs completely to madness in 1930, and the intervening 24 years correspond both to the traditional length of the Faustian pact and to one of the key multiples of the twelve-tone system of music that he develops.

Serenus Zeitblom is himself a complex figure. Although a childhood friend of Leverkühn's and a little older than him, as a retired and by no means distinguished schoolmaster, Zeitblom is always wholly in awe of him and his achievements – which produces the uniquely amusing combination of paternalism and subservience that permeates the narrative. If he is (with some reservations) a good man, sober, educated, a humanist, intent upon intellectual integrity, he is not perhaps a very good narrator – indeed he is in some respects a parody of a narrator, a biographer who spends a good deal of the opening chapters drawing attention to his own failings as a biographer, taking so long to get round to his subject, making so many false starts, interjections, distracting interpolations and apologies for doing so that the reader is torn between frustration and amusement. His opening words are 'Mit aller Bestimmtheit will ich versichern, daß es keineswegs aus dem Wunsche geschieht, meine Person in den Vordergrund zu schieben, wenn ich . . .' (p. 9) – a sentence that instantly achieves the opposite of its stated aim and takes some eight laborious lines to reach grammatical completion. There is similar awkwardness evident on a structural level: Zeitblom does not think it appropriate to write long chapters; he also considers it bad form to let a single topic extend over more than one chapter; but doing justice to Leverkühn's oratorio *Dr. Fausti Weheklag* means he has to break one or other of these rules so he divides his chapter into three, Chapters '34', '34 continued' and '34 conclusion'.

What should one make of Zeitblom? He can be rather narrow-minded – he has no time at all for the natural sciences, for example (p. 28) – and somewhat self-satisfied. In the matter of the ring given to Adrian by Frau von Tolna his incomplete learning leads him to misinterpretation; and whilst Mann might have wanted to omit much discussion of Goethe in this novel, the almost total absence of references to Weimar and the Classical Age in German literary and cultural history has consequences for our view of the narrator. Personally, too, he seems somewhat unemotional, and if always loyal to his wife – whom he seems to have chosen because of her classical name rather than for reasons of love – he is not always faithful to her, and has an affair on the basis that it represents personal experience of a classical ideal of sexual liberation. This very measured approach to relationships does not apply to Leverkühn, of course, whom he not only idolises but also adores, but this is not a wholly positive feature since it inclines him to make excuses for his descent into demonic barbarism. Leverkühn clearly represents Germany in this respect, but Zeitblom himself has no less a representative function: he and Leverkühn need to be read together if what Mann called 'das Geheimnis ihrer Identität' (*Werke*, Vol. 11, p. 204) is to be appreciated.

His delusions and special pleading notwithstanding, Zeitblom's devotion is sincere, his intentions honest, and his faults perhaps compre-

hensible under the pressure of the age and in the face of genius. For all
the sententiousness potentially present in the final words of the novel, it
is difficult not to be moved by them: 'Ein einsamer Mann faltet seine
Hände und spricht: Gott sei eurer armen Seele gnädig, mein Freund, mein
Vaterland' (p. 676). The gesture is both resigned and supplicating; the
prayer applies to the man and to the nation; there is judgement in there but
there is humility, too. There are many passages in the novel where the narrator's ponderousness fails to hide the sympathy of its magisterial author.
The 'Nachschrift', for example, reflects on the end of the war, on how
writing the novel 'hat [...] mir beschäftigend über Jahre hinweggeholfen,
die in barer Muße weit schwerer noch zu ertragen gewesen wären'
(p. 669). There is more than a little of Mann himself in that, and only
a narrator credited with some integrity would be allowed to mouth Mann's
own sentiments so plainly at so crucial a juncture. Zeitblom goes on:

> Deutschland ist frei, sofern man ein vernichtetes und entmündigtes Land frei
> nennen kann, und es mag sein, daß meiner Rückkehr in den Schuldienst bald nichts
> mehr im Wege stehen wird. [...] Werde ich wieder einer humanistischen Prima den
> Kulturgedanken ans Herz legen, in welchem Ehrfurcht vor den Gottheiten der
> Tiefe mit dem sittlichen Kult olympischer Vernunft und Klarheit zu *einer*
> Frömmigkeit verschmilzt? Aber ach, ich fürchte, in dieser wilden Dekade ist ein
> Geschlecht herangewachsen, das meine Sprache sowenig versteht wie ich die
> seine, ich fürchte, die Jugend meines Landes ist mir zu fremd geworden, als daß
> ich ihr Lehrer noch sein könnte. (p. 669)

It was Philipp Melanchthon who first received the accolade *praeceptor
Germaniae*, but Mann understood himself to be Melanchthon's successor
in this respect. Words from another of his works are a surprisingly apt
description of this attitude: 'Sehnsucht ist darin und schwermütiger Neid
und ein klein wenig Verachtung und eine ganz keusche Seligkeit'
(*Werke*, Vol. 8, p. 338) – words once used of Mann's Tonio Kröger by
his own narrator, but later used by him of himself. The fusion of the
perspectives of narrator and character that took place in the 1905 story is
now movingly – but no less knowingly – re-enacted as overlaying of the
fictive narrator and the author in *Doktor Faustus* nearly half a decade
later, notwithstanding the parodic undercutting to which Zeitblom has
throughout been subjected.

Parody is not only a destructive weapon in Mann's armoury. The
specific subject of the words quoted from 'Tonio Kröger' is love. Zeit-

blom's task in *Doktor Faustus* is fulfilled 'durch Liebe, Treue und
Zeugenschaft' (p. 668); his own life has been given meaning by 'Liebe,
Spannung, Schrecken und Stolz' (p. 675) by his friend's, and the word
'Liebe' is an often-used and highly complex motif. It is an inability to
love and the consequent readiness to abjure love that prime Leverkühn
for his pact with the Devil; it is because of love for the little boy
Nepomuk Schneidewein, known as Echo, that Leverkühn's crisis is –
mythically speaking – precipitated as the pact is broken. And what Mann
defined as 'Liebe und Parodie', using the mouthpiece of Goethe in *Lotte
in Weimar*, was none other than 'Kultur'. *Doktor Faustus* is a novel
about 'Kultur' composed of 'Liebe und Parodie' – love shown by its
narrator, parody *of* its narrator by its author, but also love shown by its
author towards its narrator and his troubled country. This is one model
for understanding Mann's parody of Zeitblom in *Doktor Faustus*:

> bei allen Besinnlichkeiten [says Goethe], die die Kunst begleiten, ist [Parodie] die
> seltsamst-heiterste und zärtlichste. Fromme Zerstörung, lächelnd Abschiednehmen
> [...]. Das Geliebte, Heilige, Alte, das hohe Vorbild auf einer Stufe und mit
> Gehalten zu wiederholen, die ihm den Stempel des Parodischen verleihen. (Werke,
> Vol. 2, pp. 680–81)

However, when Mann's Goethe defines culture as 'Liebe und Parodie'
he is reflecting on the inability of Germans to understand the relationship
of laughter and respect for the sublime or the virtuous: 'Nein, auch darin
war er nicht deutsch,' he says of Schiller, 'daß er lächelte über das Vor-
treffliche. Das tut kein Deutscher. Die schauen grimmig drein dabei, weil
sie nicht wissen, daß Cultur Parodie ist – Liebe und Parodie' (*Werke*,
Vol. 2, p. 622).

There has been extensive critical debate about whether *Doktor
Faustus* culminates in a vista of damnation or whether it offers the
possibility of redemption. My preference is for a redemptive reading, not
least because Mann is, as he later confessed, so obviously 'sorgenvoll in
[Leverkühn] verliebt', which had never been true of his other fictional
protagonists (*Werke*, Vol. 11, p. 203). It has been suggested plausibly
that many readings of the novel have been steered by the 'didactic
pessimism' of the 1587 chapbook the *Historia von D. Johann Fausten*
that Mann used and by the suppression of almost all reference to Goethe.
Scholars such as Helmut Koopmann see Mann's novel as a 'Wider-

legung der Weimarer Klassik',[24] suggesting that Leverkühn deliberately sets out in his *Weheklag* to revoke the affirmation that Beethoven's Ninth Symphony represents, to unmask the redemptive ending of Goethe's *Faust* – indeed specifically to repudiate Goethe – and put a definitive end to the biblical tradition of grace. Koopmann supports his argument with a number of extra-textual comments by Mann himself, including the assertion made in a letter of 1953 that 'Mit Goethes Faust hat mein Roman nichts gemein außer der gemeinsamen Quelle, dem alten Volksbuch'.[25] There is internal evidence, too: the price Leverkühn pays for creative release is a double one, his syphilis and an embargo on love, and when he dares to show human warmth, love even, to his nephew Nepomuk, the boy dies of meningitis, symbolically suffering a fatal intensification of Leverkühn's own tendency to migraine. It has also been suggested that his relationship with Rudi Schwerdtfeger is one of love and that the violinist's death at the hands of his jilted lover, Ines Institoris, is actually engineered by the composer as a form of self-inflicted punishment for having dared to break the Devil's conditions.[26] Ritchie Robertson underlines the grindingly retributive nature of the novel's development by suggesting that 'by comparison with this devious yet inexorable tragedy [Echo's death], Goethe's *Faust*, in which the hero always gets another chance, seems almost trivial'.[27]

Others are more receptive to an argument for the presence at least of the possibility of redemption. Hans Rudolf Vaget sees a subtext on grace undercutting the theological certainties of the chapbook and brings Mann closer to Goethe after all.[28] Susan von Rohr Scaff goes much further, insisting on the duplicity of the figure of the Devil in this novel and on 'Leverkühn's transcendence of the pact through love', a love 'subtly revealed in the Faust cantata and the mythical events surrounding its composition', which intimate that divine mercy is the 'moving force'

24   Helmut Koopmann, '*Doktor Faustus* als Widerlegung der Weimarer Klassik', in Koopmann, *Der schwierige Deutsche. Studien zum Werk Thomas Manns* (Tübingen, 1988), pp. 109–24.

25   Letter to Hilde Zaloscer of 24 August 1953, in Thomas Mann, *Selbstkommentare. Doktor Faustus und Die Entstehung des Doktor Faustus*, ed. by Hans Wysling and Marianne Eich-Fischer (Frankfurt a. M., 1992), p. 337.

26   See for example Vaget, 'Amazing Grace', p. 184.

27   Robertson, 'Accounting for History', p. 133.

28   Vaget, 'Amazing Grace'.

behind this piece of music after all and open the possibility of giving credence to the Christian view of salvation.[29]

Scholars approaching the novel from a musicological perspective almost all agree that redemption is very strongly intimated. The end of Leverkühn's final composition, the *Weheklag*, is described as a construction of 'repetitions and echoes in contrasting configurations and inversions'.[30] This work is a self-dramatisation, a composition about Faust and therefore about Leverkühn himself. The music symbolically incorporates letters from the words Hetaera Esmeralda, the name of the self-disguising butterfly Leverkühn studied as a child and the name he gave to the prostitute from whom he contracted syphilis. Soon after the publication of *Doktor Faustus* the critic Victor Oswald uncovered the hidden identity of the figure of the prostitute with that of Leverkühn's mysterious benefactress, Frau von Tolna: it is she who gives Adrian an emerald ring (echoing the 'esmeralda' in the name of the butterfly-prostitute) and who is referred to sometimes as Egeria – an etymological bridge to the family of clear-winged moths to which Hetaera Esmeralda belongs entomologically, the Aegeriidae. The low prostitute is redeemed into the eternal feminine symbolised by the Hungarian noblewoman – Zeitblom's commentary on Leverkühn's sexual liaison with her says this, but it is hard to know whether this is another example of his special pleading or whether it is true. This paradoxical transformation is paralleled by the words set in the *Weheklag*, which include 'denn ich sterbe als ein böser und guter Christ' (p. 648) – twelve syllables set on twelve tones to a row that includes the Hetaera Esmeralda encoding. Similarly, the chords Leverkühn plays on the piano in the brothel where he met her represent a progression from B Major to C Major, which is identified by Leverkühn himself as an echo of the moment in the finale of Weber's *Der Freischütz* symbolising the gift of grace bestowed upon the sinner, Max.[31] The tonal shift again articulates how the demonic and the salvific are co-present in the female figure.

29   Susan von Rohr Scaff, 'The Duplicity of the Devil's Pact: Intimations of Redemption in Mann's *Doktor Faustus*', *Monatshefte*, 87 (1995), 151–69 (p. 152). See also Stefan Börnchen, 'Tritonus der Hoffnung. Ein fiktives Intervall in Thomas Manns *Doktor Faustus*', *Orbis Litterarum*, 56 (2001), 334–54.

30   Ryan, 'The Flower of Evil', p. 48.

31   Max is also the name of the owner of the property where Adrian spends his last year and who dies almost simultaneously with his own father

As the last notes of the symphonic cantata die away, 'was übrig bleibt', Zeitblom says, 'womit das Werk verklingt, ist das hohe g eines Cellos, das letzte Wort, der letzte verschwebende Laut, in Pianissimo-Fermate langsam vergehend' (a fermata is a pause sign, holding a note for longer than its technical value). Zeitblom continues,

> Dann ist nichts mehr, – Schweigen und Nacht. Aber der nachschwingend im Schweigen hängende Ton, der nicht mehr ist, dem nur die Seele noch nachlauscht, und der Ausklang der Trauer war, ist es nicht mehr, wandelt den Sinn, steht als ein Licht in der Nacht. (p. 651)

He acknowledges that the 'dunkles Tongedicht' apparently allows no hint of 'Vertröstung, Versöhnung, Verklärung', but wonders nonetheless whether 'aus tiefster Heillosigkeit, wenn auch als leiseste Frage nur, die Hoffnung keimte [...] die Hoffnung jenseits der Hoffnungslosikeit, die Transzendenz der Verzweiflung'. Zeitblom may be providing an explanation to show his hero most positively – Koopmann rather cynically calls this 'humanistic opportunism'[32] – but his words are especially credible here because what he describes is an instance of enharmonic change, when one note changes function without changing pitch.[33] This is how the high G at the end of Leverkühn's piece, which in Zeitblom's description is an expression of mourning for a lost soul, can simultaneously be an image of light in the darkness, just as Esmeralda can be Frau von Tolna. This may be Zeitblom's attempt to rescue hope from disaster, but it is also precisely what Leverkühn himself was describing in their very first conversation about music, when three notes in a chord can change their key aspect depending on the context that another note provides for them. Leverkühn deliberately produced this

32   Helmut Koopmann, '*Doktor Faustus*: A History of German Introspection', in *Thomas Mann's 'Doctor Faustus'. A Novel at the Margin of Modernism*, ed. by Herbert Lehnert and Peter C. Pfeiffer (Columbia, SC, 1991), pp. 17–31 (p. 22).

33   C sharp and D flat, for example, are enharmonically equivalent: they are the same pitch (in the equal temperament system that Western music has used since the early 1900s) but have different names and function differently within tonal systems. Enharmonic tones and intervals often serve as pivots in modulation: in Chopin's famous 'Raindrop Prelude' for example, the repeated note that symbolises the raindrop is initially an A flat, but in bar 29 it becomes a G sharp, identical in pitch and the same note on the piano keyboard, but shifting the key of the music from D flat major to C sharp minor.

ambiguity in the violin concerto for Rudi Schwerdtfeger, which is based on triads from three different tonalities simultaneously. His lapidary definition of the nature of his art was 'Musik ist Zweideutigkeit als System' and the full meaning of the final moments of the cantata lies in the simultaneity of Zeitblom's positive interpretation and its opposite.

This is not to say that *Doktor Faustus* is a Goethean novel after all, or that Leverkühn is snatched from damnation by a Hungarian incarnation of the eternal feminine. Neither does it imply the necessity of damnation by withholding the very concept of salvation, however. The relationship Adrian Leverkühn has with Esmeralda can also rightly be described as one of love. Ryan suggests that Thomas Mann reflects his own 'fathomless despair' in this novel,[34] but she also shows how Mann's 'non-directed irony [...] leaves the reader in an agony of evaluation' because of the 'mesh of equivocality that constitutes the terms in which the novel is couched'. According to *Die Entstehung des Doktor Faustus*, Adorno himself urged Mann to tone down the optimism of the section on the *Weheklag* and remove the last forty lines, 'in denen es nach all der Finsternis um die Hoffnung, die Gnade geht'; Mann reflects, 'ich war zu optimistisch, zu gutmütig und direkt gewesen' (*Werke*, Vol. 11, p. 294). But Adorno did not believe in the redemptive capacity of music.[35] Mann instinctively disagreed, but under pressure from Adorno he allowed his instincts to be modified into what he calls a 'behutsame Form' (ibid.), albeit with real benefit to the trembling equipoise of love and parody, devastation and optimism, tragedy and beauty that constitutes the compelling yet often harrowing experience of reading *Doktor Faustus*. It is perhaps this ambivalent honesty, over and above its monumental scope, ambition and complexity that make *Doktor Faustus* one of the most conspicuously significant features of the landscape of twentieth-century German fiction.

---

34 Ryan, 'The Flower of Evil', p. 55.
35 On Mann's relationship with Adorno and their implicit aesthetic and theoretical disagreements, see Herbert Lehnert, 'Zur Biographie Thomas Manns: der Adorno-Komplex', *Orbis Litterarum*, 60 (2005), 219–38.

JULIAN PREECE

Grass, *Die Blechtrommel*

1959, the date of publication of Grass's first – and still most acclaimed – novel, represents a major caesura in the author's life.[1] In his controversial autobiography, *Beim Häuten der Zwiebel*,[2] he narrates his first three decades up to the point at which that life became more or less public property, and in an earlier memoir, the chapter '1959' in *Mein Jahrhundert*, in one magnificently swirling sentence Grass endeavours to capture the effects its reception had on him and his previously unsuspecting young wife Anna. Although he had won the *Gruppe 47* prize the year before (when he read extracts from his 'novel in progress'), he now went overnight from being an obscure bohemian poet and playwright, graduate of the Düsseldorf Art Academy and husband of a trainee ballerina, to national, and soon international, fame. In this collection of 100 fictional stories and personal reminiscences which each correspond to a year of the last century, the memoirs are often more powerful than the more purely fictional stories. As he and Anna dance away the night at a publisher's impromptu ball, he recalls the voices in the background, as if they were bellowing at them from the edge of the dance floor: 'Erfolg! Böll, Grass, Johnson machen das Rennen...'; 'Billard, Mutmaßungen, Blechtrommel...'; 'Jetzt endlich ist sie da, die deutsche Nachkriegsliteratur...'; 'Trotz Sieburg und FAZ, jetzt ist der Durchbruch gelungen...'; 'Dreißigtausend!'; 'Oskar!'; 'Oskar tanzt'.[3] But Grass himself is the greatest mythologiser of *Die Blechtrommel*, as he mentions it, or its central character, in almost every other work of fiction he has published.

Grass was soon declared to be the voice of new post-war German literature. He had attained what had not been achieved by either Heinrich Böll or Uwe Johnson, who both published significant novels the same year

1   All quotation from the *Werkausgabe*, ed. by Volker Neuhaus and Daniela Hermes, Vol. 3 (Göttingen, 1997).
2   Further quotations from *Beim Häuten der Zwiebel* (Göttingen, 2006).
3   *Mein Jahrhundert* (Göttingen, 1999), pp. 212–14.

(*Billard um halb zehn* and *Mutmaßungen über Jakob* are the titles he refers to above), nor would his success be matched by Ingeborg Bachmann, Martin Walser, or Hans Magnus Enzensberger, to name three other prominent literary contemporaries who had already begun to make their names: he had written a novel with broad, if not quite popular appeal, which earned the critics' immediate respect while making waves outside what Enzensberger, in his enthusiastic review, labelled the 'Sardinentümpel [...] unserer domestizierten Literatur'.[4]

The great post-war literary accounts of the Nazi period, which mark most of the pinnacles of creative achievement in the post-war German novel, had not yet been written: Jurek Becker's *Jakob der Lügner* (1969), Johnson's *Jahrestage aus dem Leben der Gesine Cresspahl* (1970–83), Peter Weiss's *Die Ästhetk des Widerstands* (1975–81), and Christa Wolf's *Kindheitsmuster* (1976), all appeared over the twenty-five years which followed. Only Alfred Andersch had made a serious attempt at tackling the subject in *Sansibar oder der letzte Grund* (1957), an exciting existentialist adventure novel loosely inspired by Hemingway and Camus and set in 1937 in the tiny Baltic port of Rerik. Grass and Andersch immediately took against each other when they first met, and Grass had no time for Andersch's novel, sensing perhaps the plot's moral dishonesty when set against its author's own actions in the 1940s (which has been the subject of a scathing attack by W. G. Sebald).[5] Andersch had seen the inside of Dachau for a few weeks in 1934 on account of his Communist sympathies. After his release he had married a wealthy Jewish woman whom he divorced in the early 1940s. She did not survive the Holocaust and after Andersch's death it was revealed that he had applied to join the *Reich-schriftumskammer* and had stated on his application form that he was 'geschieden' – which was not quite true, as the divorce did not go through for another couple of weeks. Had he said that he was married to a Jew he would not have been accepted. In his novel Andersch presents the Nazis as anonymous background figures referred to as 'die Anderen', denoting their distance from the three men and a boy at the novel's centre who unite to rescue a young Jewish woman and a wooden statue from

4   'Wilhelm Meister auf Blech getrommelt', in Gert Loschütz (ed.), *Von Buch zu Buch: Günter Grass in der Kritik. Eine Dokumentation* (Neuwied, 1968), pp. 8–12, (p.8).
5   'Der Schriftsteller Alfred Andersch', in *Luftkrieg und Literatur. Mit einem Essay zu Alfred Andersch* (Munich and Vienna, 1999), pp. 121–60.

the clutches of the Nazis. The impression given by the novel is that everyone in Rerik worth writing about is working with the resistance, which is clearly absurd. In total contrast, there are no resistance figures in *Die Blechtrommel*.

As the first full post-war decade neared its end, the 'Flakhelfergeneration', who were old enough to remember the Nazi years as adolescents, but too young to have incriminated themselves during them, signalled their impatience with the moral platitudes of Konrad Adenauer's *Wirtschaftswunder* years. *Die Blechtromnel* appeared on the threshold of a new decade which would change and define the old Federal Republic, and even mark the early years of the new post-reunification Republic more than any other. Indeed, Harro Zimmermann sees its influence stretching into the present and forming the basis of its author status as a public figure:

> Sein Roman *Die Blechtrommel* warf ein grelles Licht auf den bundesdeutschen Kulturprovinzialismus der fünfziger Jahre und signalisierte den intellektuellen Aufbruch der jungen Demokratie. An Günter Grass hat der nachkriegsrepublikanische Zeitgeist das Sprechen gelernt, an seiner Gegenrede arbeitet er sich nun seit fünf Jahrzehnten ab.[6]

Grass's political campaigning on behalf of Willy Brandt, which began as a reaction to the building of the Berlin Wall two years later, marked him out as new and challenging to larger sections of the West German public. In the general election campaign in 1965, having quickly followed up *Die Blechtrommel* with *Katz und Maus* (1961) and *Hundejahre* (1963), he toured the country as if he were standing for office himself, creating a stir wherever he spoke because he was not afraid to speak bluntly and address questions which did not tend to get aired publicly. There were court cases, and the withdrawal of the 'Bremer Literaturpreis' for *Die Blechtrommel* after the intervention of local politicians amid accusations of blasphemy and pornography, which *Katz und Maus* attracted in even greater measure.[7] And even to this day, as far as I am aware, there is a sequence of several seconds from Volker Schlöndorff's film of *Die Blechtrommel*, released twenty years after the novel, which cannot be shown in the UK.

6   Harro Zimmermann, *Günter Grass unter den Deutschen. Chronik eines Verhältnisses* (Göttingen, 2006), p. 9.
7   See Heinz Ludwig Arnold and Franz Josef Görtz (eds.), *Günter Grass: Dokumente zur politischen Wirkung* (*Text & Kritik*, 1971).

Grass's response to anyone who claimed to be offended by his account of teenage boys playing with themselves in *Katz und Maus*, an activity which had been depicted on stage at the turn-of-the-century in Wedekind's *Frühlings Erwachen*, or to Oskar's interrogation of the Jesus statue, is that the real obscenity and offence against religion had taken place else-where and was of a wholly different magnitude. Grass won out against his accusers. In 1960 the Bremen senators' prudishness may have denied Grass the prize money, but their city-state lost out in the bad publicity the scandal generated. Bremen subsequently reformed the rules governing the choice of prize-winner in order to prevent state interference. The reform indicates that the scandal took place in a democratic liberal state; the reasons for not awarding Grass the prize in the first place belong to an era which preferred to repress figures like Wedekind. One thing was certain: no other new author had caused quite such an upheaval in the brief history of the FRG. Liberal trends in German society were, however, on Grass's side: he was not attacked on these grounds for his novels of the next decade, *Aus dem Tagebuch einer Schnecke* (1972) and *Der Butt* (1977), both of which contain equally explicit episodes.

Die Blechtrommel's status as a cultural artefact which is known to far more than those who have read it – as witness the misleading claims which are made on its behalf in the media whenever its author becomes the subject of controversy – is uncontested. The novel is indisputably a land-mark in German cultural history, even in more general social and political history, but what will concern me equally in this essay is what makes it distinctive as a literary work of art, as a novel in the German tradition.

A 'landmark' novel must clearly be one which joins the canon; this is itself a dynamic and ever-evolving entity that nations, themselves defined by their having a literature, discover have special importance to them in periods of renewal, or change, or when their very existence is under threat. The Polish nation, for example, survived solely in its literature through the long nineteenth century when it had ceased to exist as a state – indeed, its founding classics did not get written until this time. Germany too had a national literary culture before unification in 1871. After losing a fifth of its pre-1939 territory as a consequence of National Socialism and finding at least another fifth in a separate republic under the control of the Soviet Union, 'Germany' had reached another such point in 1959. The ten-year-old Federal Republic needed a new work like *Die Blechtrommel*, just as the rest of the western world, locked in a potentially lethal struggle with Soviet

Communism, was pleased to point to evidence of post-Nazi cultural renewal. Ideologically Grass's novel transmitted values and an interpretation of recent events which the liberalising forces in the FRG, which were challenging Adenauer's hegemony, could identify with. The novel mocked both nationalist myths about the moral decency of everyday folk and their non-complicity in atrocities, as well as the legitimacy of claims to the lost territories east of the Oder–Neiße, which the Federal Republic did not renounce until the era of *Ostpolitik* under Willy Brandt. In the same way the Republic needed the novel's author to declare himself for Brandt, the ex-emigré and anti-Nazi resistor whose victory in the pivotal elections of 1969 indicated that the western part of Germany had reached a certain self-confidence and maturity. It is not just from journalistic laziness that Grass is still associated with his most famous character when he is involved in a public controversy. Novel and author helped shape the direction in which history and society were travelling.

Grass, incidentally, has been at his most effective in his dialogue with his compatriots. He has conducted this either in literary works or in speeches and articles, and particularly when his nation has been engaged in reflection on identity and direction – as it was in the 1960s and again during reunification in the period 1989–91. Such 'reflection' does not have to take place in tranquillity: with Grass it is more usually part of a noisy argument characterised by resentment and high emotions on both sides, and sometimes things are said which are later regretted. For the twenty years after the *Machtwechsel* of 1969, after he had been denied a role in Brandt's government, Grass was looking for a public function, but he had difficulty finding one with respect to Third World hunger or the anti-missile movement. He found it again in 1989–91, though, in his speeches criticising the ways reunification was being handled by Helmut Kohl. Over the following fifteen years three of his books, in 1995 the mammoth *Ein weites Feld*, in 2002 *Im Krebsgang*, and in 2006, *Beim Häuten der Zwiebel*, have touched a nerve because of how they explore national self-understanding. With *Im Krebsgang* he was swimming, unusually for him, with the tide. While one part of this *Novelle* narrates the horrific sequence of events on a freezing winter's night in the Baltic Sea when the *Wilhelm Gustloff*, which was laden with German refugees, was torpedoed by a Soviet submarine, the other circles around the meaning and interpretation of these events in contemporary Germany. The strand of interpretation which triumphs is that ordinary Germans were victims, not just of the Nazis but of the Allies too, a theme which had merely been implicit in his writing up to then. Interestingly, it is reported at the Günter Grass Stiftung in Bremen that the overwhelming majority of emails received after Grass's revelation of his SS secret past commented on his bravery for owning up at this stage of his life, with all that he had to lose.

From a literary critical point of view, more pertinent than the sex and blasphemy allegations against *Die Blechtrommel* were the disagreements over the meaning of the novel's grotesquely fascinating narrator, who insists that he deliberately stopped his growth at the age of three in order to retain his child's shape and size and keep his distance from the un-appealing adult world, which would collapse about his ears in an orgy of killing and destruction before he reached the age of twenty-one. Did he embody the sordidness and petty cruelties of the period narrated in the novel (1899–1954) and which resulted in the deaths of so many millions? Or was he a rare voice of compassion, indicating by his refusal to grow and participate fully in life under the Nazis that he was protesting against the world around him? Oskar Matzerath lives his artist's life in parallel to the rise and fall of the Nazis and the destruction which they unleashed, always acting on his own preferences and priorities. He affects to be unmoved by death and more concerned that he will have to look for a new source of drums when the Jewish toyshop-owner Sigismund Markus commits suicide rather than face those who ransack his premises on the *Kristallnacht* in November 1938. Nearly ten months later, on the last day of August 1939, it is because he needs to have a drum repaired by the caretaker in Danzig's Polish Post Office that he drags Jan Bronski, one of his two 'mutmaßliche Väter', into the hastily fortified building, from where Bronski is captured the following day by the victorious Germans and summarily executed. Both 'fathers' shared a passion, which was un-consummated in the case of Markus, for Oskar's mother Agnes, who predeceased them. Oskar, whether selfishly interested in his drums or not, gives moving accounts of the deaths of both of them. He sides with victims and fellow outsiders, such as Herbert Truczinski or Schugger Leo or Klepp and Vittlar in the post-war sequence. It is not because of a fascination with death that there are so many memorable depictions of individual demises, but out of respect for the life that has been ended, or ended itself in the cases of Agnes, Herbert, Markus, and the Matzerath family neighbour, Albrecht Greff. The novel narrates only three births or conceptions in the course of its 700 pages, compared with the deaths of twenty-three named individuals along with the unnamed, innumerable others. *Die Blechtrommel* also contains one of the first accounts of the death camps through the fevered reminiscences of Marius Fajngold, who had escaped from Treblinka where he had worked as a disinfector and lost his very numerous family.

While Oskar works for Goebbels between 1943–44 on a tour of France which takes him to Paris and the Normandy beaches, at other times he challenges Nazi values and practices, nowhere more spectacularly than in the pre-war chapter 'Tribüne'; here the assembled throng at the party rally dance to the tune which he drums from beneath the podium rather than responding to the cues of the local party leader. Oskar also parodies Hitler's cult of death in the black mass escapade shortly before the fall of Danzig to the Red Army, for which he is arrested and put on trial. But on both occasions he denies any political motivation.

If stylistically Grass can be defined by his gift for parody, politically he is perhaps more than anything a survivor. To come through times of great violence requires both luck and opportunism. For example, in *Beim Häuten der Zwiebel* the author reveals that he was lucky not to have learnt how to ride a bicycle because had he been a cyclist he would have been shot to pieces like his six comrades who were trying to pedal to safety from the abandoned cycle shop somewhere in eastern Germany where they found themselves trapped by the Soviets (pp. 147–50). He was lucky on other occasions to be standing out of the way of bombs or bullets which killed those next to him. Oskar imitates this luck when he lets his great love Roswitha Raguna return to the Normandy chateau for a breakfast cup of coffee rather than fetching one for her, only to see her blown to pieces by an American shell. Oskar sees less fighting than Grass, however – and from a biographical point of view it is interesting that, while Grass adopts and adapts so much of his own experience in his first novel, he brackets out his military episodes entirely. Harry Liebenau, the narrator of the second book of *Hundejahre*, has more attached to him, though in his case too there is no suggestion of involvement with an SS division.

Oskar is an everyday opportunist, who astutely changes allegiance on two occasions when the arrival of the invader signals a sudden change of regime. It has often been noted that he helps dispatch both his presumed fathers: first the Polish Bronski by fetching him to work on that fateful last August day in 1939, and then the German Matzerath in the family cellar in January 1945. He has a classic father complex, which is no less stereotypical than his complex over his mother and which is indicated by his often expressed wish to return to the warmth and security of the womb and his tendency to seek out other locations which are similarly protective. These Freudian clichés are advertised too openly for them to be of much help in interpreting the novel. Psychoanalysis uncovers hidden, repressed, or unacknowledged desires and Oskar's are actually the very opposite with respect to his parents. Our cultural obsession with the Oedipus Complex may have obscured understanding of the father-killing sequences, one placed at the beginning of the war, the other at the end. Both times Oskar curries favour with the forces which are now in power by performing a manoeuvre which all survivors were obliged to emulate. In *Ein weites Feld*, where the twentieth-century hero and his nineteenth-century counterpart 'make arrangements' with a succession of regimes (as the German verb 'sich arrangieren' has it), Grass chooses riding in the paternoster lift in the former 'Haus der Ministerien', once the Luftwaffe Headquarters, now central office for the operations of the 'Treuhand'. Several reviewers of the novel cited this conceit as evidence of Grass's belief in the circularity of history and thus a prediction that just as national unification in 1871 had led to two world wars, so unification 120 years later would result in catastrophe for Germany and her neighbours.[8] The Paternoster is more likely to signify changes of direction as at the top and the bottom the cabins shift several metres to the left or right before beginning their progress back up or down the building. Occupants are warned that it is unsafe to remain inside and that they should alight at the lowest or highest floor before the change in direction occurs. Fonty, alias Theo Wuttke, the central figure of *Ein weites Feld*, has been using the lift for as long as it has been in operation and has proved himself adept at surviving all the changes, both in direction and in regime.

Oskar is no less cunning when it comes to saving his own skin. He is ashamed of the way that he betrayed Jan Bronski to the German soldiers from the 'Heimwehr' when they storm into the room where Oskar, Jan, and the caretaker Kobyella have been playing skat. He does not own up to it in his first account of the incident, only in the second when, as, on other

8   For instance, Andrea Köhler, 'Die Deutschstunde: Günter Grass' Gründerzeitepos *Ein weites Feld*', *Neuer Zurcher Zeitung*, 23 August 1995, reprinted in *Der Fall Fonty. Ein weites Feld von Günter Grass im Spiegel der Kritik*, ed. by Daniela Hermes (Göttingen, 1996), pp. 92–93.

occasions when his behaviour has been incriminating, he corrects himself at the beginning of the next chapter:

> Oskar [stellte sich] schutzsuchend zwischen zwei onkelhaft gutmütig wirkende Heimwehrmänner, imitierte klägliches Weinen und wies auf Jan, seinen Vater, mit anklagenden Gesten, die den Armen zum bösen Mann machten, der ein unschuldiges Kind in die Polnische Post geschleppt hatte, um es auf polnisch unmenschliche Weise als Kugelfang zu benutzen. (p. 318)

While Oskar is taken away in a car to a hospital, Jan is shot and buried in an unmarked grave. Five years and five months later at the end of the war, when he hands over the party badge to Alfred Matzerath after the Red Army soldiers have found them cowering in their cellar, he enacts essentially a similar gesture.

As well as its status in national culture, a landmark novel may re-write literary tradition by re-invigorating it; in turn, it is itself read by later authors and makes an impact on their work as they react against it or seek to emulate it in some way. In these respects it may seem that *Die Blechtrommel* has taken over more readily than it has – so far at least – given back. In a way this is perhaps usually the case: after *Werther* or *Buddenbrooks*, to name two other 'first' novels which their authors are often said not to have surpassed, other novelists have to write in a different way to get noticed or be taken seriously. On the other hand, both these novels fed back into tradition, making their landmark status clear through subsequent intertextual allusion. Both are arguably present in *Die Blechtrommel* (which features a love triangle that results in a suicide, and which chronicles a family's decline from 'business' to 'art').

Some of Grass's first readers also noticed echoes of the seventeenth-century author Johann Christoffel von Grimmelshausen, whose *Simplicissimus Teutsch* chronicles the fortunes of its hero from boyhood to early adulthood against the backdrop of what had been until 1944–5 the most deadly and destructive conflict fought on German soil, the Thirty Years' War. Grass confirmed the significance of the *Simplicianische Schriften* in *Das Treffen in Telgte* (1979), which in part mythologises his own debut at the *Gruppe 47* and consequent impact on literary culture, and *Beim Häuten der Zwiebel*, where Grimmelshausen is mentioned more often than any other author.

The outward similarities between *Die Blechtrommel* and *Simplicissimus* have often been pointed out: they both have an episodic structure

and feature a first-person narrator-hero who looks back at his own life
and narrates it up to the point where he started writing (in other words
the 'erzählte Zeit' catches up with the 'erzählende Zeit'). The central
figures play a number of roles, which suggest that their identity may
be unstable or that their authors had an understanding of character which
was anti-evolutionary and unorganic. In both there is violence, striking
visual imagery, sudden juxtapositions, and death is omnipresent. Oskar
Matzerath and Simplicissimus both write their memoirs far removed from
society and the world: Simplicissimus on his deserted island in the southern
oceans, Oskar from his asylum bed. Both are thus detached and
unintegrated, as traditional picareseque heroes and heroines usually are,
in contrast to their counterparts in *Bildungsromane* who, according to the
classic template at least, become productive members of society who have
achieved self-understanding and social acceptance after recognising the
meaningfulness of their sequence of adventures and mishaps.

Grass's recollection of surviving war in *Beim Häuten der Zwiebel* is
mediated through Grimmelshausen's account of Simplicissimus evading
death in similarly hostile circumstances and against similarly high odds.
Putting them side by side and imagining how Grass, who assures us that he
devoured *Simplicissimus* several times as a teenager in the early 1940s,
came to formulate his two accounts of battle, the second of which he
experienced first hand, is reminiscent of a clever conceit in *Der Butt*.
In the notorious 'Vatertag' chapter his Simplicissimus runs away from
the battle to observe how 'alles Geschehen schon vorgedruckt sei' by
comparing the slaughter in front of his eyes with the description of warfare
in the German translation of Philip Sidney's novel, *Arcadia* – which had
recently been discovered to be the literary model for Grimmelshausen's
rhetorical, but realistic, account of Wittstock.

In order to convey an idea of how this works I will compare three
passages. The first is from the beginning of *Simplicissimus*, at the point
when the farmstead where the hero has been brought up is attacked by
soldiers; the latter assault the inhabitants, destroy the buildings, and steal
the food. The second passage is taken from the account of the fall of
Danzig when Alfred Matzerath is shot by a nervous Red Army soldier, a
'Kalmuck' from the Asian steppes whom the Soviet High Command used
for the most perilous missions. Meanwhile Oskar's one-time married girlfriend, the now widowed Frau Greff, is gang-raped. The third is from his
recently published memoir, and it describes how he was one of the lucky

few who survived a surprise mortar attack in the woods on the edge of the Lausitz. Once again, it is the everyday details that the narrator notices, the eruption of deadly violence into mundane routines.

Von den gefangenen Weibern / Mägden und Töchtern / weiß ich sonderlich nichts zu sagen / weil mich die Krieger nichtzusehen liessen / wie sie mit ihnen umbgiengen: Das weiß ich noch wol / daß man theils hin und wider in den Winckeln erbärmlich shreyen hörte / schätze wol / es sey meiner Meuder und unserem Ursele nit besser gangen / als den andern. Mitten in diesem Elend wendet ich Braten / und halff Nachmittag die Pferd träncken / durch welches Mittel ich zu unserer Magd in Stall kam / welche wunderwercklich zerstrobelt außsahe / ich kennete sie nicht / sie aber sprach zu mir mit kränklicher Stimme: O Bub lauff weg / sonst werden dich die Reuter mit nemmen / guck daß du davon kommst / du siehst wol / wie es so übel: mehrers konte sie nicht sagen.[9]

Was man nicht alles tut, wenn das Schicksal seinen Auftritt hat! Während mein mutmaßlicher Vater die Partei verschluckte und starb, zerdrückte ich, ohne es zu merken oder zu wollen, zwischen den Fingern eine Laus, die ich dem Kalmücken kurz zuvor abgefangen hatte. Matzerath hatte sich quer über die Ameisenstraße fallen lassen. Die Iwans verließen den Keller über die Treppe zum Laden und nahmen einige Päckchen Kunsthonig mit. Mein Kalmücke ging als letzter, griff aber keinen Kunsthonig, weil er ein neues Magazin in seine Machinenpistole stecken mußte. Die Witwe Greff hing offen und verdreht zwischen Margarinekisten. Maria hielt das Kurtchen an sich, als wollte sie es erdrücken. Mir ging ein Satzgebilde durch den Kopf, das ich bei Goethe gelesen hatte. Die Ameisen fanden eine veränderte Situation vor, scheuten aber den Umweg nicht, bauten ihre Heerstraße um den gekrümmten Matzerath herum; denn jener aus dem geplatzten Sack rieselnde Zucker hatte während der Besetzung der Stadt Danzig durch die Armee Marschall Rokossowskis nichts von seiner Süße verloren. (pp. 518–9)

War das der Junge, der vorhin noch gekonnt mit der Mundharmonika?
Kenntlich der Landser, auf dessen Gesicht der Rasierschaum trocknete...
Dazwischen krochen überlebende oder standen erstarrt wie ich. Einige schrien, obgleich nicht verwundet. Jemand greinte wie ein Kleinkind. Ich blieb in naßgepißter Hose lautlos und sah nahbei den geöffneten Leib eines Jungen, mit dem ich gerade noch weißnichtwas gequasselt hatte. Die Eingeweide. Sein rundes Gesicht, das im Moment des Todes geschrumpft zu sein schien...
Aber das, was hier im einzelnen geschrieben steht, habe ich ähnlich bereits woanders, bei Remarque oder Céline gelesen, wie schon Grimmelshausen bei der Schilderung der Schlacht von Wittstock, als die Schweden die Kaiserlichen in Stücke hauten, überlieferte Schreckensbilder zitierte... (p. 142)

9   *Der Abentheuerliche Simplicissimus Teutsch und Continuatio des abentheurlichen Simplicissimi* (Tübingen, 1967), p.19.

In the passage from *Die Blechtrommel* Grass gives an impression of how death, rape, and the fall of a city in war (what enters popular speech if not the history books as 'Schicksal'), makes its appearance in very un-heroic circumstances. Oskar is distracted from watching his father get shot by the louse he finds on the soldier's collar, while the ants are oblivious to what has just happened. Maria has apparently been saved Frau Greff's fate because three-year-old Kurt, who Oskar claims as his child, is sitting on her lap, which is a detail Grass must have picked up from eye-witnesses or rape survivors, such as his own mother, who suffered as Frau Greff did. Simplicissimus is similarly obtuse in his account of greater barbarity, going about his daily chores as if nothing untoward is happening and describing the maid who must have just been raped as 'wunderwercklich zerstrobelt'. In both novels the horror is conveyed all the forcefully because the effect is dispassionate. In the third, most recent passage, what appear to have been literary conceits in *Die Blechtrommel*, that death suddenly interrupts daily routine, were derived from experience. In both passages Grass mentions other authors, however, to indicate the constructed literary quality of his account.

Going back to Grimmelshausen hardly appears progressive, but it was in fact a sign of *Die Blechtrommel*'s newness. Usually classified, if not dis-missed, as little more than popular 'chap-books' full of ribald folksy humour, Grimmelshausen had not been identified as the author of the *Simplicianische Schriften* until the 1830s, and it was not until the later part of the twentieth century that critical interpretation of these remarkable novels was wrested from the medieval allegorists. His influence on German literature was delayed, diverted, repressed even. By aligning himself with Grimmelshausen in *Das Treffen in Telgte*, Grass is stretching German understanding of literary history, which has often struggled with the Baroque, as well as saying that he belongs himself on the periphery, as an outsider. This is not necessarily where one may expect to encounter an author of a 'landmark novel'.

Many other authors left their mark on *Die Blechtrommel*: Goethe, (but *Wilhelm Meisters Lehrjahre* rather than *Die Wahlverwandtschaften*, which helps Oskar learn to read), Jean Paul, and Nietzsche, whose opposition between Dionysiac and Apollonian (in *Die Geburt der Tragödie*) is parodied by Oskar. But in such circumstances the author is sometimes the last person to trust, and Grass arguably muddied the waters in a much quoted lecture he was invited to give on the tenth anniversary of the death of the twentieth-century modernist he claimed had taught him the most, which he entitled 'Über meinen Lehrer Döblin' (1967). Here he wanted to write his own literary history by distancing himself from the classical centre occupied by the unfashionable Thomas Mann and by claiming descent from an 'outsider' instead. In a comment in an interview he sums up his lineage:

> Es kommt [...] sehr stark von jener europäischen Romantradition her, die vom pikaresken Roman herreicht mit all seinen Brechungen, Rabelais und den Löchern dazwischen, der verspäteten Übersetzung ins Deutsche und der Neudichtung Fischarts; da ist der erste große Roman Grimmelshausens, dann die anderen europäischen Beziehungen zu England, Sterne, und hier unmittelbar auch wieder der Einfluß von Goethe zu Jean Paul, und jetzt weiter gefolgert von Sterne zu Joyce und von Joyce zu Dos Passos und zu Döblin in Deutschland, die gleichermaßen dann auch wieder Bezug zu Jean Paul haben – das sind die Traditionen, in denen ich mich verstehe.[10]

What these share is an attitude to language and an anti-realist stylistic inventiveness. Yet Thomas Mann, in particular *Doktor Faustus* and *Mario und der Zauberer*, and the Kafka of *Der Proceß* are more significant in terms of content and motifs than any of these. Elias Canetti was convinced that the hunchbacked dwarf character Fischerle in *Die Blendung* had helped Grass with Oskar.[11] What Grass discovered he could do through his narrator Oskar Matzerath was to imitate and to parody, and his narrative skates along the top of just about every text which Grass has read. This includes culturally influential *Trivialromane* such as Felix Dahn's nationalistic and once immensely popular *Kampf um Rom*, an historical warrior epic set in the Visigoth era and first published in 1878, and René Fülop-Müller's *Rasputin und die Frauen*, which Oskar's mother and her friends swoon over.[12] It is an epoch of literary 'Mief' (that word for choking suburban narrow-mindedness we cannot easily translate and which Grass has often invoked), which he sweeps away.

If a second qualification for classic or landmark status is that the novel influences what comes after it, the picture with respect to Grass's novel is

10   'Gespräche mit Günter Grass', *Text und Kritik: Günter Grass* (1978), pp. 1–39, (p.6).
11   See Sven Hanuschek, *Elias Canetti: Biographie* (Munich and Vienna, 2005), pp. 488–9.
12   See Jean-Marie Valentin, 'Les Orgies de Raspoutine. Günter Grass, lecteur de René Fülop-Müller', *Revue d'Allemagne*, 14 (1982), 683–708.

less clear. Siegfried Lenz's historical epic, *Deutschstunde* (1968), is thought to stand in its debt. Lenz adapts Grass's narrative premise by placing his narrating central figure in an institution, from where he looks back at his youth in Nazi Germany. In *Ansichten eines Clowns* (1963), Böll explores how an alienated performer engages, or more often fails to engage, with contemporary West German society in the early 1960s. Böll can have been no more than prompted by Grass, however, to think of a clown. A novel which interests me rather more than either of these is Johnson's four-volumed *Jahrestage* (1969–83), which echoes one element of Grass's basic narrative premise by alternating between the 'Erzähl-gegenwart' and 'erzählte Vergangenheit', which is repeated in turn by Christa Wolf in her autobiographical *Kindheitsmuster* (1976). Johnson's under-rated masterpiece is a reaction against the style and tone of *Die Blechtrommel*. Johnson favours sober realist detail based on documentary research and makes links only after carefully weighing up the evidence, rather than the at times random, absurdist approach adopted by Oskar. Grass did not invent 'Vergangenheitsbewältigung', but he wrote its first masterpiece. Moving into the 1980s, Patrick Süskind's *Das Parfum* (1985), the only other novel in English translation said to have made a profit in the USA, would have turned out differently had it not been for *Die Blechtrommel*. Oskar's sense of smell is not quite as developed as Jean Baptiste de Grenouille's, but he traces his erotic progress from his memories of the different fragrances emitted by the women in his life. *Die Blechtrommel* does stand out, however, from that line of German twentieth-century novels whose hero murders one or more women, as Oskar is announced to be innocent of the killing of Schwester Dorothea, for which he is tried and imprisoned. From the 1990s there is Thomas Brussig's best-selling *Helden wie wir* (1995), which Grass was even moved to endorse. Once again Brussig plays off private history against public in an ironic, deeply sarcastic voice.

It is always *Die Blechtrommel* rather than any other of his many other works which German authors refer to, but the above list, though hardly complete, falls short of a literary dynasty. Perhaps, however, such an expectation is too high. In the twentieth century it was only Brecht who had pupils in what one could clearly recognise as a 'school'. Curiously, though, Grass's legacy does seem greater in English, although British and American novelists have been more likely to react to *Katz und Maus* and *Hundejahre*, *Der Butt*, *Das Treffen in Telgte*, even *Die Rättin*.

A study published in German in 1997 listed Ishmael Reed, Thomas Berger, Bernhard Malamoud, and Eva Figes, next to the well-known cases of Salman Rushdie and John Irving, whose *Midnight's Children* and *The World According to Garp* are unthinkable without *The Tin Drum* (which has always struck me as a rather different novel to *Die Blechtrommel*).[13] I have also found a number of echoes and borrowings in Ian McEwan (*Black Dogs* and *Hundejahre*), Graham Swift (*Waterland* and *Die Blechtrommel* and even more *Katz und Maus*), and Anthony Burgess (*Earthly Powers* and *Der Butt*).[14] Rushdie modelled not only significant aspects of *Midnight's Children* on *Die Blechtrommel*, but the first two stages of his literary career. He remembers the lessons he learnt, the last one being: 'which I got from that other, immense work, *Dog Years*: When you've done it once, start all over again and do it better'.[15] Grass did this with *Hundejahre*, and it was what Rushdie would do with *Shame* (1983). Grass repaid Rushdie's flattery of imitation by portraying Rushdie as Mister Chatterjee in *Unkenrufe* (1992), and making a number of interventions on his behalf after the fatwa issued against *The Satanic Verses* (1988) in 1989. With the exception of the polyglot Burgess and ex-German student Irving, all these authors read their Grass in Ralph Manheim's translations, whose English version of *Die Blechtrommel* captures and represents the energy and sheer edginess of the original very distinctively. Its occasional divergences from Grass's German, not to mention what appear to be unfortunate omissions, will not mar the new translation which is due on the fiftieth anniversary of *Die Blechtrommel*'s publication in 2009. Such is Grass's interest in his reputation abroad that he has organised briefings for his translators since the late 1970s, and such is his novel's international status that he has commissioned new translations of it into all major European languages. Manheim's version, for all its apparent errors and gaps, will be hard to beat as it is a contemporary classic in its own right. It is noticeable that its impact on the British novel was delayed until the early 1980s, when a new generation of writers turned their attention to subject matter such as history and politics and how they intertwine with individual

13   See Henrik D. K. Engel, *Die Prosa von Günter Grass in Beziehung zur englischsprachigen Literatur* (Frankfurt a. M., 1997).
14   For further details, see my study 'Günter Grass und die britische Gegenwartsliteratur. Eine Skizze', *Sprache im technischen Zeitalter* 37 (1999), 438–53.
15   'Günter Grass' (1984), *Imaginary Homelands: Essays and Criticism 1981-1991* (London, 1992), pp. 273–81 (p.277).

lives in ways which had not been explicit in British fiction for many years.

In terms of theme and content, the Nazi past, which was not so very past in 1959, Grass was a pioneer; formally and aesthetically the novel's status is less clear. Oskar's narrative voice is characterised by sarcastic dismantling; he sits on top of so much literary tradition which he refuses to take seriously that what he started could not be continued by another. But he gave German writing back its confidence, its place in world literature, and did so with a sureness of touch. Five years later Grass entitled a lecture on his current work-in-progress, a play about Brecht putting on a performance of *Coriolanus* at the time of the 17 June Uprising in East Berlin in 1953, 'Die Vor- and Nachgeschichte der Tragödie des Coriolan von Livy und Plutarch über Shakespeare zu Brecht und mir'. Perhaps *Die Blechtrommel*'s lasting achievement in the current context is that it cleared so much away and thus gave others space in which to flourish. 'Wir sind wieder wer', a German politician claimed at the height of the *Wirtschaftswunder*. In literary terms, it was Grass who made this true.

Notes on Contributors

ELIZABETH BOA is Emeritus Professor of German at the University of Nottingham. She has published books on Wedekind, on Kafka and on *Heimat* discourse, and numerous essays in feminist criticism of German literature from the eighteenth century to the present day.

NICHOLAS BOYLE is Schröder Professor of German in the University of Cambridge and President of Magdalene College. He has published numerous articles on the classical period of German literature and studies of modern political, philosophical, and literary culture, and he is currently working on the third volume of his literary biography of Goethe.

CAROLIN DUTTLINGER is a Lecturer in the University of Oxford and Fellow and Tutor of Wadham College. Her main research interests are in twentieth-century German literature and thought. She is the author of *Kafka and Photography* and is currently working on a project exploring the role of attentiveness ('Aufmerksamkeit') in German literature, thought and culture.

PETER HUTCHINSON is Reader in German in the University of Cambridge and Director of Studies in Modern Languages at Trinity Hall. He has published widely on aspects of German literature from the eighteenth century to the present day (especially on the period since 1945), and has edited a number of studies of German literature.

DAVID MIDGLEY is Reader in German in the University of Cambridge and Fellow of St John's College. He has written extensively on German literature and thought of the period since the unification of 1871, with a special focus on literary Modernism. He has published widely on cultural change in twentieth-century Germany, with a particular interest in the relation between scientific thought and literature.

ROGER PAULIN has recently retired as Schröder Professor German of German in the University of Cambridge, where he remains a Fellow of Trinity College. He has published several pieces relating to *Werther*, as well as numerous items on poetry, drama and fiction in German literature from the Baroque to the nineteenth century.

JULIAN PREECE is Professor of German at the University of Wales Swansea. He is the author of two monographs, *The Rediscovered Writings of Veza Canetti: Out of the Shadow of a Husband* and *The Life and Work of Günter Grass: Literature, History, Politics*. He has been an editor of the Leeds (formerly Bradford) Series in Contemporary German Literature since 1994 and has also edited *The Cambridge Companion to Kafka*.

RITCHIE ROBERTSON is Professor of German in the University of Oxford, where he is a Fellow and Tutor of St John's College. He has published extensively on German and Austrian literature, and his books include *Kafka: Judaism, Politics and Literature*; *Heine*; and *The 'Jewish Question' in German Literature, 1749–1939*. He has edited *The Cambridge Companion to Thomas Mann* and (with Katrin Kohl) *A History of Austrian Literature 1918–2000*.

RONALD SPEIRS is Head of the School of Humanities and Professor of German in the University of Birmingham, specialising in German literature from 1870 to the present day. He has written or edited three books on Brecht, one on Kafka and one on Thomas Mann, co-edited volumes on Fascism and European Literature and Germany's Two Unifications, and edited and translated work by Max Weber and Friedrich Nietzsche.

MARTIN SWALES was formerly Professor of German at University College, London. He has written several pieces on Keller as well as on the *Bildungsroman*, and numerous books and articles on a range of aspects of German literature from the classical period to the present day. He is particularly well known for his work on Goethe and Thomas Mann.

ROBERT VILAIN is Professor of German and Comparative literature at Royal Holloway, University of London, and has a particular interest in twentieth-century German and French literature. He has published a book on Hofmannsthal's poetry, a Bibliography of the works of Yvan Goll, and numerous articles on early twentieth-century literature. He has been Co-Editor of *Austrian Studies* since 2002.

ANDREW WEBBER is Reader in German in the University of Cambridge and Fellow of Churchill College. He has published a number of books and articles on aspects of German and Austrian culture, as well as on theory and film literature. He has a particular interest in psychoanalysis and in theories of gender and sexuality, and has translated the Schreber Case for the new Penguin edition of the works of Freud.

CHARLOTTE WOODFORD is a Fellow and College Lecturer in German at Selwyn College, Cambridge, and teaches German literature and history after 1500. Her areas of particular interest are the nineteenth century and the early modern period. Her current research focuses in particular on women's writing, and on the influence of sentimentalism on German fiction written between 1880 and 1910.

Britische und Irische Studien zur deutschen Sprache und Literatur